ROCK CLIMBING
CONNECTICUT

Second Edition

David Fasulo

FALCONGUIDES ®

GUILFORD, CONNECTICUT
HELENA, MONTANA

For the people I love—
Lisa, Kyle, and Kevin

FALCONGUIDES®

An imprint of Rowman & Littlefield
Falcon, FalconGuides, and Outfit Your Mind are registered trademarks of Rowman & Littlefield.

Distributed by NATIONAL BOOK NETWORK

British Library Cataloguing in Publication Information available
Library of Congress Cataloging-in-Publication Data available
ISBN 978-1-4930-0990-9 (paperback)
ISBN 978-1-4930-1513-9 (e-book)

∞™ The paper used in this publication meets the minimum requirements of American National Standard for Information Sciences—Permanence of Paper for Printed Library Materials, ANSI/NISO Z39.48-1992.

WARNING:

Climbing is a sport where you may be seriously injured or die. Read this before you use this book.

This guidebook is a compilation of unverified information gathered from many different sources. The author cannot assure the accuracy of any of the information in this book, including the topos and route descriptions, the difficulty ratings, and the protection ratings. These may be incorrect or misleading and it is impossible for any one author to climb all the routes to confirm the information about each route. Also, ratings of climbing difficulty and danger are always subjective and depend on the physical characteristics (for example, height), experience, technical ability, confidence, and physical fitness of the climber who supplied the rating. Additionally, climbers who achieve first ascents sometimes underrate the difficulty or danger of the climbing route out of fear of being ridiculed if a climb is later down-rated by subsequent ascents. Therefore, be warned that you must exercise your own judgment on where a climbing route goes, its difficulty, and your ability to safely protect yourself from the risks of rock climbing. Examples of some of these risks are: falling due to technical difficulty or due to natural hazards such as holds breaking, falling rock, climbing equipment dropped by other climbers, hazards of weather and lightning, your own equipment failure, and failure or absence of fixed protection.

You should not depend on any information gleaned from this book for your personal safety; your safety depends on your own good judgment, based on experience and a realistic assessment of your climbing ability. If you have any doubt as to your ability to safely climb a route described in this book, do not attempt it.

The following are some ways to make your use of this book safer:

1. Consultation: You should consult with other climbers about the difficulty and danger of a particular climb prior to attempting it. Most local climbers are glad to give advice on routes in their area, and we suggest that you contact locals to confirm ratings and safety of particular routes and to obtain firsthand information about a route chosen from this book.

2. Instruction: Most climbing areas have local climbing instructors and guides available. We recommend that you engage an instructor or guide to learn safety techniques and to become familiar with the routes and hazards of the areas described in this book. Even after you are proficient in climbing safely, occasional use of a guide is a safe way to raise your climbing standard and learn advanced techniques.

3. Fixed Protection: Because of variances in the manner of placement, and weathering of fixed protection, all fixed protection should be considered suspect and should always be backed up by equipment that you place yourself. Never depend on a single piece of fixed protection for your safety because you never can tell whether it will hold weight, and in some cases, fixed protection may have been removed or is now absent.

Be aware of the following specific potential hazards that could arise in using this book:

1. Misdescriptions of Routes: If you climb a route and you have a doubt as to where the route may go, you should not go on unless you are sure that you can go that way safely. Route descriptions and topos in this book may be inaccurate or misleading.

2. Incorrect Difficulty Rating: A route may, in fact, be more difficult than the rating indicates. Do not be lulled into a false sense of security by the difficulty rating.

3. Incorrect Protection Rating: If you climb a route and you are unable to arrange adequate protection from the risk of falling through the use of fixed pitons or bolts and by placing your own protection devices, do not assume that there is adequate protection available higher just because the route protection rating indicates the route is not an "X" or an "R" rating. Every route is potentially an "X" (a fall may be deadly) due to the inherent hazards of climbing—including, for example, failure or absence of fixed protection, your own equipment's failure, or improper use of climbing equipment.

There are no warranties, whether express or implied, that this guidebook is accurate or that the information contained in it is reliable. There are no warranties of fitness for a particular purpose or that this guide is merchantable. Your use of this book indicates your assumption of the risk that it may contain errors and is an acknowledgment of your own sole responsibility for your climbing safety.

CONTENTS

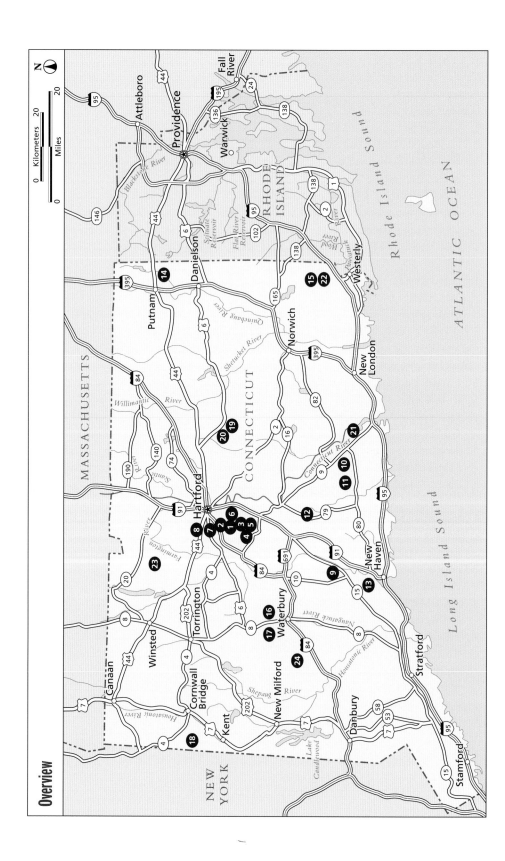

Overview

ACKNOWLEDGMENTS

Writing this guidebook required the contributions of many Connecticut climbers and outdoor enthusiasts. The names listed include individuals involved in the first edition (2002) as well as the second edition. The following editors, writers, and contributors have my sincere gratitude: Jeff Seargent, John Peterson, Lisa Pesci, Chuck Boyd, Bob Clark, Michael Kodas, Chad Hussey, Bob Dest, Leslie Brown, Claude Mallegol, Austin Zinsser, Tim Linehan, Dave Theriault, Carol Parker, Martin Torresquintero, Mike Barker, Debbie Smith, Gary St. Amand, Mike Stokes, Jeff Hogan, Ian Howat, Bill Sullivan, Mike Heintz, Jim Wilcox, Jason Pressler, Sam Slater, Rick Palm, Bill Lutkus, Anne Parmenter, Ann Coleson, Norm Zimmer, Don Pelletier, John MacLean, Scott Zanelli, Al Carilli, Nicole DeLisi, Jonathan Webster, Bill Ivanoff, Henry Barber, Greg Shyloski, Dan Yagmin, Mike Mobley, Kevin Sweeney, Christopher Beauchamp, Scott Sampietro, Stewart Sayah, Sam Streibert, Will Adsit, Morgan Patterson, John Peterson, Nate McKenzie, and Brian Phillips.

INTRODUCTION

Welcome to the steep and intricate climbing that abounds in Connecticut. While the state lacks the vertical height of many popular areas in other parts of the country, the rewards of Connecticut climbs are in the intricate face holds that rely on technique rather than brute strength. Steep and sustained climbing, coupled with often intimidating protection, allow for adventurous climbing. *Rock Climbing Connecticut* is written for the experienced rock climber. If you are new to the sport, you will need qualified instruction on rock climbing to understand, and safely use, this guide.

GEOGRAPHY

The traveling climber will find that the Connecticut basalt crags, known locally as Traprock, provide some of the best face climbing to be found anywhere. Traprock comes from the word *trappa*, a Swedish word for "steps," and is a reference to the shape of the boulders. Connecticut has one of the largest Traprock ridgelines in the country. These ridges were formed as volcanoes spread lava across the countryside. Once the lava cooled, the basalt layers cracked and tilted upward. Over time layers were sheared off and carried away during the Ice Age. The rock rusted, owing to the iron content, resulting in the beautiful orange color.

Aside from Traprock, Connecticut contains several small crags comprised of metamorphic gneiss that is classified in various forms throughout the region. For instance, the rock at Chatfield Hollow is a type of metamorphic rock called Monson gneiss. The rock was lifted as a result of collisions between North America and the European and African continents, creating north–south hills and valleys running throughout Connecticut. Millions of years of erosion and glacial ice have exposed the ledges, and the melting of glacial ice 17,000 years ago deposited several glacial erratics in the surrounding area. The abundance of boulders scattered throughout Connecticut offers many bouldering opportunities throughout the state.

As you explore Connecticut's woodlands, you will note something else about the natural surroundings: many dead hemlock trees. The hemlock woolly adelgid was discovered in Connecticut in 1985 and spread through cultivated and forest hemlocks, causing the dieback of branches and death of trees. As the years pass, these little buggers will surely have an effect on the landscape.

LEARNING TO ROCK CLIMB

Do not try to learn the ropes on your own. Get involved with an established group to learn from a mentor(s), or hire an American Mountain Guide Association (AMGA) certified guide. Local guides can be found online at amga.com. A single day with a guide can save you months or even years learning safe methods to climb outdoors and maybe even save your (and your partner's) life. Also, do not be too proud to graciously accept feedback, or politely critique others, with regard to anchor and belay systems. We are just trying to keep one another safe while enjoying Connecticut's high and wild places.

Justine Pasniewski on *YMC*, Ragged Mountain PHOTO DAVID FASULO

ABOUT THIS BOOK

For climbers many of the leads in Connecticut are quite bold and require expert use of leader protection. Connecticut is not a place to lead at your limit until you get a feel for the routes and protection. Due to the often-intimidating protection and small crags, toproping is very common in Connecticut. However, as of 2015 there are opportunities for sport climbing throughout Connecticut.

Rock Climbing Connecticut is a select guide to Connecticut climbing. It is not a comprehensive guide to every rock climb or area in Connecticut. Many of the Connecticut crags are not listed because of access problems or a lack of high-quality climbs. Also, if you believe that you have found a virgin crag and line, chances are that the route has already been ferreted out since in most areas a route exists every 5 feet or so. This second edition has included more climbs and in many cases the first ascent history.

ACCESS TO CLIMBING AREAS

Where can you climb in Connecticut? Climbing is permitted on the portion of the Main Face of Ragged Mountain that is owned by the Ragged Mountain Foundation. The conservation easement on the property stipulates rock climbing is an acceptable activity. Every other area in this guide, however, is written for historical purposes and does not guarantee permission of the landowner, town, state, or park or forest supervisor concerning access. "Historical purposes" indicates an attempt to document areas that have been frequented by climbers for decades and to document the difficulty of the ascents.

Access to climbing areas in Connecticut can and does change depending on the landowners' and/or supervisors' wishes. *Rock Climbing Connecticut* is not an invitation or excuse to trespass. There are many great climbing areas in Connecticut; unfortunately, some of them are located on private or town property that is no longer open to climbers. Many longtime climbers will be disappointed that some of the best, but now closed, areas are not included in this guide. Others may wonder why areas that are currently closed are included. The fact is that if all the closed areas were omitted from this guide, fewer climbers would be motivated to solve access problems to these areas.

This guide lists:

1. A climbing area that is officially open for climbers for generations to come. This includes the portion of the Main Face at Ragged Mountain located on Ragged Mountain Foundation property.

2. Climbing areas that are located on state property. These areas include West Rock Ridge State Park, Ross Pond State Park, Chatfield Hollow State Park, Sleeping Giant State Park, Pine Ledge (Cockaponset State Forest), Whitestone Cliff (Mattatuck State Forest), Jericho Cliff (Mattatuck State Forest), High Ledge (Pachaug State Forest), Selden Neck State Park, and Bear Rock Ridge (Cockaponset State Forest). According to the previous State Park & Forest Regulation (1993):

"Section 23–4–1(dd): Rock and ice climbing are potentially dangerous sports which pose a risk of injury. All rock and ice climbers are responsible for assessing the safety of the climb for themselves and for any minor accompanying them, relative to the climber's skills, having regard to the condition of the terrain, weather and the climber's experience and equipment. The State provides no supervision, inspection or maintenance of the rocks, ice or cliffs, and State personnel are not authorized to instruct or advise climbers and are not responsible for warning of dangerous conditions. Weather conditions can make the rocks too hazardous to climb. Rock and ice climbers shall assure that their activity does not damage any natural resources."

However, rock climbing is not referenced in the most recent State of Connecticut Regulation: Department of Environmental Protection Sections 23–4–1 through 23–4–5, July 27, 2007. As the author understands it, the previous rock-climbing language was more of a policy statement than an enforceable regulation. Therefore, rock climbing is not currently (as of 2015) included in the regulations.

3. An area that is unique, since it is located on Mashantucket Pequot Tribal Nation (MPTN) property. This federally recognized Native American nation consists of 1,250 acres, including the nearby resort properties. When contacting the MPTN legal department in January 2014, the following access statement was considered accurate: "Lantern Hill is currently (2014) open to the public and Foxwoods has provided trail markers for various loops from the casino. With regard to rock climbing on Lantern Hill, the Mashantucket Pequot Tribal Nation does not explicitly permit or deny rock climbing on Lantern Hill."

4. Climbing areas located on national park property. This includes the crags of St. Johns Ledges.

5. A climbing area located on private property, Pinnacle Rock in Plainville, that has seen regular use for decades, however, written permission to climb in this area has never been granted by the landowner. This area is listed for historical purposes only and is not an invitation to trespass. It should be noted that the landowner for Pinnacle Rock has graciously granted access for trail work and cleanups sponsored by the Ragged Mountain Foundation (RMF) and outdoor retailers such as Eastern Mountain Sports dating back to 1999. More recently "Adopt-a-Crag" events in 2012, 2013, and 2014 were co-sponsored by the Access Fund and the RMF at Pinnacle Rock. These events bring together climbers and hikers to remove trash that accumulates in this area, remove graffiti, and stabilize the trails. Do not contact the landowner(s) in an attempt to secure access on an individual basis. Instead, work with the RMF to build positive relationships in the hopes of securing long-term access.

6. Climbing areas located on town property in towns that do not have an official written stance on rock climbing. For example, in 2001 the town of Farmington stated "As for whether you should be climbing on Town-owned property, the Town has no direct position. Rock climbing is neither encouraged, nor discouraged." Town of Farmington property includes Will Warren's Den and Rattlesnake Rock. Town of Southington property includes the Fire Wall, Low Voltage Crag at Electric Rocks, and a few small crags south of the Low Voltage Crag. The town of Southington does not explicitly permit or deny rock climbing. However, the Parks and Recreation Department gave permission "to secure

Stewart Sayah on the first ascent of *Swamies and Overhangs,* Grond Cliff, 1982
PHOTO STEWART SAYAH COLLECTION

fixed anchors" at the Fire Wall in 2008 to climbers. Town of Woodbury property includes a section of Orenaug Park.

7. Climbing areas located on Land Trust properties. These areas include Diamond Ledge, Fifty-Foot, and Wolf Rock. Climbers have been frequenting these areas on a regular basis for decades. With regard to rock climbing, these land trusts neither explicitly permit nor deny rock climbing.

8. Climbing areas that have an ordinance regulating rock climbing. Rock climbers have been frequenting these areas since the 1930s, however, on June 1, 1992, the city of Meriden passed an ordinance regulating rock climbing within city limits. Within this guide this ordinance affects the East Peak crags, Washington's Head, and the Evening Wall. The Meriden ordinance states: "All rock climbing is prohibited in any park area except with the written consent of the Director of Parks and Recreation and appropriate insurance waiver." The author contacted Parks and Recreation in August 2001 and was given verbal consent to climb on East Peak as long as "pitons were not left behind." When calling in regard to the insurance waiver in September 2001, the author was informed that climbing is not permitted in Meriden—subject closed. Climbers should not contact the city on an individual basis because it will inflame the situation. To the

author's knowledge the ordinance has never been enforced at the above-mentioned areas. In the future, outdoor organizations can, it is hoped, amend the Meriden ordinance to once again allow climbing on the many historic crags. For the time being, consider East Peak, Washington's Head, and the Evening Wall closed and the information regarding these areas for historical purposes only. Washington's Head is located on Town of Meriden open-space property, but its use is dictated by the Meriden Parks and Recreation ordinances.

9. Climbing areas that are currently closed to climbers but access to which is being negotiated. These areas include the property owned by the New Britain Water Company (NBWC) and include Split Rock, and Owl's Lair. Aside from areas mentioned in this book, there are many longtime favorite crags on NBWC property, such as Grond and Spider Wall, which will, it is hoped, be opened in the future. The areas included in this guide are located away from NBWC reservoirs and do not rely on parking located on NBWC property. As of 2015, access is being negotiated with the Ragged Mountain Foundation. For the time being, information regarding these areas is included for historical purposes only.

Finally, an area that is truly missed by many is the Small Cliff at Ragged Mountain. For many years the Ragged Mountain Small Cliff was the traditional gathering spot for Connecticut climbers. The first comprehensive guidebook of Connecticut rock climbing, *A Guide to the Main and Small Cliffs at Ragged Mountain, Southington, Connecticut*, was published in 1964 and included this historic site. Since then, at least four other guidebooks have described the climbing at the Small Cliff. However, with the loss of the parking lot on Carey Street, its popularity decreased. In September 1999 the cliff was closed to climbers. One of the landowners (the area is comprised of two separate private parcels) feels that its popularity has taken a toll and that the area needs to be closed for an unspecified period of time to allow it to regenerate to its more natural state.

Liability is often noted as the primary concern of landowners who allow rock climbing on their property. The Connecticut Recreational Use Act, which was strengthened in 2011, gives landowners who allow free access to their property a layer of liability protection. The complete Connecticut Recreational Use Act is listed in the appendix and should be used as a tool to promote access.

Some history with regard to the recreational use act is helpful in understanding some of the changes in access. The earlier version of the recreational use act was weakened due to the Connecticut Supreme Court's *Conway v. Wilton* decision. This decision set a precedent that municipalities (not private landowners) could be found liable for injuries sustained on municipal property open for public recreation. It was this court decision that led to climbing bans on Metropolitan District Commission (MDC) properties in West Hartford and Barkhamsted, as well as increased restrictions on New Britain Water Company properties. However, the Connecticut Recreational Use Act, essentially, Connecticut General Statues sections 52–557f through 52–577i, was amended in 2011 by Public Act 11–211. This was in response to the court finding the MDC liable for injuries to a bicycle rider on MDC property. The amendment specifically includes municipalities, political subdivisions, water districts, and others among entities immune from liability for recreational use of their property. This amendment, it is hoped, will be a useful tool to renegotiate access to various climbing areas in Connecticut.

Preserving and protecting Connecticut's Traprock ridges benefits climbers, hikers, and all those who appreciate these magnificent landscapes. Many of the Traprock ridges are accessed by the Metacomet and Mattabesett Trail systems. These trails provide beautiful vistas and border most of the best climbing areas in the state. In an effort to protect these trail systems and the Traprock ridges, the state legislature passed the Ridgeline Protection Act in 1998.

Spearheaded by Norm Zimmer, the Ridgeline Protection Act enables local governments to enact zoning and conservation regulations to limit residential and commercial use on designated Traprock ridges and setback areas, which includes "the area bounded by (A) a line that parallels the ridgeline at a distance of one hundred fifty feet on the more wooded side of the ridge, and (B) the contour line where a ridge less than fifty percent is maintained for fifty feet or more on the rockier side of the slope." (Public Act 95–239)

In a ceremony held on May 16, 2001, Governor Rowland honored the Blue-Blazed Hiking Trail System as one of Connecticut's first officially designated greenways. Also receiving greenway designation was the Metacomet Ridge, the striking Traprock ridge that runs northward through the center of the state (CFPA, 2001). Also worth noting is Public Act No. 14–231, approved on June 13, 2014, which allows, among other things, greater flexibility when selling or donating water property lands to nonprofit land trusts.

Beyond bureaucracy, the best way to ensure access is to own the property or have input on the conservation easement. In July 1999 the Ragged Mountain Foundation set a new standard for access: ownership of the Ragged Mountain Main Face as well as fifty-five adjoining acres. Ragged Mountain is one of the few climbing areas in the country actually owned by local climbers, thus ensuring responsible stewardship.

Currently, organizations such as the Ragged Mountain Foundation, the Connecticut chapter of the Appalachian Mountain Club, and the Access Fund are working to reopen Connecticut climbing areas that have been closed over the years. Working with the landowners, owning the property, and developing access-friendly conservation easements are a good start. Do your part by getting involved.

A BRIEF HISTORY OF CONNECTICUT CLIMBING

Connecticut is an area rich in climbing history. Climbing legends such as Fritz Wiessner, Roger Whitney, Betty Woolsey, Charles Houston, and William House established routes as early as the 1920s. During the 1930s at Ragged Mountain, first ascents included *Ancient Way,* 5.4, by Betty Woolsey, Roger Whitney, and Donald Brown; and *Juniper Wall,* 5.7, by Fritz Wiessner, Betty Woolsey, and Bill House.

During the 1930s some of the nation's most difficult free ascents were established in Connecticut by Fritz Wiessner. At Ragged Mountain these ascents included *Tower Crack,* 5.7+, *Wiessner Crack,* 5.8+, and *Vector,* 5.8. Legend has it that Wiessner led *Vector* with a single piton placement, creating the country's first 5.8, and according to Waterman (1993), "completed what probably remained the hardest single pitch lead in the country for almost twenty years." Most climbers feel that *Vector* and *Wiessner Crack* are still intimidating, even with sticky rubber

Sam Streibert on *Bombay,* Ragged Mountain, 1966 PHOTO SAM STREIBERT COLLECTION

and modern camming devices. At East Peak, Fritz Wiessner and Percy Olton climbed the steep and strenuous *Rat Crack,* 5.7.

As early as 1925 the Chin section at Sleeping Giant State Park was explored by climbers such as Hassler Whitney, Roger Whitney, Tom Rawles, and Steve Hart. These early climbers formed the original Yale Mountaineering Club (Waterman, 1993). During the 1930s Fritz Wiessner left his mark at Sleeping Giant with his ascent of *Wiessner's Rib,* 5.6. Since modern climbing techniques were not fully developed, the early pioneers used limited protection and lived, literally, by the adage "The leader must not fall."

In 1953 a climbing accident occurred at Sleeping Giant (during a safety conference for northeastern climbing clubs) and the area was closed to climbing temporarily. The climbing scene shifted to Ragged Mountain, and its first climbing guide, *A Guide to the Main and Small Cliffs at Ragged Mountain, Southington, Connecticut,* was published by John Reppy and Sam Streibert of the Yale Mountaineering Club in 1964. The Yale Mountaineering Club updated this guide in 1973, and it was copyrighted with the quote "Every Goddamned Right Reserved."

During the 1950s and 1960s, Sam Streibert, John Reppy, Dick Williams, and Layton Kor added classics such as Broadway, *YMC (Yale Mountaineering Club), Kor Crack, Unconquerable Crack, Bombay,* and *Subline* at Ragged Mountain. In 1964 Reppy and Streibert free-climbed Connecticut's first 5.9, *Shadow Wall* at the Ragged Mountain Small cliff. During the 1960s John Reppy also began to pioneer the use of nuts where pitons traditionally had been used for protecting climbs. According to the 1964 guidebook to Ragged Mountain by Reppy and Streibert, "The vertical cracks present problems for leader protection; one solution is the use of a nut sling, (a large hex nut threaded on a loop of rope), as an artificial chockstone." Ragged Mountain, as well as the Shawangunks of New York, were areas in which "clean climbing" was pioneered. Prior to this style the placement and removal of pitons caused scars in the rock that remained visible for many years.

During the 1970s the equipment available for climbers improved, the free-climbing standards were being pushed, and the climbers of this era exhibited great talent and vision. Top-level free climbers such as "Hot Henry" Barber visited Connecticut and produced free ascents of demanding lines such as *Subline, Anticipation,* and *Hot Rocks* at Ragged Mountain. Sam Streibert was also climbing well, with first free ascents of *Cat Crack* and *Reflections of Fall* at East Peak. In 1971 Dennis Merritt and Sam Streibert free-climbed Connecticut's first 5.10, Aid Crack at the Ragged Mountain Main Face.

Connecticut also possessed an abundance of local talent, and notable ascents of the 1970s at Ragged Mountain included *Visions* by Harry Brielman and Bill Lutkus; and *The Ragged Edge* by Jim Adair, Sam Slater, and Bruce Dicks. One of Connecticut's best routes, *Dol Guldur* at East Peak, was freed by Tony Trocchi and Mike Heintz. This was a period of great adventure, and many other fine routes were established then as well.

Throughout the 1980s the new route activity continued, and several climbs were established on the many small crags throughout Connecticut. Climbers such as Bill Sullivan, Mike Lapierre, Bob Clark, Ken Nichols, Mike Heintz, Al Rubin, and Chad Hussey established numerous routes, offering a greater variety for Connecticut climbers. *Traprock: Connecticut Rock Climbs,* by Ken Nichols, was published in 1982 and carefully documented many of Connecticut's Traprock climbs.

Eric Bader, *St. Valentine's Day Massacre*, Winter Wall, 1976 PHOTO STEWART SAYAH

During the 1980s a larger number of climbers were entering the sport, and each weekend climbers would congregate at the Small Cliff to climb, pose, meet partners, and socialize. The new route activity of the 1970s and 1980s provided a greater variety of routes and crags, which helped to disperse climbers away from Ragged Mountain. The Ragged Mountain area exhibited, and continues to exhibit, stress from overuse. This stress includes trail erosion, wear on trees due to toprope anchors, and issues related to parking due to the increasing number of climbers.

Beginning in the 1980s, in an effort to limit the amount of fixed protection in Connecticut, several routes were first led using tied-off hooks. These routes had been previously toproped, and the climbers were completing the first lead ascent. In this guide most of the routes led with tied-off hooks are listed as R/X for the protection ratings. Connecticut climber Ken Nichols was the leading proponent of this method and kindly invited others to participate on first ascents. The author had the opportunity to be a part of the first hook-led ascents of *Atlantic Hurricane* at Ragged Mountain FA: Ken Nichols, Bob Finch, David Fasulo, Chad Hussey, Jim Wilcox, Wes Beman, Al Rubin (1985), and *Fishhook* at West Peak, FA: Ken Nichols, David Fasulo (1987). However, after being on the sharp end while aid climbing routes with hooks it is the author's belief that the use of tied-off hooks is not appropriate for free climbs. While the use of tied-off hooks was inspired by an effort to reduce the amount of fixed protection, the end product was a route with inadequate protection, forcing toproping of the route to become the norm. Furthermore, this style also resulted in routes such as *Atlantic Hurricane,* in which bolts were placed, which are useless to most climbers. The upshot of hooks is that the bolts have been kept to a minimum, helping to preserve the aesthetic nature of the many small crags.

One of the first ascents that characterized the climbing scene in the 1980s was *Bleu Cheese,* on the Green Wall at Rattlesnake Mountain. It is a climb established on a small Traprock crag, located off the Metacomet Trail, nestled in a tranquil hemlock grove. *Bleu Cheese* was bolted on the lead and first ascended by longtime—and continually active—local climber Bob Clark. Although this climb is insignificant on the national level, it is a fine example of the spirit of exploration during this period. To close out the 1980s, Bill Lutkus upped the free-climbing standard by free-climbing May Day, 5.13, at Ragged Mountain in 1989.

The 1990s was a period of much change in Connecticut. The first indoor climbing gym was opened—Prime Climb in Wallingford—and was soon followed by other climbing gyms. The gyms provided Connecticut climbers with a safe haven from poor weather, a social gathering place, and a central location for slide shows and climbing clinics. The gyms also opened up the sport to more people, resulting, naturally, in a greater impact on Connecticut's limited climbing resources.

It was also during the 1990s that Connecticut's premier climbing area, the Ragged Mountain Main Face, was acquired by the Ragged Mountain Foundation. Originally, the Nature Conservancy was contacted in regard to preserving the Stanley Hart property that contains a majority of the Main Cliff at Ragged Mountain, as well as Hart Pond and 55 adjoining acres. Noting the recreational value of the property, the executive director of the Nature Conservancy wrote to the Appalachian Mountain Club in 1982 about a joint preservation

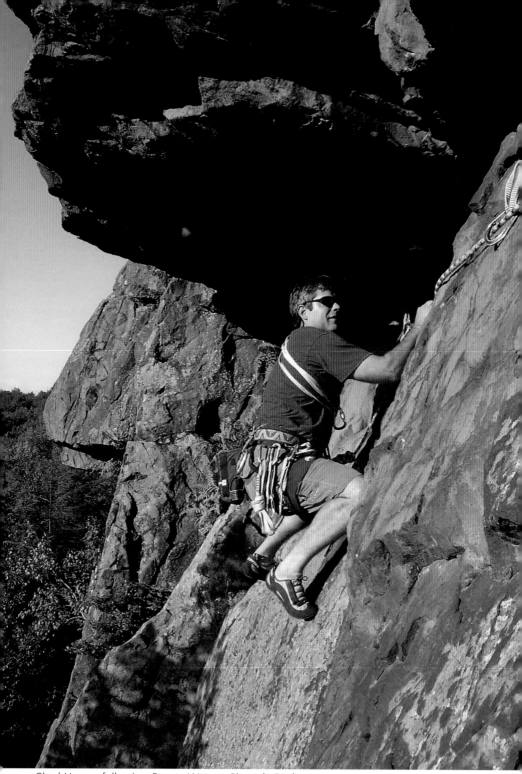

Chad Hussey following *Dream Weaver*, Pinnacle Rock PHOTO BOB CLARK

effort. After a biological survey for rare plants and animals, the lands would be transferred to the Appalachian Mountain Club to be used for camping, hiking, and climbing. The two organizations collaborated to secure the permanent conservation of the former Stanley Hart property. In December 1989 the property was transferred to the Nature Conservancy. The plan called for a caretaker, a campground, and a nature center.

Apparently, the Appalachian Mountain Club had experienced operating deficits from some of its newer facilities. While the Connecticut chapter of the Appalachian Mountain Club was enthusiastic about assuming ownership, headquarters was not. The Connecticut Mountaineering chair, Ed Budzik, formed a committee to examine the transaction. When the committee realized that the Appalachian Mountain Club would not accept the gift, they recommended that a local organization be formed to assume the stewardship role. Without the public standing and resources of the AMC, the new team scaled back the original plan to fit the character of the newly developed residential neighborhood. At this point local climbers and hikers, spearheaded by Leslie Brown, formed the Friends of Ragged Mountain, which later became the Ragged Mountain Foundation.

After nearly a ten-year formal and informal stewardship process, the former Stanley Hart property was transferred to the Ragged Mountain Foundation on July 9, 1999, and the Berlin Land Trust became the holder of the conservation easement. After serving as treasurer, the author served as president of the RMF shortly after the transfer; however, it was the tireless efforts of former presidents Leslie Brown, Walt Hampton, Gary St. Amand, and longtime board member Jeff Sargeant (as well as several other volunteer board members) that led to the successful acquisition of the property. The group also received support from the Appalachian Mountain Club, Connecticut Forest & Park Association, and the Access Fund.

Some, however, have called the 1990s the "Dark Ages" of Connecticut climbing. Access, most notably restricted parking (the loss of the parking lot at the base of Pinnacle Mountain as well as the Small Cliff parking at Ragged Mountain) and climbing bans, had become major issues at popular climbing areas. Areas that were once very popular, such as Short Mountain, the Spider Wall, and the Ragged Mountain Small Cliff, were closed to climbers.

The last decade was also a period when disagreements among climbers attained a new level. Some of the hostility that reared its ugly head in the 1990s had been festering since the 1970s. The complete story would require several pages of text for a fair and balanced account. The June/July 1991 issue of *Climbing* magazine and the May/June 1991 issue of *Rock & Ice* magazine provide further detail. In essence, two issues were debated among climbers: parking at Ragged Mountain and fixed protection.

When the former Stanley Hart property was transferred to the Ragged Mountain Foundation, the Deed of Conservation Restriction stipulated, among other things, that a parking lot would not be permitted on the property. With regard to bolts at Ragged Mountain, the Deed of Conservation Restriction section 2.9, July 1999, states: "There shall be no use of bolts for rock climbing on the Protected Property, except as provided in 3.6." Section 3.6 states, "The right to take action to prevent the erosion of any slope on the Protected Property and to protect public health and safety, including the replacement of bolts previously placed on the climbing routes located on the Protected Property."

Kayla Pelletier sending PHOTO HUNTER PEDANE PHOTOGRAPHY

Statewide, there are climbers who feel that fixed protection, specifically bolts and pitons, should only be placed on the lead without the use of aid. Aid means hanging from climbing gear, placed while on a toprope or on rappel. Conversely, there are climbers who feel it is appropriate to place fixed protection on aid. In the 1970s at Ragged Mountain, a few routes had bolts placed on aid and were regularly used for years. These routes included *No Parking, Bombay Direct,* and *Vajolet Corner.* Other routes, which had fixed protection placed on rappel, were stripped of the fixed protection after the first ascent and reascended with protection placed without aid. At Ragged Mountain these routes included *Visions* and *Vanishing Point.*

Some climbers were appalled that a bolt or piton could be chopped or removed from a route. They were also agitated by threats that if bolts or pitons were placed on rappel, they would be removed. Conversely, some climbers were appalled that a bolt or piton would be placed on aid or on rappel and were advocating an ethic of purely ground-up ascents in Connecticut.

In 1991 the route *Volcanic Eruption* was rappel-bolted and led. The bolts on this route were removed shortly after by the first-ascent party. Some believe that bolting *Volcanic Eruption* was a step into the future and produced one of the finest sport climbs in the Northeast. Others believe that the bolts disregarded an established set of climbing ethics in Connecticut, permanently damaged Connecticut's limited climbing resources, and marred the environment.

Differences in opinion escalated with regard to the vision of the former Stanley Hart property and fixed protection. In late March / early April 1993, virtually all of the fixed protection—bolts and pitons—on the popular climbs were stolen.

In fall 1999, and in accordance with the conservation easement on the former Stanley Hart property, most of the original bolts were replaced on Ragged Mountain. Shortly after the replacement of the fixed protection, the bolts were again stolen, and holds were chopped off the route *Vanishing Point.* It was, and continues to be, a difficult situation. The stolen protection (most of which was placed free and on the lead) represents a serious threat to public safety, and the chiseling of holds off of routes and destruction of the rock is clearly unacceptable. As of 2015 fixed protection throughout Connecticut continues to be replaced by local climbers and again stolen or damaged—truly a sad and pathetic state of affairs, hence the "Dark Ages" continue to linger on in Connecticut.

As time marched on, the 1990s brought about higher free-climbing standards. Talented local climbers such as Bill Lutkus, J. D. Mackie, Sam Slater, Ken Nichols, John MacLean, and Bruce Jelen established routes to the 5.12 and 5.13 levels. In 1993 J. D. Mackie succeeded on the often-tried *Wall of Horrors,* 5.13–, at Ragged Mountain. Sam Slater added *In the Presence of God,* 5.13–, and *Lightning Strike,* 5.13, at East Peak.

The new millennium has brought fresh talent and ideas to the Connecticut climbing scene. With this new talent, bouldering has become the rage and has inspired a new level of energy and enthusiasm. While Connecticut will never have "big wall" routes, the abundance of boulders opens up opportunities for new problems and exploration. As of 2015 the established boulder problems in the region are vast, and the Internet is the best source for keeping up-to-date on bouldering. As with rock climbing, issues with access at bouldering areas are already a concern.

As of 2015 there are changes in terms of fixed gear in Connecticut. In August 2008 climbers obtained permission from the town of Southington to "secure fixed anchors" at the Fire Wall. Shortly after bolts and anchors were installed on rappel at the Fire Wall, and rappel placed bolts and anchors were placed on select crags throughout the state. From 2009 to 2014 Christopher Beauchamp established several sport routes at the previously neglected Pine Ledge and Bear Rock, as well as sport and mixed routes at the Wintergreen Wall and Selden Neck. From 2012 to 2014 climbers such as Greg Shyloski and Dan Yagmin established very difficult sport climbs at Chatfield Hollow and the Fire Wall. From 2010 to 2013 Brian Phillips established popular sport routes at Ross Pond and Pine Ledge. During this time period bolts and anchors were also placed on the towering walls of West Rock and other crags throughout the state.

Historically, differences in opinions led to much of the fixed protection in Connecticut being removed, whether placed in accordance with Connecticut climbing ethics or not. In April 2013 an article entitled "Ceasefire," by Brian Phillips, appeared in *Rock & Ice* magazine discussing the changes in Connecticut climbing. "Ceasefire" provided a sampling of sport routes in Connecticut and pointed out that toproping has become common practice at several crags—partly due to the stolen fixed protection. According to Phillips, "Most climbers never repeat these run-out climbs on lead because they aren't foolish enough to put their life in jeopardy or spend the rest of their life disabled for the second or third repeat of an ascent on some obscure climb." "Disabled" was in reference to a climber with whom the author climbed the Regular Northwest Face on *Half Dome VI* 5.9 A2 in the 1990s. Sadly, the same climber fell

Chris Beauchamp sport climbing at Selden Neck PHOTO DAVID FASULO

to the ground while attempting to lead a poorly protected route in Connecticut, breaking his back, and is severely disabled as a result of the fall. The accident exemplifies that many of the leads in Connecticut can be complex and at times dangerous.

A related issue to sport climbing, that being fixed anchors, has instigated a separate debate. On most of the new sport routes, fixed anchors are placed at the top for lowering. However, in an effort to increase safety and reduce erosion, some areas have seen the addition of fixed anchors on routes that have been regularly climbed for years using natural anchors. The debate on the responsible use of anchors throughout Connecticut will need to consider the environmental impact, public safety (hikers as well as climbers), aesthetics of the crag, and impact on access.

The future of Connecticut climbing will, more than likely, be focused on preserving the aesthetic nature of the crags and ensuring access to these areas. Climbers may disagree on the use of fixed protection; however, much of the beauty of the Connecticut crags can be attributed to the minimal use of fixed protection. The use, and misuse, of fixed protection and anchors will undoubtedly continue as the years pass. Access is a major issue. The future legends and heroes of Connecticut climbing will be the individuals who are responsible for regaining, and then protecting, access to Connecticut's high and wild places.

AUTHOR'S NOTE

Unfortunately, at the time of this writing, much of the fixed protection—pitons and bolts—has been stolen from many Connecticut crags, a potential disaster for the unsuspecting leader. At the Ragged Mountain Main Face alone, the following routes have been compromised because of missing bolts: *The Cage, No Parking, Obsession, Bombay Direct, Pork Barrel Project, For Madmen Only, Terminal Velocity, Vajolet Corner, Lavaredo Corner, Knight's Gambit, Skull and Bones, Atlantic Hurricane, Hemlock Groove,* and *Vanishing Point.*

Routes with missing pitons, considered by many climbers to be important at the Ragged Mountain Main Face, include *Visions, Ash Tray, YMC Route* (start), Broadway (lower section/hole), *The Ragged Edge,* and *Vanishing Point.* To some the need for the missing pitons is debatable. For example, the expert leader can lead *YMC* and *Broadway* without the missing pitons, although they were in place for many years. Also, many of the original pitons were in such poor condition that they would not have held a fall.

In 1998, however, I was watching a climber lead *Broadway* at Ragged Mountain. He had taken a multiday leading course in Colorado earlier in the season and had led a few routes at Ragged that day. While testing a piece of gear at the "hole," 30 feet off the deck on *Broadway,* the piece popped out and he fell. On the way down the protection he placed lower on the route caught his ankle and flipped him upside down. The young climber, who was getting married the next weekend, landed headfirst right in front of me.

The climber had a large frame, and I noticed his body compress on his head and neck as he hit the ground. I thought he was dead. His helmet broke off a corner of a sharp boulder, and he was knocked unconscious.

We alerted 911, and when he awoke we stabilized his injuries as best we could. The climber was evacuated using a specialized wheeled litter and was "lucky" to escape with some broken bones and a strained back. The moral of the story: Traditionally, there has been a fixed piton (replaced with a new piton and again stolen in 1999) in that location that would probably have prevented that accident. Replacement of pitons is an issue that deserves dialogue.

CAMPING IN CONNECTICUT

The safest bet is to utilize a state park campground. Among these, Hammonasset State Park in Madison is probably the traveling climber's best bet. Hammonasset has quick access to Route 80 and I-95, a good beach, and some bouldering on the eastern end of the beach. Private campgrounds are also available throughout the state, and the Internet can inform on many options.

FIRST ASCENTS AND ROUTE RATINGS

This second edition of *Rock Climbing Connecticut* contains information on first ascents for historical purposes. However, many of the routes have a complex history. A single route may have a first-aid ascent, first toprope ascent, first lead ascent, and first revised lead ascent (original versus present route). Other routes may have a first recorded ascent (FRA), meaning the route was more than likely ascended prior to the first "recorded" ascent listed. To streamline the guide, the route that makes the most sense to the author (original versus revised and very subjective) is described and credited as the first ascent.

Rating climbs is a subjective game. A 5.10 face in Connecticut may feel like a 5.11 face in other states. Typically, climbs are rated by the first ascent party, and in Connecticut some climbs may reflect grading practices from the 1960s and '70s. According to the first guide to Ragged Mountain by John Reppy and Sam Streibert, published in 1964, "The NCCS (National Climbing Classification system) has been used to indicate the difficulty of the climbs. In this system free climbs are graded from F 1 to F 10 according to difficulty, while climbs utilizing aid are classed from A 1 to A 5. It is hoped that the grades used at Ragged will correspond fairly closely to those used in the Shawangunks." *The Climber's Guide to Ragged Mountain*, second edition (1973), helped to solidify some of the grades at Ragged Mountain. According to the 1973 guide, "The list of climbs in order of difficulty represents a compromise among the opinions of a number of climbers whom were polled." Most of the previously recorded grades remain, but some of the grades have been changed (upward) by the author. If you feel the grade is not accurate, a pen is best to change the grade.

With regard to names, a majority of the climbs in this book have kept their commonly known names, and local climbers have edited the book to improve accuracy. Some of the names, however, were simply made up.

Quality Rating

Starred routes (★) are routes of exceptional quality.

Protection Rating

Note: Not all routes have protection ratings. You will need to use your own judgment for these routes.

G	Generally good protection for the leader (typically not listed next to the route name to streamline the guide).
PG	Fair protection.
R	Poor protection—serious potential for injury or death.
X	Terrible protection—a fall will result in serious injury or death.
R/X	Led using tied-off hooks. This is not a recommended practice for protecting free climbs. Hooks are scary enough while aid climbing.
TR	Lack of protection requires that a toprope be used.
x	A small x on the line drawing refers to a fixed bolt.
(bolt missing)	Assume an X rating if the bolt is not in place.

Difficulty Rating

Routes are rated using the Yosemite Decimal System. Free climbs are graded from 5.0 to 5.15.

Free Climbing Rating

5.1–5.5	Beginner
5.6–5.9	Intermediate
5.10–5.12	Advanced
5.13–5.15	Extreme

Map Legend

Transportation

⟨95⟩	Interstate Highway
⟨1⟩	US Highway
⟨3⟩	State Highway
⟨12⟩	Local Road
= = = =	Gravel Road
- - - - - -	Trail

Symbols

⎍	Cliff
❶	Climbing Location/Pitch Number
⬭	Crag/Boulder
┇	Gate
▲	Mountain Peak/Summit
🅿	Parking
■	Point of Interest/Structure

Water Features

⬭	Body of Water

Land Management

♠	State Park

Topo Legend

o	Natural gear belay stance
x	Single piece of fixed protection (bolt or piton)
xx	Fixed belay or rappel station

RAGGED MOUNTAIN (SOUTHINGTON)

The Main Cliff at Ragged Mountain is home to some of the best and most popular rock climbs in the state. Technical rock climbers have been frequenting Ragged Mountain since the 1930s. Originally, the crack systems at Ragged were used for ascents and allowed reasonable protection. Eventually, climbers ventured out into the thin cracks and blank faces. Due to the texture of the rock, most climbs utilize a variety of intricate face holds. These routes offer some of the best face climbs to be found anywhere in the country.

There are two trails that access the top of the cliff: the North Gully Trail and the South Gully Trail. The gullies are connected via the Undercliff Trail at the base of the cliff and the Metacomet Trail on top of the ridge. To help reduce erosion, the Ragged Mountain Foundation and its members constructed a stone stairway on each gully. These projects required several work parties and two years of effort. Do your part by picking up trash, staying on trails, using gear for anchors to reduce the impact on trees, volunteering for work parties, and getting involved with the RMF.

Directions: Directions are provided to the junction of Reservoir Road and Route 71A (see map). From there two access points are described.

From Hartford: Take I-84 West to exit 35 (left exit for Route 72 East), then take exit 7 (Route 372). Take a right off the exit and continue on Route 372 East for 1.5 miles, after which you will veer right onto Route 71A. Follow Route 71A south for 3 miles to Reservoir Road. If traveling I-91 South, take exit 22N to Route 9 North, and follow directions from Old Saybrook.

From Waterbury: Take I-84 East to exit 35 (left exit for Route 72 East), then take exit 7 (Route 372). Take a right off the exit and continue on Route 372 East for 1.5 miles, after which you will veer right onto Route 71A.

From Old Saybrook: Take Route 9 North to exit 24. Go to the stoplight at the end of the ramp; turn left at the light on Route 71A South (Chamberlain Highway). Proceed 0.9 mile to the West Lane entrance on your right. Follow West Lane past a stop sign to the parking pull-out on the right, or continue 2 miles to Reservoir Road.

Approach: There are two official access points to the Ragged Mountain Foundation property.

1. The Metacomet Trail (blazed in blue) via Carey Street in Southington: This is the most popular official access point for the Main Face, but parking is not optimal. Limited parking is located along Sheldon Road and Moore Hill Drive in Southington.

Ragged Mountain PHOTO DAVID FASULO

The presence of nonresident vehicles in this family neighborhood is stressful to relations with local property owners. Do not park in no-parking areas or in front of mailboxes, always carpool, and be quiet and considerate to the homeowners. Timberlin Park (listed below) is a convenient carpool location.

From one of these roads, hike across Andrews Street to Carey Street. Follow Carey Street east for about 5 minutes to a private driveway on the left. The abandoned parking lot just before the driveway, closed to climbers and hikers in the 1990s, is a good landmark. From Carey Street follow the private driveway past a small orchard. You will encounter the Metacomet Trail on the right after a short walk up the driveway. About 6 minutes of hiking up the drive-way / Metacomet / Blue Blaze Trail will bring you to the junction of the Undercliff Trail (unmarked). Go left on the Undercliff Trail for 5 minutes to reach the base of the Main Face. You will reach the Small Cliff (closed

as of 2015) if you have missed the Undercliff Trail and have gone too far.

This access utilizes private property. So far, climbers and hikers have had the good fortune of this access owing to the kindness and tolerance of local property owners. Do your part to maintain the goodwill between the local property owners and the climbing and hiking community.

2. Ragged Mountain Memorial Preserve entrance off of West Lane: This area contains a small parking lot. There are no immediate threats of a closure to this area. This is a pleasant but long (about 1 hour) approach that offers fine views, and the trail passes over several small crags with many established lines. Using this lot will help maintain goodwill with the local property owners who are concerned with climbers and hikers parking in their neighborhoods.

To get to West Lane from Reservoir Road, follow Route 71A North for 1.1 miles and turn left on West Lane.

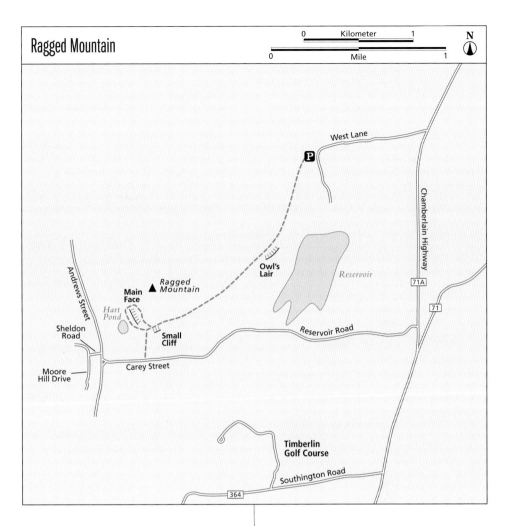

If coming from Route 9, take exit 24 (Kensington). Take a left off the ramp onto Route 71A South and continue 0.9 mile to a right turn on West Lane. Once on West Lane, continue straight past a stop sign to the Ragged Mountain Memorial Preserve parking area on the right.

Blue Blaze / Red Dot trail: From the Memorial Preserve boulder / plaque, follow the wide fire road / trail. Veer left after 1 minute onto the Blue Blaze / Red Dot Trail on the left. After 15 minutes you will reach a cliff overlooking the reservoir. The trail crosses a riverbed twice, and 30 minutes later you will reach a cliff with a detached tower known as the Clock Tower. Less than 5 minutes from the Clock Tower, you will reach another tower called the Lost Owl Spire, as well as a view of West Peak in Meriden. This spire is the west side of the Owl's Lair cliff. Continue along the trail to an open area with a large flat boulder—this is the top of the main section of Owl's Lair. The unmarked trail near the boulder is used to descend to the base of Owl's Lair—35 total minutes for the approach to Owl's Lair.

To reach the May Crack Block and base of the Small Cliff: From Owl's Lair continue on the Blue Blaze / Red Dot Trail; you will pass over a crag (Citadel) in 5 minutes. Continue for 2 more minutes to a junction with an unmarked trail on the left. Leave the Blue Blaze / Red Dot Trail and continue on the unmarked trail, aka Undercliff Trail. After 1 minute you will reach May Crack Block. This crag is easily identified by the striking hand crack. Continue on the Undercliff Trail for 1 minute to the base of the Small Cliff. The time from West Lane to the Small Cliff is 40 to 50 minutes. If you remain on the Blue Blaze / Red Dot Trail, you will go to the top of the Small Cliff. The trail then intersects with the blue-blazed Metacomet Trail.

To continue to the Ragged Mountain Main Face: Top of Small Cliff to Main Face—follow the blue-blazed trail for 10 minutes to a T junction. Go right at the junction (30 seconds) and you will be at the top of the route YMC. Bottom of Small Cliff to Main Face—Walk down the gully on the west end of the Small Cliff. Hike downhill for 2 minutes to the junction with a trail on your right (Undercliff Trail) just before a stone driveway. Follow this trail northwest for 5 minutes to the junction of the South Gully Trail.

3. Timberlin Park in Berlin—carpool location. For years climbers utilized a parking area at Timberlin Park in Berlin and hiked to Carey Street. However, the trail access seems to change. A blazed trail may exist to Carey Street, but the description is not included in this edition. It is possible to hike the Blue-Blazed Metacomet trail to Ragged Mountain from this parking area, but it is a long and arduous approach. The gate for the park closes at sunset, so plan accordingly.

From Route 71 (Chamberlain Highway), follow Route 364 West for 0.6 mile to the Timberlin Park entrance. Follow the road past the golf course and continue into the park, veering left. Follow the road to the end and turn around in the loop.

The climbs are listed here from left to right.

The Girdle Traverse (5.9 / 5.10) is for the adventurous. In 1973 Henry Barber and Sam Streibert climbed a traverse of Ragged, which begins on End Run and finishes up at Carey Corner. The climb generally stays high and is completed in approximately seven pitches.

Main Cliff

1. The Cage (5.10+ PG / R ★; bolt missing 2015) This climb ascends the right side of the imposing north wall. Climb steep cracks on the right side of the wall to a rest. Hand-traverse left under the roof (crux) to a ledge with a bolt. Climb the roof above, traverse right (approximately 5 feet), then climb to the top. The original route was ascended by Sam Streibert in 1965 and rated A3. FFA: Ken Nichols, 1974.

1a. Uncaged Variation (5.11 R / X) From the crux roof continue straight up the inside corner instead of traversing left under the roof. FA: Tom Egan, 1973. FFA: Ken Nichols, 1988.

1b. Breakout Variation (5.9+ R) Instead of traversing right after the second roof, continue straight to the top. FA: Greg Newth, Nancy Emro, 1975.

2. End Run (5.4 ★) Begin on the north face and ascend a ramp running left to right to the outside corner. Traverse right around *North End* across ledges to a right-facing corner and wide crack, which leads to the top.

3. No Parking (5.10 PG; bolt missing 2015) Around the corner from the *End Run* ramp, on the left end of the Main Face, is a short overhanging wall. Ascend the middle of the wall past a bolt. Either continue up *North End* or belay on the ledge above. To descend, traverse right across ledges. FA: Greg Newth, 1976.

4. North End (5.9– PG) Begin on the steep left-facing corner to the right of *No Parking*. Climb the corner; continue up and left, past a ledge, to another steep corner (the first left-facing corner to the right of *The Cage*), which is followed to the top. Protection can be strenuous to place on the upper corner. A piton (could be missing) was used to protect the top for many years. FA: John Reppy, Sam Streibert, 1963.

John Reppy on the first ascent of *North End*, 1963 PHOTO JOHN REPPY COLLECTION

move. Descend from the ledge by traversing right. A second pitch (5.9 R) can be added by climbing the face to the left of *Outside Edge*. FA: Sam Streibert 1964. FFA Layton Kor, Sam Streibert, 1964.

8. Hangover (5.9) The left-facing corner system to the right of *Lana Crack* and left of *Aid Crack* is climbed to the ledge. FA: Ajax Greene, Ken Nichols, 1993.

9. Hangnail (5.9+) Another short route. Climb the face to the right of *Hangover* and left of *Aid Crack*. FA: Mike Heintz, Chad Hussey, Ken Nichols, 1981.

10. Aid Crack (5.10) A short but popular route. Climb the prominent thin crack to the ledge. FA: Phil Nelson 1964. FFA: Dennis Merritt, Sam Streibert, 1971.

11. Julia (5.11 TR) Climb the short, smooth face 5 to 6 feet to the right of *Aid Crack* to the broken ledges. Named for Jim's wife and chairperson of the James Wilcox Memorial Award committee. The committee provides grants in conjunction with the Ragged Mountain Foundation honoring the adventurous spirit of climbing. FA: Jim Wilcox, 1992.

12. Sisu (5.8+ R) Typically climbed as a variation to *Owl Perch*. The original line climbs a short crack to the right of *Aid Crack* to a ledge. Climb up and right following a left-facing corner (formed by the left edge of the *Owl Perch* overhang) to a traverse right to the upper-corner system of *Owl Perch* (poorly protected). Continue traversing right through a crack on a left-facing corner past a piton (missing in 2015) to an airy mantel. Continue up the face to the top. *Sisu Direct* (5.8+ ★ R): A more popular combination is to climb *Owl Perch* past the first overhanging corner. At the top of the corner, traverse right into *Sisu* at the crack breaching the

5. Taurus (5.9 PG / R) Probably best climbed in two pitches. Climb the face between *North End* and *Lana Crack* to the notch. Continue up the prominent corner system to a ledge (the base of the final corner on *End Run*). Work up the face to the left of the *End Run* corner / arête to a hand traverse that leads left to a finish on *North End*. FA: Sam Streibert, George Eypper, 1970.

6. Megalosaurus (5.9– TR) The face left of *Lana Crack*. FA: Jim Wilcox, Blake Della Bianca, Marc Pelletier, Bob Clark, Bill Lutkus, 1988.

7. Lana Crack (5.9–) Climb the slightly overhanging finger / hand crack to a strenuous last

Ragged Mountain and Crack Face

steep left-facing corner. Poorly protected after the mantel move. FA: Mike Heintz, Mike Hassey, John Sahi, 1980.

13. Owl Perch (5.8 PG ★) Steep and intimidating. Take your time placing the necessary protection before launching over the initial overhanging corner, as accidents have occurred on this climb. Scramble up ledges to the left of *Cemetery Vault* and *Easy Rider* to an overhanging buttress. Climb the overhanging corner / crack system on the right of the buttress to a stance. Continue straight up the corner system to the top. FA: Bert Arsego, John Reppy, 1955.

14. Hard Rider (5.11+ R) Starting left of *Easy Rider*, climb up the face and through the roof between *Owl Perch* and *Easy Rider*.

15. Easy Rider (5.11 R / X ★) Begin at the 10-foot-high hand crack to the left of *Cemetery Vault*. Continue up the face, ascending a ledge system, up and right, to the top of the flake. Work over the huge roof above (off the left side of the flake), and follow a crack through more hangs to the top. FA: Sam Slater, Ken Nichols, Mick Avery, 1984.

16. Trojan Horse (5.11 R / X) Begin at the tree just left of *Cemetery Vault*. Climb a broken left-facing corner system to the top of the flake (original first pitch belay). Climb the overhang to the right of *Easy Rider* at the overhanging right-facing corner. Continue straight up, passing overhangs to the top. The original route (5.9 R 16v.) avoids the first overhanging wall by climbing up *Cemetery Vault* above the roof, then traverses left to finish on *Easy Rider*. FA: Ken Nichols, Mike Heintz, 1981. FA revised route: Ken Nichols, 1996.

17. Cemetery Vault (5.8 PG) On the right side of the broken recess, follow double cracks (strenuous to protect) to a stance below the left-facing corner / crack / ramp system. Climb the corner / crack to the top. FA: John Reppy, Bert Arsego, 1955.

The following short climbs begin on the ledge system above *Aid Crack*. To reach the base, follow ledges and corners up and right from the start of *Easy Rider*.

A. Vicious Animal (5.10+ R) Start at the left end of the overhang and climb the face to the left of *Outside Edge*. FA: Ken Nichols, Rick Palm, 1994.

B. Outside Edge (5.5 or 5.9+ R) Climb the face just left of the *Jam Corner* arête. Either step off and left from the *Jam Corner* ledge (5.5) or begin below the overhang below (5.9+). FA: Ken Nichols, Rick Palm, Matt Rugens, 1994.

C. Jam Corner (5.4) Climb the wide crack in the corner on the left side of the recess.

D. Eternity (5.10+ TR) The face between *Jam Corner* and *Obsession*. FA: Mike Heintz, 1989.

E. Obsession (5.11– R / X; bolts missing 1978) Start atop the left edge of the block on the ledge. Climb the thin face and finish on the shallow left-facing corner. Bolts were placed on this route and later removed. FA: Bruce Dicks, 1978 (two bolts placed by another climber). FA: Ken Nichols, Chad Hussey, 1985 (using tied-off hooks).

F. Poison & Passion (5.12 TR) The face between *Obsession* and *Sweat Slot*. FA: Mike Heintz, 1989.

G. Sweat Slot (5.5) The off-width crack in the center of the recess.

H. Cowabunga (5.10 R) Ascend the face to the right of *Sweat Slot* and left of *Frostbite*, and continue up the left-facing corner system. FA: Ken Nichols, Bob Clark, Mike Lapierre, Roy Charette, 1981.

I. Frostbite (5.9+ PG / R) A strenuous short climb. Ascend the steep dihedral that forms the right end of the recess. FA: Larry Winship 1968. FFA: Henry Barber, Ajax Green, 1973.

J. On Edge (5.8+ R) Traverse out right from the start of *Frostbite* and ascend the thin face. FA: Ken Nichols, Bob Clark, 1981.

18. The Fall of the House of Monticello (5.11 TR) The steep wall and arête formed by the *Cemetery Vault* corner. Climb the center of the wall, passing a short, broken, left-facing corner. After the corner, move left to the arête; climb it to the top. FA: JD Mackie, 1990. To enjoy the arête at a 5.9 rating, *Cenotaph Corner*, traverse right to the arête from the start of the ramp on *Cemetery Vault*. FA: Ken Nichols, Bob Clark, 1985.

19. Sandbag (5.11 TR) Start at the left-facing corner between *The Fall of the House of Monticello* and *Duck Soup*. Up the large corner to a stance. Then up the steep corner / arête until a few feet from its end, then climb up and right to finish on *Duck Soup*. FA: Ken Nichols, 1984.

20. Duck Soup (5.11; bolt missing 2015; R / X ★) Very good climbing. This route begins on a ledge up and right from *Cemetery Vault* on top of the northern slab. Ascend the steep face (beginning at a small left-facing corner [5.9] or at a thin crack on

the left [5.7]) to a ledge and a rest. Work up the left-leaning crack on the overhanging wall. Near its top an awkward reach enables you to surmount the lip of the wall. Continue straight up to the top. The bolt placed for the hook ascent is missing (2015). FA (toprope): Jim Adair, 1970. FA: Ken Nichols, 1987. *Horse Feathers* variation (5.11 TR): Instead of moving left at the top of the corner / crack, move up and right up the steps.

21. Cro-Magnon (5.11 TR) Climb the steep face between *Duck Soup* and *Neanderthal Wall*. After the first ledge, climb the short right-facing / arching corner up the face above. FA: Ken Nichols, 1996.

22. Neanderthal Wall (5.9+ R) To the right of *Duck Soup* and left of the wall / cave formed by the northern slab, ascend the face to the right end of the *Duck Soup* ledge. Climb a short right-facing corner; when it ends traverse right to a crack and a right-facing corner. Meander up the steep face directly above. FA: Greg Newth, Jeff White, 1977.

23. Stone Age (5.9 R / X) Starting on the right end of the ledge, climb the face between *Neanderthal Wall* and *Marlinspike*, ascending a small left-facing corner system (which comes within a few feet of *Marlinspike* just before the angle lessens). Continue straight up the face above. FA: Ken Nichols, Marco Fedrizzi, 1984.

The following climbs begin on top of the northern slab.

24. Marlinspike (5.8+ ★) The crack beginning from the top left of the northern slab. FA: Sam Streibert, Marlin Scully, 1963.

Ragged Mountain Main Face

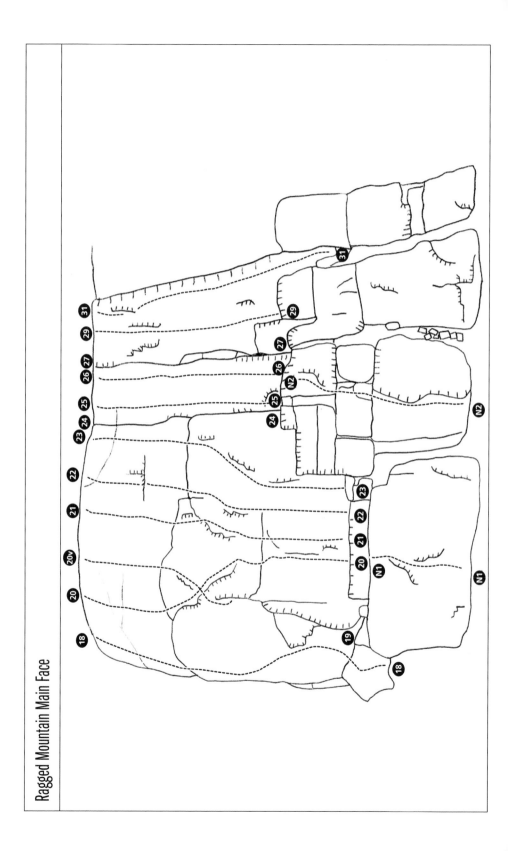

25. Future Shock (5.9+ R ★) Climb the face to the right of *Marlinspike*, heading for an overlap approximately 10 feet right of *Marlinspike*. FA: Doug Madara, Mick Avery, 1977.

26. Tiger Country (5.9+ R) The face to the left of *Double Crux*. FA: Ken Nichols, Sam Slater, Chad Hussey, 1982.

27. Double Crux (5.8 PG) The prominent crack between *Marlinspike* and *Ancient Way*, which begins on top of the northern slab and passes a small overhang on the left at midheight. In 1988 the author came across rock music stars David Lee Roth and guitarist Steve Vai climbing in this area while taking a break from their tour. The many attractive groupies were not a common sight at Ragged. FA: Sam Streibert, Pete Trafton, 1963.

28. Galactic Recession (5.10+ TR) The face between *Double Crux* and *Modern Times*. FA: Ken Nichols, 1996.

29. Modern Times (5.10– R / X) The face between *Double Crux* and *Ancient Way*. Begin on the shallow right-facing corner to the right of *Double Crux*. Climb straight up, then trend right to finish on the left-facing corner system. FA (toprope): Mark Delany, 1973. FA: Ken Nichols, Chad Hussey, 1984.

30. Holy Burning Schnikes (5.10 TR) The face between *Modern Times* and *Apean Way*, finishing on the small left-facing corner of the left-hand *Apean Way* finish. FA: TR Rob LeMire, 1996.

31. Apean Way (5.10 TR ★) The face climb just left (west face) of *Ancient Way*. At midheight you can either continue straight up the face (10+) or trend left and finish up the line of the small left-facing corner (10–). FA: Paul Niland, 1981.

N1. Slabby Face (5.3) The short route up the slab is good for small children.

N2. Northern Slab Route (5.4) The route up the center of the northern slab. *War Eagle* variation (5.7R): To the left of this route, and to the left of a crack, ascend the face past blocks and the face above to the top of the ledge. Named after a peculiar climber from the 1980s.

The following climbs begin on top of the central slab.

C. Central Slab Route (5.4 ★) The route up the center of the central slab. The top of the slab contains an off-width crack, which requires a large piece of gear. To avoid the off-width, traverse left to the gully.

32. Ancient Way (5.4 ★) A natural line and one of the best of its grade. Starting between the northern and central slabs, ascend the right-facing corner system. FA: Betty Woolsey, Roger Whitney, Donald Brown, 1935.

33. Pork Barrel Project (5.9+ R; bolt missing 2015) Begin to the right of *Ancient Way* and left of the birch tree. Climb the thin face, passing a "protruding square," and continue up, aiming for a left-facing corner. Follow the corner, then continue straight up the face. FA: Ken Nichols, Bob Clark, 1982.

34. Pyrrhic Victory (5.10 TR) Climb straight up the face between *Pork Barrel Project* and *Right Under*, passing a few feet right of the *Pork Barrel* corner. FA: Ken Nichols, 1994.

35. Right Under (5.9+ R) Climb the face a few feet to the right of the birch tree. Start at a very small crack (about head height) and continue straight up, passing a shallow left-facing corner system. FA: Brian, Mark Delany, 1973.

36. Leftover (5.8+ PG ★) Approximately 10 feet left of *Deception*, climb the face and shallow crack system to the top. Well protected after a boulder problem start. FA: Sam Streibert, John Dowd, 1964.

37. Deception (5.8) The hand / off-width crack starting from the right side of the central slab. FA: Sam Streibert, John Reppy, 1963.

38. Land-o-Lakes Butter Bank-Busting Sweepstakes (5.10 R ★) The steep and sustained face 5 to 10 feet right of the *Deception* crack. The climb begins on the low ledge between the central and southern slabs. As of 2015 there are about four pitons missing, including a RURP for the crux. FA: Mike Heintz, Ken Nichols, 1981.

39. Lottery Ticket (5.10+ TR) Starting in the blocky area between the central and southern slabs, climb the face between *Land-o-Lakes Butter Bank-Busting Sweepstakes* and *Bloody Sunday*. FA: Ken Nichols, 1994.

The following climbs begin on top of the southern slab.

40. Bloody Sunday (5.9– PG / R) Step off the top left corner of the southern slab to an overlap. Climb straight up the thin crack to the small ledge. Continue straight up the thin crack, splitting the headwall. Somewhat intimidating. FA: Sam Streibert, Steve Arsenault, 1971.

41. Cicada (5.10 TR) Start 9 to 10 feet left of May's Way and climb straight up the face. Midway up trend right a couple feet and up the face to the top. FA: Ken Nichols, 1994.

42. Sunday Bulge (5.6 R) From the start of *May's Way*, climb the left diagonaling ramp / corner system to a ledge beneath a thin crack splitting the headwall. Climb the right diagonaling ramp to a left-facing corner and finish up the face above. FA: John Reppy, Harold May, 1963.

43. May's Way (5.5) Above the southern slab climb the obvious left-facing corner and crack system. At midheight, if you choose, you can escape right on a ramp at 5.2.

44. Barracuda (5.10 R / X) Climb the arête to the right of *May's Way* to the ledge, step right, and continue up the face above. FA: Ken Nichols, Marco Fedrizzi, 1984.

Ragged Mountain Main Face

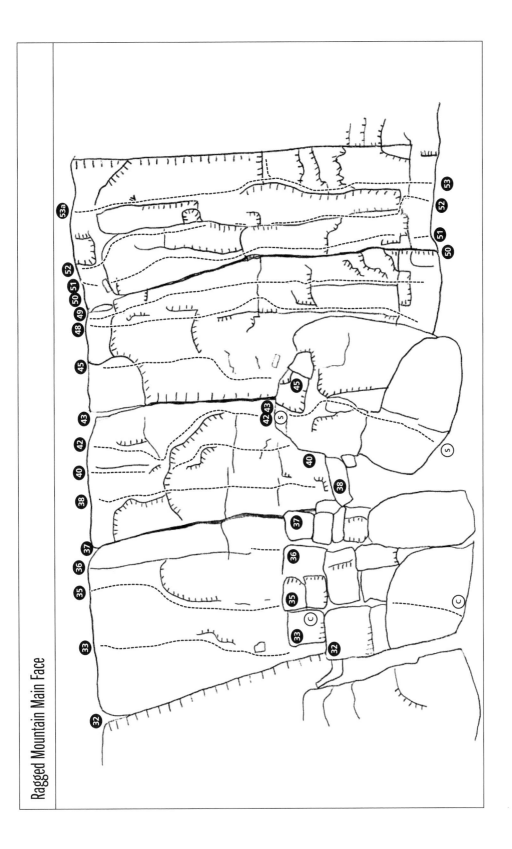

45. Chopper Flakes (5.8+ PG / R) From the top right of the southern slab and left of *Visions*, step onto the face and climb past flakes to buckets formed by a detached flake. Continue past a small ledge and right-facing corner to the ramp. Finish on the ramp. FA: Ken Nichols, Bob Clark, 1981.

The following climbs ascend the southern slab.

S. Southern Slab Route (5.3) Ascend the line up the center of the slab.

46. VMP (5.9+) Start on the south face of the slab. Climb the crack on the left side of the steep wall. FA: John Shelton, Tony Julianelle, 1972.

47. Southside (5.10 R) The crack on the right side of the steep wall. Boulder straight up and then trend right. If you continue straight up, it is 5.8+. FA: Sam Streibert, 1966.

The following climbs begin to the right of the southern slab.

48. Visions (5.11+ R ★; fixed protection missing 2015) Start left of *Unconquerable Crack* and just right of the base of the southern slab. Climb a short left-facing corner and continue up a thin crack to another left-facing corner. Work up and right a few feet (you can continue up the crack at 5.11) to a stance, and then continue up the face, trending left slightly, to a small ledge and a rest. Continue up the shallow corner and face above—sustained. Holds have broken off since the first ascent, changing the grade from the original 5.10+ rating. FA: Harry Brielman, Bill Lutkus, 1979.

49. Double Vision (5.12 TR) Climb up the middle of the roof and continue up the thin crack to a stance. Continue up the face midway between *Visions* and *Unconquerable Crack*. FA: Ken Nichols, 1984.

50. Unconquerable Crack (5.9+ ★) One of the best lines in Connecticut. Follow the steep hand and off-width crack. Well protected with a good selection of stoppers and camming units. FA: Sam Streibert, John Reppy, 1963. FFA: John Reppy, Sam Streibert, 1964.

51. Ashtray (5.11+ R ★; fixed protection missing 2015) Launch over the overhanging flake to the right of *Unconquerable Crack* and left of *Subline*. Work up the face to a stance just right of *Unconquerable Crack* in a left-facing corner system. Climb the left-facing corner system, and continue up the face to the left of *Subline* to the top. FA: Sam Slater, Harry Brielman, Chad Hussey, 1984.

52. Subline (5.11– PG ★; protection generally good but strenuous to place) One of the best lines in Connecticut. Work past the overhanging flake to a thin crack (a knee lock and small camming unit are helpful for the start). Continue up the crack and corner system to the top. This is also a very good climb to practice aid climbing. If aid-climbing the route, do not use a hammer! The route goes clean at C1+. *Historical note:* In the 1970s Henry Barber, who first climbed the route free, was one of the best free climbers in the world. One of his more famous climbs was his on-site first ascent of *Butterballs* (5.11) in Yosemite Valley. *Butterballs* is a stunning finger crack that rebuffed attempts at a free ascent by Yosemite locals and visiting climbers until "Hot Henry" sent it in 1973. FA: Sam Streibert, John Reppy, 1963. FFA: Henry Barber, Bob Anderson, 1972.

53. Bombay (5.9) Start at the overhanging flake and work right into the large right-facing corner. At the top of the corner,

Anne Parmenter following *Bombay Indirect* PHOTO BOB CLARK

move right under the small roof and continue up the large right-facing corner. FA: John Reppy, Bob Durham, 1965.

53a Bottom Line Variation (5.10 PG / R) After the initial corner on *Bombay*, continue straight up the steep face instead of moving out right. Follow the right-facing corner system and face to the top. FA (toprope): Jim Adair 1977. FA: Ken Nichols, 1983.

53b Bombay Direct Variation (5.10– ★) Starting to the right of *Bombay*, ascend overlaps and a vertical crack (bolt missing 2015, but still well protected) that leads to the prominent right-facing corner on the upper section of *Bombay*. FA: Ken Nichols, Jim Fitzpatrick, 1975.

53c Calcutta Variation (5.11 TR) The left side of the arête formed by the upper *Bombay* corner. FA: Ken Nichols, 1985.

53d Bombay Indirect Variation (5.10– PG / R) Climb the overhang left of *Main Street* and up a corner. Traverse left following a crack to *Bombay*. Finish up *Bombay*. FA: Ed Webster, Casey Newman, 1975.

54. Indian Empire (5.11 TR) Start between *Bombay Direct* and *Old Man of Ragged*. Climb past the overlaps and straight up the face, finishing left of the final corner on *Old Man of Ragged*. FA: Ken Nichols, 1996.

55. Old Man of Ragged (5.11 TR ★) Interesting and sustained climbing. Pull the

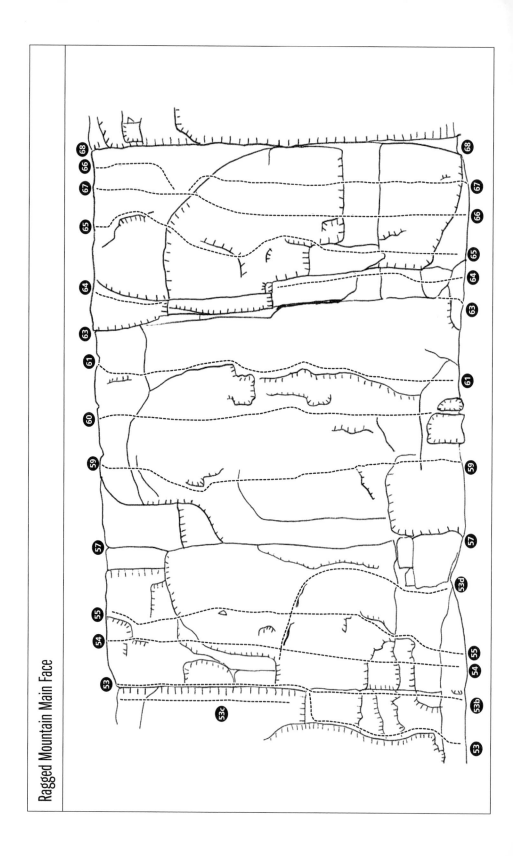

roof approximately 10 feet to the right of *Bombay Direct* and move slightly right. Work up the face to about midheight, where you encounter a triangular hole. From this point jog left and then continue up the face past a shallow crack. FA: Ken Nichols, 1992.

56. Fountain of Youth (5.9+ TR) Climb the face to the left of Main Street, past the overhang, to the left-facing corner on *Bombay Indirect*. When *Bombay Indirect* heads left, continue up and right, following the left side of the *Main Street* arête. FA (toprope): Ken Nichols, 1992.

57. Main Street (5.6 PG) To the right of *Old Man of Ragged*, climb the obvious crack / chimney system that widens at the top. If you begin on the left side (north) of the block, the initial crack is 5.8. Most people scramble up from the right side of the block. FA: Fritz Wiessner, Roger Whitney, Charles Houston, 1935. *Historical note:* In 1938 Houston, while attempting the first ascent of the Abruzzi Ridge on K2, climbed one of the most difficult sections of the route—the *House Chimney*. Houston and Paul Petzoldt came within 700 meters of the summit but were turned back due to weather. However, the *House Chimney* has been used by every subsequent expedition on the Abruzzi Ridge (Fay, Bent, et al, 2002).

58. Big Bang (5.10 TR) Starting about 4 feet to the right of the *Main Street* arête, climb straight up the face, finishing on the right side of the short arête on *Main Street*. FA: Ken Nichols, 1994.

59. Steady State (5.10– R / X) From the left side of the blocks leaning against the cliff—10 feet right of *Main Street*—climb the face past a small ledge, aiming for a small left-facing corner and overlap. Follow the

path of least resistance straight to the top. FA: Ken Nichols, Marco Fedrizzi, 1984.

60. Continuous Creation (5.10+ R / X) Better than it looks. Start from the middle of the block leaning against the wall. Climb the face to the left edge of the overlap. Continue up the shallow corner system and face on the left to the ledge. Go straight up the headwall to the top. FA: Ken Nichols, Sam Slater, 1983.

61. For Madmen Only (5.9 R; bolt missing 2015) Fifteen feet left of *Wishbone*, climb the right-facing corner system to a small roof. Continue up the right-facing corner system to the ledge. Move a few feet left, work past the bulge, then climb back right and up the face. FA: Bob Anderson, Sam Streibert, Al Rubin, 1973.

62. Insanity Defense (5.9+ R / X) Climb straight up the face midway between *For Madmen Only* and *Wishbone*. FA: Ken Nichols, Howard Carney, 1994.

63. Wishbone (5.7+ ★) Begin up the wishbone-like overlaps and prominent crack system, which leads to a large left-facing corner and crack system. FA: Sam Streibert, 1965.

64. Kor Crack (5.9 ★) Don't be lured onto this route without a large piece of gear for the wide crack past the roof. Begin on *Wishbone* and move right into the crack system that cleaves the overhang. Once past the overhang the difficulty eases and follows a wide crack. The roof (crux) is well protected; getting to the roof can be strenuous to protect. *Historical note:* Layton Kor made several notable first ascents in Colorado, California, and the Southwest deserts during the 1960s. FA: Layton Kor, John Reppy, 1964.

65. Foobah (5.9+ R) To the right of *Kor Crack*, a boulder problem over the corner of

Jim McCarthy on *Bushy Groove*, 1964
PHOTO SAM STREIBERT

the roof leads to a left-facing corner. Climb up to and around this corner on the right, and continue straight up the face. FA: Doug Madara, Jim Adair, 1976.

66. High Anxiety (5.11 TR) Climb the overlap and face between *Foobah* and *Suspense* to the overhang. Over the overhang, aiming for a short right-facing corner. When you reach the left-trending ramp / ledge, traverse up and right 4 feet and finish up the steep face. FA: Ken Nichols, 1996.

67. Suspense (5.9 R) Approximately 10 feet to the left of the *Bushy Groove* corner, climb the low overhang and slab above. Continue past the next overhang and up the face to a left-leaning ramp. Follow the ramp and short

face to the top. FA: Ken Nichols, Mike Heintz, Bill Ivanoff, Chad Hussey, 1981.

68. Bushy Groove (5.8 ★) A neglected climb. Climb the prominent left-facing corner system to the top. FA: John Reppy, 1955.

69. Slingshot (5.9+) A good boulder problem (or mini TR) for the crack climber. Climb the overhanging hand / off-width crack on the block to the right of *Bushy Groove* and underneath *Juniper Wall*. FA: Sam Streibert, 1964.

70. Taproot (5.9+ R / X) Climb the crack between the main wall and *Slingshot* block. Climb the face and arête to the ledge on *Juniper Wall*. Finish up *Juniper Wall*. FA: Mike Heintz, Ken Nichols, 1981.

71. Juniper Wall (5.7 PG ★) Begin to the right of the *Slingshot* block. Climb the crack and corner system to the ramp. Move up and left on the ramp to its top and the base of a steep headwall. A long reach gains a crack system and face, which is followed to the top. The crux can be strenuous to protect (pitons missing for many years), and a ledge awaits you if you blow it. FA: Fritz Wiessner, Betty Woolsey, Bill House, 1934. *Historical note:* Fritz Wiessner is credited with the first recorded technical rock climb in the Shawangunks in 1935. *Mad Dog* variation (5.10+ R): Climb the face above the *Slingshot* block between *Taproot* and *Juniper Wall* to the ledge. FA: Bill Lutkus, 1984.

72. The Prince (5.9 R) Begin at the hairline crack just to the right of *Juniper Wall*. Climb up the face to the ledge. Continue straight up the vertical crack to the top. Poor protection getting to the crux. FA: Sam Streibert, John Reppy, 1965.

73. Bald-Faced Hornet (5.11 R / X) Starting at the left edge of the block, just left of

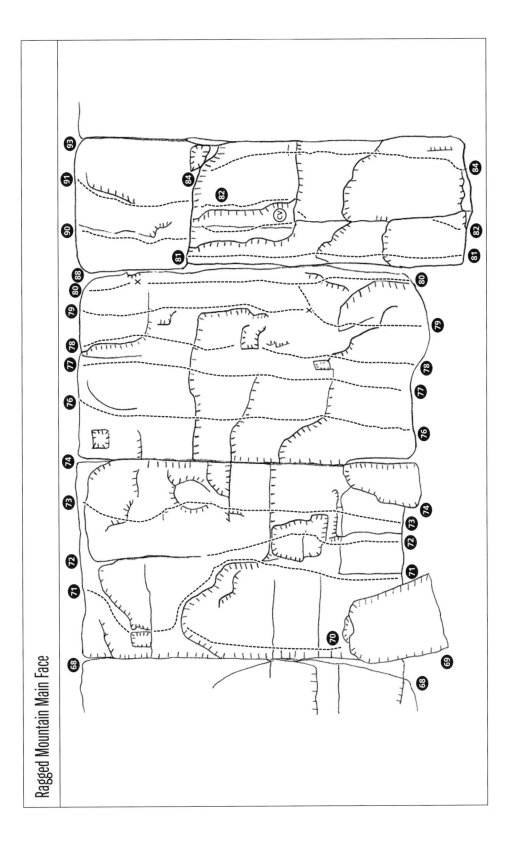

Bill Lutkus on *Vector* PHOTO DAVID FASULO

Vector, climb the face to the circular hole. Climb up and left to a small overhang and left-facing corner. Move up, then right, and continue up the face. FA: Ken Nichols, Marco Fedrizzi, 1984.

74. Vector (5.8 ★) Start behind the free-standing block. Climb the prominent left-facing corner and crack system that passes an overlap at two-thirds height. Legend has it that Fritz Wiessner led this line using only one piton for protection. According to Waterman (1993), "Fritz went up twice to try it but each time turned back, reluctant to commit himself to such a strenuous and unprotected sequence of moves. On the third occasion he made the commitment and completed what probably remained the hardest single pitch lead in the country for almost twenty years." Keep that in mind at the crux, while you are stuffing in camming units, standing in sticky rubber shoes, tied into a state-of-the-art dynamic rope, and comforted by a padded harness. FA: Fritz Wiessner, Roger Whitney, 1935.

75. Laughingstock (5.10– TR) Climb the center of the slab just right of *Vector*. Ascend the face between *Vector* and *The Last Laugh*. FA: Ken Nichols, 1992.

76. The Last Laugh (5.10 R) The original fixed bashie used for the crux has long since disappeared—not that it was reliable in the first place. Approximately 5 feet to the right of *Vector*, climb straight up the face, aiming for a curving crack near the top of the cliff. Good climbing on the crux section. FA: Jim Adair, Bruce Dicks, 1978.

77. Calculated Risk (5.9 R) The face between *The Last Laugh* and *Side Entry*, which avoids the final corner on *Side Entry*. FA: Ken Nichols, Mike Day, David Fasulo, Jim Wilcox, 1992.

78. Side Entry (5.7+ PG) An intimidating route on shaky rock. Start approximately 15 feet to the right of *Vector*, aiming for a protruding block. Step right from the block and work over the shaky overlap. After the overlap step right again and finish up a right-facing corner to the top. FA: Sam Streibert, John Reppy, 1963.

79. Terminal Velocity (5.9+ PG; bolt missing 2015) Approximately 10 feet to the left of the *Vajolet Corner* start, ascend the steep face past a bolt and a thin crack to a stance at the base of a right-facing corner near the top. Finish on the face to the left of the corner (first ascent line) or the short face to the right of the corner. FA: Chris Plant, Chad Hussey, Ken Nichols, 1983.

80. Vajolet Corner (5.10– PG / R ★; bolt missing 2015) This is an excellent route with sustained climbing. Work up the face just left of *Wiessner Slab* to the arête. Continue up the arête; pass a bolt and the crux, where continually challenging moves lead to the top. Small gear is helpful getting to the bolt. FA: Sam Streibert, Dennis Merritt, 1971. *Rebate* variation (5.8+ PG): An enjoyable variation is to climb *Terminal Velocity* to the bolt (missing 2015). From the bolt, thin face climbing leads right to join the normal route (5.10).

The Wiessner Slab

The next four routes climb Wiessner Slab, the low-angle slab that is detached from the main wall. To descend from the top of the slab, the climber must either rappel or continue to the top via another route, *Knight's Move* being the easiest. There has been a swaged cable attached to a block to allow climbers to rappel the slab, but you should not count on it being there.

81. Left Edge (5.6 R) Face-climb the left side of the slab. FA: Ed Webster, Ken Nichols, 1974.

82. Wiessner Slab (5.3 ★) Begin at the center of the slab and ascend the main crack system to a ledge midway. Move right to a shallow left-facing corner and follow it to the top. FA: Fritz Wiessner, Bill Burling 1933. *Crack* variation (5.3 ★): Instead of moving out right to the shallow corner, continue straight up the main crack system, which is better protected.

83. Lunar Eclipse (5.8 R) Over the overhang and up the face between *Wiessner Slab* and *Right Edge*. FRA: Ken Nichols, Paul Maresca, Mike Day, Ron Reichler, 1989.

Kevin Fasulo on the *Wiessner Slab* PHOTO DAVID FASULO

84. Right Edge (5.7 PG ★) Climb the right edge of the slab to a stance below a smooth wall. Place protection and conquer the low-angled crux with the gear just below your feet. FA: Bob Harding, Al Rubin, 1972.

85. Southern Exposure (5.10+ TR) The diagonal crack on the right (southern) side of the *Wiessner Slab*. FRA: Howard Carney, 1996.

The following routes begin from the top of Wiessner Slab.

86. Hot Rocks (5.10– PG / R) From the left side of *Wiessner Slab*, climb the steep crack system on the south face, next to the *Vajolet Corner* arête. Protection is strenuous to place. FA: Henry Barber, Ajax Green, 1972.

87. Cutting Edge (5.11 R) Start just left of *Tower Crack* on the south-facing wall. Climb the steep and intricate face. FA: Bill Lutkus, Chad Hussey, Jim Wilcox, 1988.

88. Tower Crack (5.7+) Good training for Devil's Tower in Wyoming, and may have assisted Fritz Wiessner on his subsequent first free ascent of Devil's Tower. On June 28, 1937, Fritz, along with William House and Lawrence Coveny, made the first free ascent of Devil's Tower, placing only one piton en route. The tower had been previously summited in 1893 by means of a 350-foot-long "ladder" made of wooden wedges. *Tower Crack* ascends the off-width crack and corner and the junction of the south-facing and west-facing walls. FA: Fritz Wiessner, Percy Olton, William Burling, 1933.

89. Un Petit Peu (5.12– TR) The difficult face between *Tower Crack* and *Faceout*. FA: Chris Tacy, 1990.

90. Faceout (5.8 PG) Begin approximately 5 feet to the right of *Tower Crack*. Climb the face to the flake and thin crack above (piton missing 2015). FA: Sam Streibert, John Parker, 1964.

91. Jessica (5.8+ R) Climb the face between *Faceout* and *Wiessner Crack*, which leads to a small corner leading to the top. FA: Bob Clark, Bill Sullivan, 1981.

92. Nux Vomica (5.11+ TR) The technical face between *Jessica* and *Wiessner Crack*. FA: Harry Brielman, 1990.

93. Wiessner Crack (5.8+ PG ★) Climb the prominent left-facing dihedral at the right end of the recess. The original guide from 1964 states, "The shallow cracks pose a problem for piton placement." Even with modern gear, awkward to protect for the inexperienced leader. A difficult climb at the time of the first ascent. FA: Fritz Wiessner, Hassler Whitney, Roger Whitney, 1934. *Historical note: Vector* is often noted as the first 5.8 in the United States. However, *Traprock Connecticut Rock Climbs* by Ken Nichols (1982) indicates *Wiessner Crack* was climbed (free?) a year before Wiessner's ascent of *Vector*.

94. Knight's Move (5.4 ★) Exciting and exposed. Although not difficult, care should be taken when protecting the second for the awkward step from *Wiessner Slab* to the traverse ledge. From the top of the *Wiessner Slab*, traverse under the block on the right edge of the slab to reach a traverse ledge. Follow this ledge to a short crack (crux), which leads to a ledge and the final corner / crack.

Kalmia Buels on *Wet Wall* PHOTO DAVID FASULO

The following routes begin to the right of *Wiessner Slab*.

95. Laverado Corner (5.7+ R ★) Start just right of *Wiessner Slab* on the main face and ascend left-facing corners, just to the left of *Knight's Gambit*, to the *Knight's Move* ledge. Climb the jammed block or the face to the right (5.8+ *Knight's Gambit* bolt missing 2015), and continue up the face and arête to the top. FA: Sam Streibert, Al Rubin, Tony Julianelle, 1972.

96. Knight's Gambit (5.7+ PG ★; bolts missing 2015) Enjoyable and exposed climbing on the upper face. To the right of Laverado Corner, move up and right, passing a bolt. Work up the corner (small TCU helpful at a horizontal crack) and small overhang to the Knight's Move ledge. Climb the face and left-facing corner to the right of the bolt to a left-facing flake. Follow cracks and corners to the top, trending a little left at the finish. FA: Sam Streibert, Ed Arens, 1964.

97. Ferret (5.10– R) Starting behind the hemlock tree, climb the face to the right of *Knight's Gambit* to the *Knight's Move* traverse ledge. Follow the shallow, poorly protected, right-facing corner between *Laverado Corner* and *Knight's Gambit* (5.8+) to the top. The corner above the traverse ledge makes a good variation to *Knight's Gambit*. FA: Mike Guravage, 1983.

98. En Passant (5.9 R) The face left of *Wet Wall* follows small, sharp holds to an overlap. When you reach the ledge at the base of the final corner on *Knight's Move*, step left and climb the face left of the arête. FA: Harry Brielman, George Cocores, 1978.

99. Wet Wall (5.6 PG ★) A good introduction to the Ragged Mountain Main Face. Approximately 15 feet left of the *Hemlock Groove* crack system, climb up and right, passing overlaps and a short right-facing corner. Head left and ascend a corner containing a crack. Climb the face to the right of the *Knight's Move* crack systems. If you are leading at this level, the bottom crux is not well protected. FA: Fritz Wiessner, Donald Brown, 1935. *Wetlock* variation (5.6 PG; 99v): After the lower crux arch on Wet Wall, move up and right to a vertical crack system that connects to *Hemlock Groove*. FA: Sam Streibert, John Reppy, 1965.

100. Islands (5.10 R / X) Climb the face and overhang left of *Hemlock Groove*. Continue up the face to the prominent crack left of the arête, then to the top of a pedestal. Finish on the face to the left of the arête. Variation (5.10 TR): Ascend the face to the second roof, over it, and up the center of the pedestal. Finish on the regular route. FA (toprope): Stewart Sayah, 1983. FA: Ken Nichols, Lanier Benkard, Lisa Pesci, Bill Lyttle, Dave Hirschler, 1996.

101. Hemlock Groove (5.6 PG) Approximately 10 feet to the left of *YMC Route* is an off-width crack with a dead tree. Follow the crack system to the top. The upper section has a bolt (missing in 2015), which protects the last 15 feet. FA: Fritz Wiessner, Henry Beers, Bill Burling, 1934.

102. Netherlands (5.10– R ★) Excellent face climbing. Start between *Hemlock Groove* and *YMC Route*. Follow the path of least resistance straight up the wall until you are at

Ragged Mountain Main Face

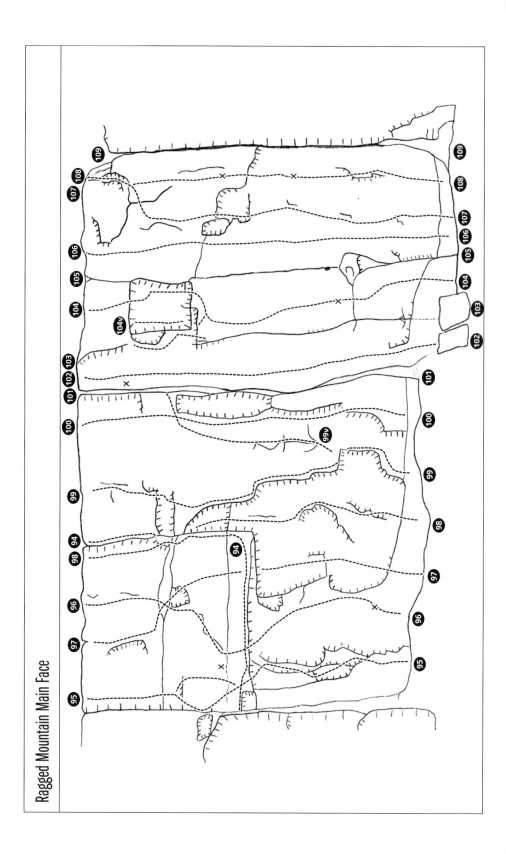

the same height as the *Skull and Bones* block. From here the climb jogs left slightly to a point where it is within a few feet of *Hemlock Groove*. Pass this section and continue up the face between *YMC* and *Hemlock Groove*. The marginal fixed protection that was once used on the route has vanished over time. FA: Harry Brielman, Ken Nichols, 1979.

103. Yale Mountaineering Club (YMC Route) (5.9 ★) A Ragged Mountain classic. Climb the crack system that leads past the left side of the large protruding block. If the piton at the start is missing, the beginning is a little run-out. However, the rest of the climb is well protected and has adequate stances to place gear. FA: John Reppy, Will McMahon, 1963. FFA: Dick Williams, John Reppy, 1964.

104. Skull and Bones (5.11 R; bolt and piton missing 2015) Start approximately 5 feet left of *Broadway* and ascend the face to a depression. Pass fixed protection (bolt and piton), trending left then straight up to the block. Traverse to the right edge of the block and work up the arête to the top of the block. Continue up the middle of the short wall above. The block has become more difficult since a large portion of the right corner fell off. FA: Ken Nichols, Mike Heintz, Bob Obrien, 1981. *Visitor Reception Center* variation (5.12+ TR): From the base of the block, work up and over the left edge of the roof. FA: TR Bill Lutkus, 1986.

105. Broadway (5.8 PG ★) Climb the crack system that leads past the right side of the overhanging block. If the pitons are missing at the hole / depression 30 feet up, the protection can be difficult to place. Good technique is helpful at the top of the block. In 1998 a climber took a headfirst ground

fall from the "hole." The leader was wearing a bicycle helmet, which chipped off a corner of a large block at the base. Although the climber sustained injuries, the helmet probably saved his life. FA: John Reppy, Gil Young, Frank Carey, 1958.

106. Times Square (5.10+ TR) Starting 5 to 6 feet right of *Broadway*, climb the face to the blocky ledge. Climb up and right, staying just left of the *Carolyn* corner and left of the arch above. FA: Ken Nichols, 1985.

107. Carolyn (5.9 X) Approximately 10 feet to the right of Broadway, work your way up the face, passing an overlap on the right to the prominent ledge. Continue up a small right-facing corner until it fades. Traverse out right, aiming for an overlap that is climbed on the right. Finish up the face above. FA: Mark Delany, April 1974.

108. Atlantic Hurricane (5.10 R / X; bolts missing 2015) Climb the face approximately 5 feet to the left of *Carey Corner* to the ledge. Continue up a thin crack to an overlap, which is followed to the right to finish on *Carolyn*. Originally led with tied-off hooks and supplemented with two bolts—one midway up the face below the ledge and one just above the ledge. FA: Ken Nichols, Bob Finch, David Fasulo, Chad Hussey, Jim Wilcox, Wes Beman, Al Rubin, 1985.

109. Carey Corner (5.8– ★) The obvious crack and left-facing corner system left of *Cygnus X-1* and right of *Broadway*. Carry a wide selection of gear, from small wires to larger camming devices. Crack climbing and stemming skills put to the test. A classic route, loved by some and loathed by others. FA: Fritz Wiessner, Bill Burling, Henry Beers, 1935.

Sam Streibert, co-author of the first climbing guide to Ragged published in 1964, on *Broadway* in 2015. PHOTO DAVID FASULO

110. Black Orchid (5.11 PG / R; pro difficult to place) From the ledge midway up *Carey Corner*, climb the thin crack to the left of the *Cygnus X-1* arête. FA: Bill Lutkus, Greg Jones, 1980s. FFA (toprope): Bill Lutkus. FA: Ken Nichols, Bill Lyttle, Howard Carney, 1997.

111. Cygnus X-1 (5.11 TR ★) An excellent and sustained line. Start approximately 5 feet to the right of *Carey Corner*. Climb over the overlap into the left-facing corner and roof. Make a long reach out right and step right around the corner to a small stance. Climb up and left, traversing just over the lip of the overhang to a stance on the arête (awkward no-hands rest). Continue up the arête to the horizontal crack. Finish up the strenuous *Ragged Edge* arête. FA: Ken Nichols, 1984. *Swan Song* variation (5.11 TR): Instead of heading right at the first roof, head left and layback over the roof to join the arête. FA: Sam Slater, 1990.

112. Golden Age (5.12 TR) A difficult link-up of two routes climbing directly up the overhanging aspects of the *Ragged Edge* arête. Start following the *Swan Song* variation of *Cygnus X-1* (left at the roof, then layback out the arête) and follow the arête until about halfway up. At an undercling, swing out left to the crack on the northern overhanging face (Black Orchid) and work a compression sequence up the *Ragged Edge* arête. FA: Morgan Patterson, 2012.

113. Crag Rat (5.11 TR) Contrived but good climbing. Best climbed from a toprope off of *Angle of the Dangle*. Start just right of *Carey Corner* and traverse up and right to the roof. Climb directly over the roof below and to the right of *Cygnus X-1* (strenuous layback-ing). Follow the right-facing corner system of *Ragged Edge* to a thin horizontal crack near the top. Finger-traverse right, following a thin crack / seam, and finish just left of *Vanishing Point* (using the crack on *Vanishing Point*).

Memorial plaque: The memorial plaque is dedicated to Ragged Mountain climber Jim Adair. Jim was the first to ascend many of Connecticut's most classic and daring lines—including the breathtaking *Ragged Edge*—exhibiting great vision and talent. Tragically, he was killed in a climbing accident on Sentinel Rock in Yosemite Valley, California, in 1978. Jim's ashes were spread on top of Ragged Mountain, and his parents erected the memorial plaque. In June 1997 the plaque was stolen. In spring 2000 the Ragged Mountain Foundation, along with the Adair family, replaced the plaque, using a replica of the original.

114. Ragged Edge (5.10+ PG / R ★; rated R if the fixed pitons are missing) A bold and significant ascent of the times in 1977. Begin at the memorial plaque and work up left to an overlap, then up left again to a small ledge. Climb up a small right-facing corner and traverse left to the more prominent right-facing / left diagonal corner system, passing fixed pitons to a horizontal crack with a fixed piton (missing 2015). Traverse left to the arête and climb this, with much exposure, to the top. FA: Jim Adair, Sam Slater, Bruce Dicks, 1977.

Justine Pasniewski, *Carey Corner* PHOTO DAVID FASULO

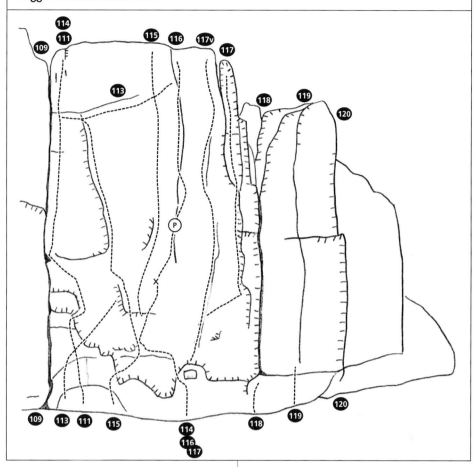

Angle of the Dangle Direct Start (5.7+ ★): *Vanishing Point* and the Ragged Edge start from a stance below the memorial plaque to the right of the large hemlock. Many climbers, however, prefer to begin these routes on *Angle of the Dangle*. The beginning is bouldered until you can place a TCU in the overlap.

115. Angle of the Dangle (5.11 or 5.12– TR; rating dependent on the top sequence)

From behind the large hemlock tree, boulder up and across a left-facing corner to the base of an overlap. Climb past the overlap to a small ledge. Ascend the shallow corners and face to the left of the *Vanishing Point* crack. Holds within inches of the crack make the route 5.11. Staying farther to the left ups the grade to 5.12–.

116. Vanishing Point (5.10+ PG ★; bolt and piton missing 2015)

Begin at the memorial plaque and work up left to an overlap. From the overlap climb up and left to a stance at the base of a tiny left-facing corner. From here climb diagonally up and right, passing a bolt, and into a thin crack with a piton. Follow the finger crack to the top. The original bolt on *Vanishing Point* was placed on rappel in 1976. This bolt was removed, replaced again, and later chopped. A new bolt, also placed in 1976, was placed on the lead. The new bolt was stolen in the early 1990s. It was replaced, along with the crux piton, in 1999. Shortly after being replaced, all protection on the route was again stolen, and holds (approximately eight) were chopped off the route. FA: Bruce Dicks, Mike Heintz, Mick Avery, 1976.

117. Vanishing Gutter (5.6 PG / R) Climb the face above the memorial plaque until you can traverse right to a right-facing corner. Ascend the corner system to the top. FA: Bruce Dicks, Jim Adair, 1977. *Pointless* variation (5.10+ TR) Instead of traversing right to the corner system, ascend the face to the right of *Vanishing Point* and left of *Vanishing Gutter*. FA: TR Brian Delany, 1972.

118. Green Gutter (5.5) The inside corner to the right of *Vanishing Gutter*. FA: Fritz Wiessner, 1930s.

119. Once Is Enough (5.10 R) The steep face and incipient crack to the right of *Green Gutter*. The fixed protection is long gone. FA: Bruce Dicks, 1976.

120. Thwart (5.7) The short corner on the southern (right) side of the Main Face. FA: John Reppy, Sam Streibert, 1965.

The Main Face Boulders

The stretch of rock outcroppings scattered between the Main Face and the Small Cliff offers a variety of bouldering possibilities.

Ragged Mountain Small Cliff, Outcrop, and Other Crags

The Small Cliff is the 50-foot crag located between the Outcrop and May Crack Block. In September 1999 the area was closed by one of the private landowners for an unspecified period of time to allow the area to regenerate (see "Access to Climbing Areas" in the introduction). Also of note is the once popular Outcrop Crag. Located on private property, this is the small but steep outcrop of rock located northwest of the Small Cliff. From the base of the Small Cliff (*Anticipation* and *Roundabout* routes), walk through the talus that dips down to the base of the Outcrop. The Outcrop has been frequented by climbers since Sam Streibert ascended the route *Cracker Jack* in the 1960s. Popular routes included *Cliffhanger* (5.11) on the south face and the 5.9 cracks on the short east-facing wall. Other once-popular crags stretching from the Small Cliff to Owl's Lair include: May Crack Block (with the striking *May Crack* [5.8]), Bloody Head Buttress, and Citadel (thirty-two established routes). Most of these areas lie on private property and are not included in this edition. Climbing at these areas was a privilege, not a right. They will, it is hoped, be officially reopened in the future.

Owl's Lair

Owl's Lair is owned by the New Britain Water Company and is not currently open (as of 2015) to climbing. This area has been frequented by climbers since at least the 1970s, and the information is included for historical purposes and in the hopes that Owl's Lair may be opened to climbers in the future. Owl's Lair is about 50 feet high, faces southeast, has some very good climbs, and was a favorite spot for climbers on cold days. From Owl's Lair, if continuing toward West Lane in Berlin, other formerly popular crags (which are not included because they are on private property) include Junkyard, Wasp's Nest, and Cathedral Rock.

Climbs are described from left to right.

1. The Good (5.8–) The short crack that begins on the left side of the main wall, about 15 feet right of the descent gully. FA: Doug Madara, Casey Newman, 1975. There is an even shorter crack to the left, *Gaunlet*, which is rated 5.6.

2. Magnum Force (5.10 TR) Climb the face to the left of *The Bad*, finishing left of the short arête near the top. FA: Ken Nichols, 1992.

3. The Bad (5.8) The left-facing corner system, which finishes at the top of the descent gully. FA: Ken Nichols, Dave Feldman, 1976.

4. The Sanction (5.10– R) The face between *The Bad* and *The Ugly*. FA: Ken Nichols, Tim Jones, David Fasulo, 1987.

5. The Ugly (5.7 PG) The rabbly crack and left-facing corner system to the right of *The Bad*. FA: Ken Nichols, Dave Feldman, 1976.

6. The Enforcer (5.11 R ★; fixed pitons missing 2015) A steep and strenuous line. Scramble up the ledge to the base of a thin crack on the steep wall to the left of *Serendipity*. Follow the crack and face above to the top. FA: Ken Nichols, Marco Fedrizzi, 1984.

7. Pale Rider (5.11 TR) The face between *The Enforcer* and *Serendipity*. FA: TR Chris Tacy, 1991.

8. Serendipity (5.5 ★) The prominent left-facing corner system. FA: Casey Newman, Doug Madara, 1975.

9. De Sade (5.12– TR) Begin on *Serendipity* and climb the roof to the left of *Mad Crack* using a crack. Continue up the overhanging south face, avoiding the *Serendipity* arête. FA: JD Mackie, 1992.

10. Mad Crack (5.9+) Climb the short face to the right of *Serendipity* and continue up the hand crack, which splits the overhang. From the ledge move right, climb a left-facing corner to a ledge, move right again, and finish up another left-facing corner. FA: Doug Madara, Casey Newman, 1975. Variation (5.10+): After the first left-facing corner, continue straight up the face instead of traversing right to the final corner.

11. Sabertooth (5.10+ R ★; bolt missing 2015) Climb *Mad Crack* through the roof to the ledge. Work up the arête and face to the right. FA: Chris Tacy, 1992. Variation (5.10+ R): From the ledge work left around to the overhanging face and climb to the horizontal crack on the arête. FA: Ken Nichols, Chad Hussey, 1983.

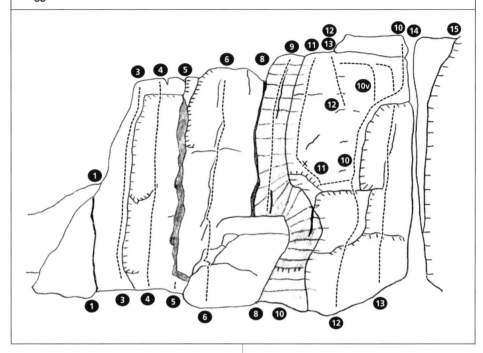

12. Hang 'Em High (5.10+TR) Cool climbing on the upper wall. Start on the face to the left of *Divide and Conquer* (about 10 feet right of the *Mad Crack* arête) and climb up the face, gaining the upper Mad Crack corner. Near the top of the corner, move left on the face and finish on *Divide and Conquer*. FA: Chris Tacy from the ledge above the overhanging crack. FA: Ken Nichols, 1992.

13. Divide and Conquer (5.10– R) Climb the face approximately 8 feet left of *Erebus* to the ledge. Finish up the final corner on *Mad Crack*, or climb the face to the left of the corner to a horizontal crack. Traverse left at the horizontal crack and scramble to the top. FA: Ken Nichols, 1983.

14. Erebus (5.6) Begin at the large left-facing corner and crack system to the right of *Serendipity*. Work up the left-hand crack

and chimney system. FA: Doug Madara, Casey Newman, 1975.

15. Cul-de-Sac (5.5) The right hand–chimney and corner system to the right of *Erebus*. FA: Gary Later, Joyce Franklin, 1977.

16. The Gray Face: There are a couple of toprope climbs on the gray face to the right of *Cul-de-Sac*. The face approximately 5 feet to the right of *Cul-de-Sac*, *Bite the Dust*, is 5.10+R. FA: Ken Nichols, 1986. The face to the right of the 5.10+ and left of the outside corner is a 5.8 TR, *Al'sheimer's Disease*, which finishes up a short corner system near the top. FA: Al Carilli, 1992.

17. Freeze-Thaw Cycle (5.9 R / X) To the right of *The Gray Face*, climb just right of the arête and left of *Talon* to the topmost ledge and finish on *Talon*. FA: Ken Nichols, Bruce Jelen, Howard Carney, Sandy Carney, 1992.

Ragged Mountain Owl's Lair

18. Talon (5.9+ R / X; bolt missing 2015) Begin at a flake on the face to the left of *Piggyback Flake*. Climb the flake and face above, aiming for a small right-facing corner that brings you to a stance. Continue straight up the face above. FA: Ken Nichols, Bob Clark, 1985.

19. Piggyback Flake (5.4) The right-facing corner and crack system, which finishes on a short left-facing corner. FA: Dave Feldman, Ken Nichols, 1976.

20. Dustbuster (5.10 R / X) Start on the right of the arching corner and work your way up to the top. FA: Ken Nichols, Chuck Boyd, 1985.

21. Cedar Shingles (5.8 R) Climb the face left of *Sore Throat* and finish on the left-facing corner. FA: Ken Nichols, Franco Ghiggeri, 1980.

22. Sore Throat (5.4) Begin at a flake on the face to the right of *Piggyback Flake*. Climb the flake and face above, aiming for a small right-facing corner that brings you to a stance. Continue straight up the face above. FA: Ken Nichols, 1980.

23. Prime Rib (5.10+ R; bolt missing 2015) A wild ride that is safer to toprope. Climb up the steep south-facing rib of Lost Owl Spire. FA: Ken Nichols, Mike Heintz, Kim Smith, 1982.

24. New Year's Resolution (5.11– TR) Follow the right edge of the *Prime Rib* arête, passing ledges, to the final face a few feet to the right of the arête. FA: Ken Nichols, 1996.

25. Happy New Year (5.9+ PG) Climb the right-center wall on the front of the spire. FA: Ken Nichols, Bill Sullivan, Mike Lapierre, Chad Hussey, Mike Guravage, 1983.

BRADLEY MOUNTAIN, SOUTHINGTON

Hidden in the woods and easily accessed from Crescent Lake Park, the Fire Wall at Bradley Mountain is the ideal spot for climbers looking for steep roofs, corners, and intricate face climbs. The Fire Wall is unique (2015) for Connecticut Traprock climbing as it contains a variety of steep traditional as well as sport and mixed (fixed gear supplemented with passive gear) climbs. Since the 1980s climbers have been climbing at the Fire Wall on a regular basis, and the parking and access from Crescent Lake Park appears to be a good situation. Climbers should keep a very low profile and work in a proactive manner to preserve access to this area. Keep your climbing equipment in packs, dogs on leashes, noise to a minimum, carpool, and obey the park rules.

Access note: On July 26, 2001, the state supreme court ruled that every municipality in Connecticut must allow nonresidents access to town beaches and parks under the free speech provision of both the federal and state constitutions. When the Southington Parks and Recreation Department was contacted in December 2001, they stated that the park is open to nonresidents.

While not a destination crag, the bouldering in the Split Rock vicinity is quite good. Split Rock, however, is located on New Britain Water Company property and is currently closed to climbers.

GPS directions: According to the town website, the GPS directions are 495 Shuttle Meadow Rd., Southington.

Directions: From the South: Take I-91 to Route 691 West (exit 5). Go around the Meriden Square Mall on the north side to Route 71 (Chamberlain Highway). Follow Route 71 North for several miles, going past Route 364. Take a left onto Reservoir Road and follow directions below.

From the north: Take I-84 to Route 372 East to Route 71A South (Chamberlain Highway). On Route 71A South, take a right onto Reservoir Road. Follow directions below.

From Reservoir Road: Continue to the end of Carey Street to the junction with Andrews Street. Take a right on Andrews and proceed to a junction with Long Bottom Road. Veer left onto Long Bottom Road and then veer right at the next junction.

Crescent Lake Park: To reach Crescent Lake Park, continue past Roger's Orchards and take a left on Shuttle Meadow Road. After a few miles the entrance to the park will be on your right.

APPROACH

A trail map can be found online to assist, but the Blue Trail is not marked. Walk to the lake and take a right (east) on the Orange / Red Trail. Follow the trail along the shore of the lake (very wet in spring—wear boots) for 13 minutes to a split (Orange Trail). Continue on the Red Trail for 1 minute to the blue-blazed trail (not the "official" blue blaze—2015) on the right. Head up the blue-blazed trail for a couple minutes (leads to large boulder in the woods) to the base of the Fire Wall. There are access trails on both ends of the cliff.

Split Rock approach: From the eastern end of the parking lot, an unmarked trail / road brings you to the Green Trail. Go left (north) on the Green Trail and follow it to the Orange Trail. Take a right (south) on the Orange / Green Trail and after a few minutes you will come to an intersection of fire roads (Bradley Junction). From the intersection continue straight (taking a left will lead

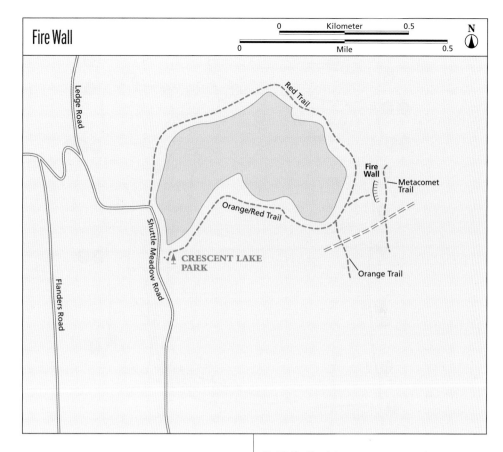

Fire Wall

		Kilometer		
0			0.5	

0 Mile 0.5

N

to the top of the Fire Wall) on the dirt road to the intersection with the gas-line trail. Continue straight on the dirt road until it splits. At the split, Split Rock will be directly in front of you. It is a 30-foot crag marked by a crack going through a low roof (5.10–).

Fire Wall

Climbs are listed from left to right.

1. Ashen Face (5.9– R / X) Climb the small left-facing corner and face a few feet to the left of the *Flaming Arrow* start. FA: Ken Nichols, Nicki Hall, 1990.

2. Flaming Arrow (5.9–) The left-facing corner and crack system. FA: Ken Nichols, Bob Clark, 1980.

3. Little Feet (5.9–; sport) A tricky start up and right to good holds and the first bolt. Continue up the face between *Flaming Arrow* and *Andiron*. FA: 2012.

4. Andiron (5.5) The largest of the left-facing corners. FA: Bob Clark, Ken Nichols, 1980.

5. Hot Feet (5.9+; sport) Climb the arête between *Andiron* and *Kindling*. FA: 2012.

6. Firewood (5.8) Up the steep corner, trend left at the roof, and follow the shallow corner to the top. FA: Ken Nichols, 1983.

7. Kindling (5.5) Up the left-facing corner, but trend right into the crack system then up the face to the top. FA: Ken Nichols, Bob Clark, 1980.

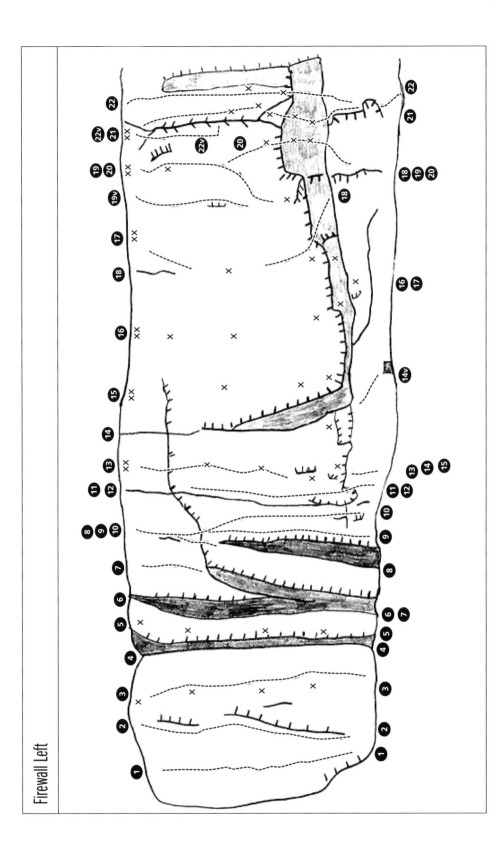

8. Hot Coals (5.6 R) The last of the left-facing corner systems on the left side. FA: Bob Clark, Ken Nichols, 1980.

9. Red Hot (5.11 TR) Climb the arête to the right of the *Hot Coals* corner and finish on *Hot Coals*. FA: Ken Nichols, 1990.

10. Incinerator (5.10+) Start about 8 feet to the right of *Hot Coals* and climb up and left, past the small overhang above a short corner. Continue up the face and finish on the upper face of *Hot Coals*. FA: Sam Slater, Mark Bourque, 1983.

11. False Alarm (5.10–) Clear the small overhang at the crack, and continue up the crack to the top. FA: Paul Niland, Ken Nichols, Al Rubin, Paul Ledoux, 1980.

12. Pyromaniac (5.11+ R / X) Climb the corner / arête just to the right of *False Alarm*, then follow the crack to the ledge. Climb up and right to the ledge and finish on the face and flakes above. Loose / broken holds may alter the start and rating over time. FA: Ken Nichols, 1983.

13. Arsonist (5.11+; mixed) Start on *Playing with Fire* (the overhang just to the right of *Pyromaniac*). Stick-clip the first bolt and climb the steep face between *Pyromaniac* and *Playing with Fire* past bolts to the ledge. Finish up the face above the ledge to anchors. FA: Ken Nichols, R / X, 1989. FA (mixed): 2012. Loose / broken holds may alter the start and rating over time.

14. Playing with Fire (5.11+; mixed) Climb up the overhang to the right of *Pyromaniac*. Move right into the left-facing corner and crack system that leads to the top. Originally rated 5.8 because it avoided the initial roof by climbing a tree (now missing). Once the tree died the start was poorly protected, but stick clipping the *Arsonist* bolt protects the start. FA (original 5.8 version): Ken Nichols, Al Rubin, Lauren Perry, 1978. FA: Sam Slater, 1983. *Squeeze Play* variation (511+ R / X): Start a few feet to the right at the block, and diagonal left over the overhang to the base of the left-facing corner. FA: Ken Nichols, Bruce Jelen, 1989 R / X. Loose / broken holds may alter the start and rating over time.

15. Retrocolor (5.11+; mixed) Follow *Playing with Fire* to the base of the corner. Step right over the corner and climb the face, passing bolts to fixed anchors. Nice section of rock guarded by the very difficult start. FA: Ryan Richetelli, 2012.

16. Spike Roof (5.12; sport) Start to the right of the *Playing with Fire* corner, and climb to the first bolt. Reach left to the "spike" and second bolt under the roof. Climb the face past three bolts to fixed anchors. FA: Dan Yagmin, 2012.

17. OC Roof (5.12–; mixed) Start on *Spike Roof*. After the first bolt head right to a second bolt and over the roof at the corner and bolt. Continue up the *Firebird* face, passing a bolt to fixed anchors. FA: 2012. *Road to Nowhere* (5.12–; mixed) variation: After the roof head right and finish on *Two Dimes for a Quarter*. FA: Dan Yagmin, 2012.

18. Firebird (5.11– R ★; mixed) A wild ride. Work up the face and thin crack to the block. Move left about 8 feet under the roof to the small right-facing corner. Crank over the roof and finish up the thin face. FA: Ken Nichols, Marco Fedrizzi, 1984. Originally R / X but the *OC Roof* bolts offer more protection.

19. Two Dimes for a Quarter (5.11– R ★; mixed) Start as for *Firebird* and head up to the roof and block. Climb up and traverse left along the corner. Crank over the roof and traverse left for a mental break. Head up and right into a left-facing corner and then to the top. FA: Sam Slater, Mike Heintz, 1983. Bolts added in 2012. 19v *Phoenix* variation: From the stance above the roof, continue straight up the face to the top. FA: Ken Nichols, 1992.

20. Iron Sheik (5.13–; mixed) Start as for *Firebird*, but move right at the roof, aiming for two bolts under the roof and left of the arête. Over the roof past a bolt joining *Two Dimes for a Quarter* and another bolt to fixed anchors. FA: Dan Yagmin, 2012.

21. El Chiste (5.12+; sport) Start on *Burned Beyond Recognition*. Climb the face to the roof, move left, then climb over the roof to the left of the *Burned Beyond Recognition* corner past two bolts. Continue up the steep face past three bolts to the right of the arête (a bit run-out after the last bolt). This was the first rappel-bolted sport route on the Fire Wall. FA: Dan Yagmin, 2012.

22. Burned Beyond Recognition (5.11 ★; mixed) The right-facing corner and roof system. FA: Ken Nichols, Marco Fedrizzi, Chad Hussey, 1984. Originally R / X but two bolts were added around 2012. *Charred Remains* variation (5.10+ TR): A few feet after the roof, traverse out left and finish up the left side of the arête. FA: TR Paul Niland, 1980.

23. Firecracker (5.9) To the right of the gully. Climb the left-facing corner and crack. FA: Ken Nichols, Franco Ghiggeri, 1980.

24. Cremated (5.10; sport) The face climb between *Firecracker* and *Funeral Pyre*. FA: TR Ken Nichols, 1989. Bolts and anchor added around 2012.

25. Funeral Pyre (5.10 R ★; bolt missing 2015) The centerline of corners and cracks. A bolt (missing) protects the moves above the ledge to a fixed anchor. FA: Ken Nichols, Mike Heintz, Kim Smith, 1982.

26. Banana Peel (5.5) Start as for *Funeral Pyre*, but when you reach the first horizontal crack, traverse right following the crack / roof / ledge system until it ends on the upper right side of the cliff. Finish up the short *Burning Ember* corner. FA: Ken Nichols, Dave Feldman, 1976.

27. Scenic Offering (5.9 ★; mixed) Follow *Banana Peel* (gear) to the base of the *Scenic Clip* variation (small roof and bolt) on *Burnt Offering*. Follow the *Scenic Clip* variation to *Burnt Offering* and the top. A link-up offering good protection and climbing throughout.

28. Burnt Offering (5.10– PG / R; mixed) Starting about 10 feet to the right of *Funeral Pyre*. Just left of the small overhang, climb up the face, passing a horizontal crack (difficult move and landing) to a bolt and then the horizontal crack / overlap. Continue up the face to the right of *Funeral Pyre* following a system of shallow corners. FA: Ken Nichols, Bob Clark, Marco Fedrizzi, Chad Hussey, 1984 with an R / X rating. Bolts added around 2012. *Scenic Clip* variation (5.9; mixed): After the upper horizontal crack / overlap, climb up and right to the small roof and bolt, then climb left to join *Burnt Offering* to the top.

29. Forrest Fire (5.8+) Starting on the right edge of a small overhang, climb up the water streak past a small left-facing corner, then left to the horizontal crack / overlap. Move left a few feet and climb past the left-facing corner to a sharp roof. Step right onto the face and up corners and ledges to the top. FA: Ken Nichols, Mike Heintz, 1982. Bolt (*Scenic* variation) added 2012.

Fire Wall Right

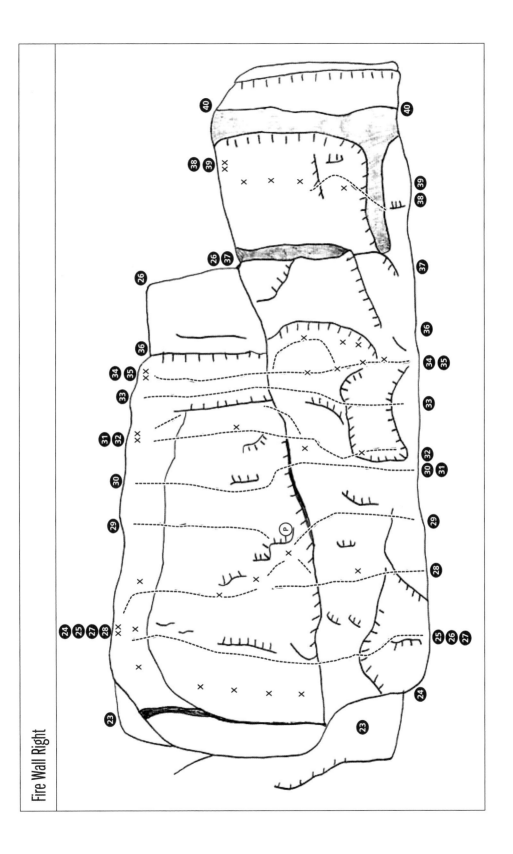

30. Flashback (5.9; mixed) Start on the left-facing corner between the overhangs. Climb up the corner to the bolt. Up the face left of a second bolt to the horizontal crack / overlap. Over the overlap, then head left to a crack corner. Up the crack past ledges to the top. FA: Ken Nichols, Jim Ratcliff, 1989. Bolts added 2013.

31. Fresh Bag (5.9–; mixed) Climb *Flashback* (better climbing and protection) or *Smoke-Out* to the horizontal crack / overlap. Climb over the right end of the overlap (committing move) and up the face past a bolt to fixed anchors. FA: Mike Mobley, 2013.

32. Smoke-Out (5.8; mixed) Up the face just to the right of the *Flashback* corner to gain the top of the corner / ledge. Up the face to the right of the bolt to the horizontal crack, then traverse right into the left-facing corner. Up the corner to fixed anchors. FA: Jim Ratcliff, Ken Nichols, 1989. Bolts added 2013.

33. Fire Escape (5.10+ R) Work up the center section of the overhang to the right of the *Flashback* corner (wide part of roof and small right-facing corner). Up the short face to the ledge. Move right and then up the steep face past ledges to the top. FA: Ken Nichols, Mike Heintz, 1982.

34. Blazing Saddles (5.10–; mixed) Start under the steep wall just left of the *Light My Fire* corner. Up the overhanging face / right-facing corner past two bolts to large holds. Move across the face past a bolt (loose hold 2015) to the arête. Up the arête past a bolt to a ledge. A camming unit protects moderate climbing to the anchor. FA: Ken Nichols, Jim Ratcliff, 1989 R / X rating. Bolts added 2013. *Dalha Wanna* variation

(5.10–; mixed): Instead of traversing right, continue straight up the face past a bolt to the ledge, then anchors.

35. Open Project (not graded; mixed) Up the steep wall past two bolts, then out right past two bolts to join *Blazing Saddles* to the top. Rating not confirmed 2015.

36. Light My Fire (5.11 R) Climb over a low overhang, then into the large right-facing corner to a small ledge. Finish on the short corner to the top. FA: Sam Slater, Mark Bourque, 1983.

37. Burning Ember (5.9) To the right of the *Light My Fire* corner, climb a crack through a roof and continue up the right-facing corner. FA: Sam Slater, John Baudean, Bob Butera, 1973.

38. Eternal Flame (5.11+ / 12–; sport) Start in the center of the wall, and work up and right at the overhang. Head up and left to the overlap and then up the center or the wall. FA: TR Ken Nichols, 1990. FSA: Greg Shyloski, 2013. *Less Than Zero* variation (5.12+): Climb the overhang and face left of the first bolt, then join *Eternal Flame* at the second bolt. FA: Greg Shyloski, 2013.

39. Ball of Fire (5.11 TR) Start on *Eternal Flame*. Work up and right, traversing to the base of the arête. Up the blunt arête, and then up the right side of the sharp arête. FA: TR Ken Nichols, 1988.

40. Fireplace (5.5) The large right-facing corner and crack system to the right of the *Burning Ember* corner. FA: Ken Nichols, 1980.

To the right of *Fireplace* is a gulley, and then a few short clean corners.

WEST PEAK, SOUTHINGTON

Electric Rocks is comprised of two separate crags, separated by power lines, at the northernmost section of the West Peak traprock ridge system. North of the power lines is the High Voltage crag, and south is the Low Voltage crag. The High Voltage crag has interesting lines and a clean and open base to belay. Climbers have frequented this crag since the 1970s, and it has about twenty-seven established routes. However, the High Voltage crag is mostly located on private property and not listed in this edition. The Low Voltage crag is a bit scruffier and is located on Town of Southington property.

There are many small crags extending south from Electric Rocks to the radio towers in Meriden. The author grew up near these crags, and before Copper Ridge Road was completed, he spent many nights camping on top of the Valley View crag (located behind a house on the northern section of Copper Ridge) and climbing the few (but dramatic) routes on this crag. Unfortunately, the Valley View crag is owned by three separate private owners. As the author understands it, the owner with the home below does not allow public access. There are also a variety of crags, with many established routes, located on the ridgeline between the northern Copper Ridge cul-de-sac and Electric Rocks. According to *Hooked on Traprock: Rock Climbing in Central Connecticut* by Ken Nichols (1995), these crags include Cedar Point (fifty-nine routes), Lower Ridge Rocks (sixty routes), Irish Corner (two routes), and Giant Corner (seven routes). Overall, the route quality on these crags is relatively low, but there a few good lines to explore. To access these crags, follow the Black Trail from Camp Sloper, take a right

on the Purple Trail, after a few minutes take a left (east) on the White Trail to the base of a short cliff, and then continue to the top of the scattered crags.

Historical note: The large but loose crag located above the southern end of the cul-de-sac on Copper Ridge is Jumping-Off Point and is located on Town of Meriden property (see "Access to Climbing Areas" in the introduction). Jumping-Off Point is so named because during the 1970s and 1980s, it was a popular launch site for hang gliders. The pilots would land their gliders in the Mountain Grove Swim Club fields, and once in a while in front of the author's childhood home. Around the age of 13, before Copper Ridge Road existed, the author led rescuers to the base of this crag after a pilot was ejected from his glider while attempting a launch. If choosing to explore Jumping-Off Point, it can be accessed by the Blue-Blazed hiking trail. An interactive map for the trail (2015) is available at www.ctwoodlands.org/bluetrailsmap.

Directions: Electric Rocks is best accessed through Camp Sloper. Camp Sloper is located close to Ragged Mountain, situated in the middle of Routes 691, 91, 84, and 372. From each of these points, the directions are somewhat different. So your best bet is to use a GPS or the Internet to customize your directions for YMCA Camp Sloper, 1000 East St., Southington, CT.

ACCESS

1. YMCA Camp Sloper: A yearly pass can be obtained for an Outdoor Center Membership allowing parking on the Sloper property. The pass can be purchased at the Southington YMCA. The Camp Director, as of 2015, has allowed limited parking at the YMCA Camp Sloper in the main parking lot for climbers (group size limited to eight but always subject to the discretion of Sloper staff) to access Electric Rocks without a pass. The Ragged Mountain Foundation purchases a day pass (2015) each year on behalf of local climbers to assist with access to Electric Rocks, and as of 2015 dashboard passes can be printed from the RMF website. Groups of eight or more are required to get a special permit. ***Please note:*** Climbers *will not* be able to access Electric Rocks through the YMCA Camp Sloper property while the day camp program is in session: Monday through Friday the last weeks of June, July, and August between 6:30 a.m. and 5:30 p.m. This policy is in place for the protection of the YMCA campers and strictly enforced by the YMCA Camp Sloper staff. Climbers can park on the YMCA Camp Sloper property on the weekends during this time, but be advised the gate opens at dawn and closes at dusk. Cars will be towed at the owner's expense if they remain in the YMCA parking lot after dusk. Climbers can park at the YMCA Camp Sloper property in the spring and fall when the gate is open during daylight hours. For more information on Outdoor Center Memberships or parking privileges at YMCA Camp Sloper, please call the Camp Office at (860) 621-8194 or visit www.ymcacampsloper.org. As of 2015 the weekends have provided ample parking for all climbers who show up and utilize the very large parking lot. If a problem arises, please contact the Ragged Mountain Foundation (raggedmtn.org).

From the Camp Sloper parking lot, follow the wide gravel trail under the power lines. The trail is blazed in black. Follow the Black Trail (passing the Yellow, Blue, and Purple Trails) to the top of the ridge under the lower lines (15 minutes). Follow the Black Trail south along the ridge and power line clearing. Shortly after entering the woods, trend right on a climber's trail to the top of the Low Voltage crag. If you remain on the black-blazed trail, it will dip down below the ridge (but you have gone too far). The best descent is the north end of the crag.

2. Copper Ridge cul-de-sac—northern end. This access point should be a last resort, for midweek summer access only. **Directions:** Use a GPS for Copper Ridge, Southington. Continued access requires extremely limited parking and a low profile (ropes in packs, out before dusk, low noise). Climbers *must* carpool. The northern Copper Ridge cul-de-sac abuts Town of Southington property (the same parcel that contains Electric Rocks) and is marked by a sign that reads "Korin Open Space." From the cul-de-sac a short trail leads to the Silver Trail. Take a right on the Silver Trail and in 5 minutes you will reach the Purple Trail. Take a right (north) on the Purple Trail and in 5 minutes you will intersect the White Trail. Continue straight on the Purple Trail for a couple minutes to the southern loop of the Black Trail (under power lines). Head up the Black Trail to the top of the ridge. Follow the Black Trail south along the ridge and power line clearing. Shortly after entering the woods, trend right on a climber's trail to the top of the Low Voltage crag. If you remain on the black-blazed trail, it will dip down below the ridge (but you have gone too far). The best descent is the north end of the crag.

Electric Rocks

Low Voltage Crag

Not the best crag in Connecticut due to loose rock at the start of many climbs, but there are some exciting arêtes as well as the rare Traprock sport climbs to be found on this 70-foot crag. *Note:* Some routes are graded a half grade harder due to loose holds / rock.

1. Hot Wire (5.6) Climb past the corner and roof systems and finish up the middle of a short buttress. FA: Ken Nichols, Harold Mullins, Bob Clark, 1980.

2. No Current (5.4) The large left-facing corner / gulley to the ledge. Step left and finish up the center of the buttress. FA: Bob Clark, 1980.

3. Kermit in the Corner (5.12; sport) Start on *No Current*, then reach right to the first bolt on the north-facing buttress and work up the slick face past two more bolts to a fixed anchor. FA: 2013.

4. Burn Baby Burn (5.11+ TR / mixed) Climb the arête to the right of *Kermit in the Corner* to the ledge (toprope). Up the corner, then move right to the base of the lower corner / arête. Up the lower, then higher arête to the top. Holds may have broken off the first arête on the upper section. FA: Ken Nichols, 1991. The upper finish, above the ledge, received two bolts 2012. The most logical lead (mixed) would be up *Electric Chair* to the ledge, then up and right on the upper arêtes.

5. Electric Chair (5.6 PG / R) The first section of the route is poorly protected. Up the chimney / crack / large left-facing corner to the ledge. Finish up the left-facing corner. FA: Chris Stone, Ken Nichols, 1975.

6. Shock Treatment (5.11+ ★; mixed) Climb *Electric Chair* to the first ledge. Head up the left-facing corner, then hand-traverse right at the horizontal crack to the second bolt, and finish up the steep vertical crack. FA: Ken Nichols, 1980. Bolts added on the traverse 2012.

6v. 2000 Volts (5.10+; mixed) Climb *Shock Treatment* to the second bolt, then continue traversing right to the fixed anchors around the corner. Up the short face to the top. FA: Ken Nichols, 1980. Bolts added on the traverse 2012.

7. End of an Era (5.13; sport) Up the north-facing buttress to the first bolt. Trend up and left and fight your way past steep rock and underclings to the fourth bolt. Work your way up into a series of powerful underclings below the fifth bolt. Diagonal up and right at the fifth bolt to the ledge on *Rare Earth*. Rest up, step left, and finish on *Shock Treatment* (bolt and crack to anchors). FA: Dan Yagmin, 2004. (*Note:* As of 2015 two bolts are placed next to each other at the fifth bolt because one was damaged.)

8. The Unseen (5.13–; sport) Up the north-facing buttress to the first bolt. Trend up and right, staying left of the arête. A boulder problem crux at the third bolt leads to the fourth bolt on *End of an Era*. Finish on *End of an Era*. FA: Dan Yagmin, 2014. (*Note:* As of 2015 two bolts are placed next to each other at the fifth bolt because one was damaged.) *The Birth of a Prince* variation (5.13; sport): The hardest of the three lines. From the fifth bolt step left to a large mail-slot undercling. Once you have gained the undercling, fire straight up to reach the hand-traverse ledge and finish on *Shock Treatment*. FA: Phillip Schaal, date unknown.

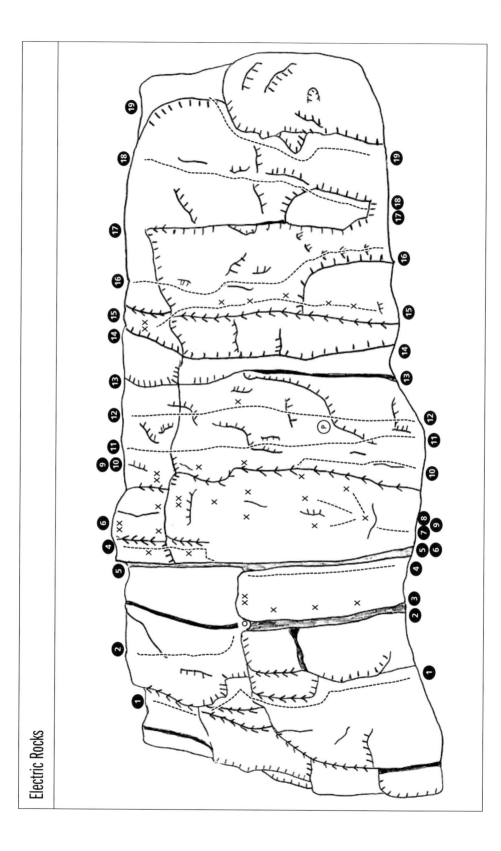

9. Rare Earth (5.10+; sport) No protection to the first bolt in the center of the slab and loose rock until the third bolt is clipped. Start as for *End of an Era* and climb to the first bolt. Head right (loose rock and off balance at second bolt) and climb the arête past four bolts to the fixed anchor. Originally rated 5.9+, but broken holds have altered the rating, and this may change with holds braking in the future. FA: (toprope) Bruce Jelen, 1991. FA (sport): 2012.

10. Earth Decay (5.9– TR) Climb just right of the arête up loose rock, and join *Rare Earth* at the second bolt. Finish up *Rare Earth*. FA

11. Ferric Oxide (5.7 R) Follow your nose through positive but loose holds, trending left to the face just right of the arête. Finish on the clean face and small left-facing corner a few feet to the right of the fixed anchors on *Rare Earth*. FA: Ken Nichols, Harold Mullins, Bob Clark, 1980.

12. Electron (5.7+ R) Climb the center of the blocky face 6 feet left of the *Nightcrawler* crack. Up the face, passing a fixed piton, then past a bolt (2015), and continue to the top passing left-facing corners. FA: Ken Nichols, Bill Sullivan, 1981.

13. Nightcrawler (5.5) The prominent crack and corner system 5 feet to the left of the *Dropout* corner. FA: Ken Nichols, Chris Stone, 1975.

14. Dropout (5.6) The large left-facing corner and chimney system. FA: Chris Stone, Ken Nichols, 1975.

15. Positron (5.11– / 10+; sport) Starting to the right of the first bolt and climbing just to the right of the next two bolts is easier (5.10+) and is the original line, but the rock is looser and scarier. Starting under the first bolt, the rock is more solid, but harder, as is staying just left of the next two bolts (5.11–). The rock is loose, and at times slippery, past the first three bolts and can be scary despite the bolts. There are hidden fixed anchors left of the final short arête. FA (toprope): Ken Nichols, 1985. FA (sport): 2012

16. Octoberfest (5.8+ R) Climb the blocky rock just right of the left-facing corner / arch. Diagonal up and left, and follow a crack and shallow corners to the right of *Positron*. FA: Ken Nichols, Franco Ghiggeri, 1980.

17. Trick or Treat (5.6) Climb the ugly-looking crack / fissure through the overhang and finish up a clean right-facing corner. FA: Chris Stone, Chris Stevenson, 1975.

18. Short Circuit (5.7+) The left-facing corner / arête just right of *Trick or Treat* to the shallow left-facing corner. Scramble to the top. FA: Ken Nichols, Bob Clark, Harold Mullins, 1980.

19. Open Circuit (5.5) The short left-facing corner and roof. Scramble to the top. FA: Ken Nichols, 1980.

EAST PEAK, MERIDEN

As per a city ordinance, there is a regulation concerning rock climbing in Meriden. Please refer to page xiii of the "Access to Climbing Areas" section in the introduction. Therefore, the information on rock climbing at East Peak is for historical purposes only and is not an invitation to trespass.

The Hanging Hills of Meriden provided some of the best climbing in Connecticut. The most notable landmark, dividing the ridges of East and West Peaks, is the Castle Craig Tower. This tower was dedicated October 29, 1900, and given to the people of Meriden by Walter Hubbard. Its observation area is 1,002 feet above sea level and provides a spectacular view. This area is part of the 900-acre aptly named Hubbard Park. Prior to 1986 the parking area near the tower was a disaster. Frequented by partygoers all day and night, the area was unsafe and unclean. The city of Meriden cleaned up the area, gated the road at night, and had a security guard stationed in the lot during the day. These efforts greatly improved the look and feel of the area.

Of special interest to climbers are the Traprock cliffs that tower above the Merimere Reservoir in Hubbard Park. This section, East Peak, is home to some of the best and most strenuous climbs in Connecticut. Climbers have been frequenting East Peak since the 1930s. Since that time East Peak, in particular the Merimere Face, has produced some of the hardest climbs in the Northeast. A chronology includes *Rat Crack*, 5.7, by Fritz Wiessner and Percy Olton in 1934; *Cat Crack*, 5.10, by Sam Streibert and Steve Arsenault in 1972; *Dol Guldur*, 5.11, by Tony Trocchi and Mike Heintz in 1976; *Volcanic Eruption*, 5.12, toproped by Ken Nichols in 1987 and led by Sam Slater in 1991; *Lightning Strike*, 5.13, toproped by Sam Slater in 1990; and *In the Presence of God*, 5.13–, toproped by Sam Slater in 1992.

While not included, it should be noted that the Castle Craig area, which borders the parking lot, was once a very popular destination and contains more than one hundred established climbs. However, despite the efforts of the city of Meriden, this area has filled with trash over time.

Directions: From Waterbury: Take I-84 East to I-691 East.

From Hartford: Take I-91 South to I-691 West. Take I-691 to exit 4. If traveling eastbound, take a left off the exit. If traveling westbound, take a right off the exit. Go downhill to Hubbard Park 0.1 mile. You can park in the main lot in Hubbard Park.

Approach: If the gate is open (usually Apr–Nov from 10 a.m. to 5 p.m.): From the entrance to the park, travel 0.2 mile to the intersection. At the intersection continue straight to a stop sign. Take a left, go through the gate, and drive up the park road. Bear left toward Castle Craig at an intersection a few miles up. Park at the lot for the castle. Walk toward the guardrails / wires (away from the castle and across the parking lot). Just on the other side is a steep gully that brings you to the Metacomet Trail.

If the gate is closed: From the entrance to the park, travel 0.2 mile to the intersection. At the intersection is a parking lot across from the pool. Park here and hike under the highway bridge on a paved / dirt road. You will pass a water tower on the left and join up with the main park road. Walk on the paved park road, then take a left onto a dirt road that skirts the reservoir. Follow the main dirt road until it bends to the left (avoiding the side trails on the left). About 100 feet from the bend, there is a faint trail that leads toward the cliff, through a talus field, to the base of *Cat Crack*.

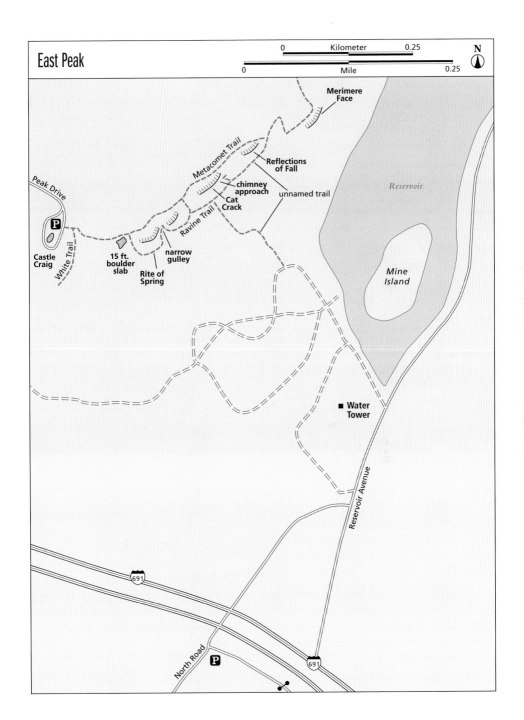

East Peak

Merimere
Face

Metacomet Trail

Reflections
of Fall

unnamed trail

Reservoir

chimney
approach

Peak Drive

Cat
Crack

P

Ravine Trail

Mine
Island

Castle
Craig

White Trail

15 ft.
boulder
slab

narrow
gulley

Rite of
Spring

Water
Tower

Reservoir Avenue

691

North Road

P

691

N

Romy Choi on *Thor's Hammer* PHOTO SCOTT SAMPIETRO

A poor trail leads left and then up the ravine trail. Some climbers gain the top by climbing a 5.1 chimney on the right end of the crag, and some exposed ledges, to the top of the cliff.

A longer but gentler approach continues on the dirt road, past a pavilion, to the White Trail, which is followed to the top to a junction with the Metacomet Trail.

East Peak

Rite of Spring Area

1. Petrouchka (5.9) The shallow corner on the face left of *Rite of Spring*. Once you hit the ledge, finish on *Rite of Spring* or the face above. FA: Ken Nichols, Bruce Bates, 1976.

2. Rite of Spring (5.10+ ★) Follow the steep crack above the cave and finish on the left-facing corner. FA: Bruce Dicks, Greg Newth, 1976.

3. Pagan Ritual (5.11 R / X ★) The technical face right of *Rite of Spring* and left of *Lunge or Plunge*. FA: Ken Nichols, Chuck Boyd, Dave Rosenstein, 1989.

4. Lunge or Plunge (5.11 R; bolt missing 2015) Begin at the right-facing corner and continue up the right side of the face. *Historical note:* First led by Chuck Boyd, a Rhode Island / Connecticut local climber who was on the team that made the first ascent of the Shipton Spire in Pakistan. FA: Chuck Boyd, Ken Nichols, 1985.

The next few climbs begin on the south-facing wall to the right of the chimney / gully.

5. Gyrator (5.12 TR) The technical face to the left of *Joel's Stroll*. FA: Bruce Jelen, 1994.

6. Joel's Stroll (5.3) The prominent crack system on the left side. FA: Joel Ager, 1980.

7. Twin Crack Left (5.4) The right-facing corner and crack system. FA: Sam Streibert, Al Rubin, 1976.

8. April Shower (5.5) The crack system between the *Twin Cracks*. FA: Ken Nichols, Franco Ghiggeri, 1980.

9. Twin Crack Right (5.7) The crack system that passes through a small roof. FA: Sam Streibert, Al Rubin, 1976.

10. Out to Pasture (5.7+ R) The arête on the south-facing wall. FA: Ken Nichols, Franco, Ghiggeri, Bob Clark, Jim Meigs, 1980.

11. Modern Eyes (5.9) The crack to the right of the *Out to Pasture* arête.

East Peak Right of Spring Area

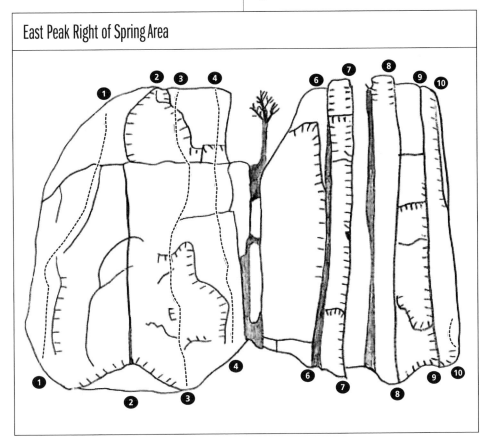

Blue Trail

Chimney

Rappel Groove Wall

The following climbs are located on the blocky sections between the chimney and the approach / descent gully. They are not the best climbs in Connecticut but are in the easy-to-moderate range, unlike many at East Peak.

12. Rhapsody in Blue (5.5) Start at the small pillar of rock and move right to the ledge. Continue up the face and the small corners above. FA: Ken Nichols, 1980.

13. Larry and Moe (5.5) Follow the corners to a ledge, move right, and finish up the right-facing corner. FA: Mike Lapierre, Jim Lombardi, Bob Clark, 1980.

14. Curly (5.9+) Climb the overlap and crack to the right of *Larry and Moe* to the ledge. Continue up the thin crack and face above. FA: Ken Nichols, Franco Ghiggeri, 1980.

15. Rappel Groove (5.5 ★) The right-facing corner. A very good intermediate lead. FA: Al Rubin, Sam Streibert, 1969.

16. Pearl Harbor (5.7+) The crack system and face climb above the "box." FA: Sam Streibert, Al Rubin, 1969.

17. Southeast Arête (5.8 R) The entertaining arête to the right of *Pearl Harbor*. FA: Ken Nichols, 1981.

18. Off the Beaten Track (5.7+) To the right of *Southeast Arête* is a left-facing corner. FA: Ken Nichols, George Mandes, 1976.

19. By the Way (5.6) To the right of *Off the Beaten Track* is another left-facing corner. FA: Ken Nichols, Al Rubin, 1977.

Dihedral Section

The following climbs begin approximately 75 feet to the right of the approach / descent gully.

20. Letterbox (5.7) The corner and chimney system formed by the blocks. FA: John Dowd, 1964.

21. Finders Keepers (5.8) Climb the arête between *Letterbox* and *Lost Corner*. At the

East Peak Dihedral Section

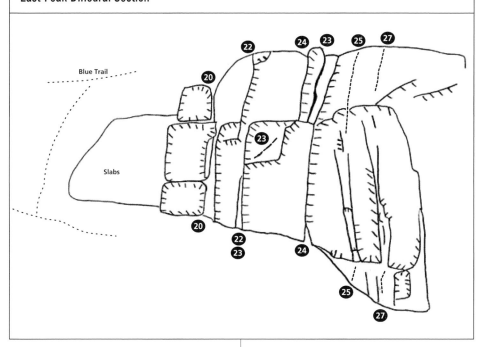

ledge, step right and continue up the arête formed by *Lost Corner*. FA: Mike Lapierre, Ken Nichols, 1982.

22. Lost Corner (5.7+ ★) Climb up the large corner system to the right of *Letterbox*. A 5.8 variation traverses right under the small corner and across the face at the top. FA: Sam Streibert, Larry Winship, 1972.

23. Crossover (5.6) Climb up Lost Corner to the first ledge. Cross over to the right and finish up the crack to the right of the corner. FA: Ken Nichols, Joel Ager, 1980.

24. Downcast (5.9 ★) Climb up the large left-facing corner, move left on the ledge (optional belay), and continue up the left-facing corner system. FA: John Dowd, Sam Streibert, 1964. *Extremely Downcast* variation (5.9 R ★; 214v): A good variation to *Downcast*. Instead of moving left to the ledge,

continue straight up the intimidating corner. FA: Jim Adair, Bruce Dicks, 1977.

25. Black Cloud (5.6) The chimney and crack system. FA: Ken Nichols, Sam Streibert, Jack Rankin, 1975.

26. Cold War (5.11 TR) Start a few feet to the right of *Black Cloud* and climb up the right side of the overhang. Climb the left side of the arête to the top. FA: Bruce Dicks, 1988.

27. Journey to the Center of the Earth (5.10– ★) Attack the roof from the left side and continue up the corner system. FA: Jim Adair, Bruce Dicks, 1977.

28. Back Alley (5.5) The large, loose corner system. FA: Bruce Bates, 1976.

Amphitheater Wall

29. The Wodniw (5.9) Start up *Back Alley* and then work right, climb through the hole, and finish up the cracks and face above. FA: Jim Adair, George Mandes, and Bruce Dicks, 1977. During a rededication ceremony for the Jim Adair plaque at Ragged Mountain in 2000, George and Bruce each wrote a letter that was read to Jim's father.

30. Say It Ain't So (5.9 R ★; bolt missing 2015) Follow the arête. A bolt was placed on rappel, and later removed to be replaced with a bolt that was placed on the lead. However, that bolt has been removed as well.

31. The Window (5.7+ R ★) Climb up the face to the ledge system, climb through the hole, and finish up a corner on the opposite side. Good climbing but a bit loose. FA: Sam Streibert, John Dowd, 1964.

32. Blank on the Map (5.10 TR) Start 5 to 6 feet left of the *Rauros* corner, and climb the face staying 4 and 6 feet to the left of *Rauros*. Finish on the final *Rauros* crack or face to the left. FA: Sam Slater, 1982.

33. Rauros (5.10+ R) Climb the prominent right-facing corner to the roof. Clear the roof and continue up the left-facing corner to a ledge. Finish up the nice crack on the left. FA: Jim Adair, Ken Nichols, Bruce Dicks, 1977.

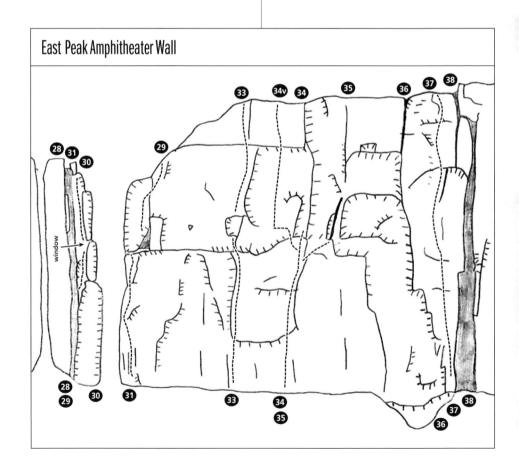

East Peak Amphitheater Wall

Sam Streibert on the first free ascent of *Cat Crack,* 1972 PHOTO SAM STREIBERT

34. Mondo Beyondo (5.9) Work up a corner system to a stance below the roof. Crank the roof and follow the corner system to the top. FA: Sam Streibert, Al Rubin, Al Long, 1975. *Warped Space-Time* variation (5.12 TR; 34v): From the stance under the roof, move left and launch over the roof at a left-facing corner. Move left again a few feet and head straight up to the top. FA: Ken Nichols, 1987.

35. Footloose and Fancy Free (5.9) Climb *Mondo Beyondo* to the stance under the roof. Move right and clear the roof at the crack that is followed to the top. FA: Bruce Dicks, Ken Nichols, 1976.

36. Grey Corner (5.9+ R ★) The right-facing corner system left of *Rat Crack*. FA: John Reppy, Alan Wedgewood, 1964. FFA: Bob Anderson, Sam Streibert, Al Rubin, 1973.

37. T-Rex (5.11 TR ★ The face between *Grey Corner* and *Rat Crack*. FA: Ken Nichols, 1987.

38. Rat Crack (5.7 ★) The prominent chimney / crack system. First ascended by Fritz Wiessner and Percy Olton in the 1930s. A very difficult climb for the times—probably one of the hardest in the country when first ascended. FA: Fritz Wiessner, Percy Olton, 1933. *Rat Race* variation (5.8): Climb the steep crack on the wall to the left. FA: Chris Hyson, Jim Wilcox, Mike Lapierre, Bob Clark, Ken Nichols, Chad Hussey, Chuck Boyd, Bruce Dicks, 1988.

39. Nitroglycerin (5.12 TR) The difficult line following the left side of the face between *Rat Crack* and *Cat Crack*. FA: Ken Nichols, 1987.

40. Toxic Shock (5.12– TR) The difficult line following the right side of the face between *Rat Crack* and *Cat Crack*. When you reach the small ledge two-thirds of the

way up, move right and finish on *Cat Crack*. FA: Ken Nichols, 1992.

41. Fly on a Windshield (A4) An early aid line up the face between *Cat Crack* and *Rat Crack*. FA: Stew Sayah, Mike Bader, 1979. Aid climbing using a hammer is not recommended (due to rock scarring) and the route is listed for historical purposes only.

42. Cat Crack (5.10 ★) The chimney to hand crack. Once you pass the loose start, this is good Yosemite training. FA: Sam Streibert, Larry Winship, 1966. FFA: Sam Streibert, Steve Arsenault, 1972.

43. Volcanic Eruption (5.12– TR ★) One of the best climbs in Connecticut. The technical lower face and pumpy upper face between *Cat Crack* and *Dol Guldor*. First toproped, it was later bolted on rappel and led with only four bolts (the first bolt broke while being placed). The bolts were removed shortly after, and the rappel-placed bolts on this route sparked a tremendous amount of debate among climbers in Connecticut. FA (toprope): Ken Nichols, 1987. FA (sport): Sam Slater, Harry Brielman, Mick Avery, 1991.

44. Dol Guldor (5.11+ PG ★; bolt missing 2015) The start has thin protection and the finish is "sporty" above the roof. Another one of the best climbs in Connecticut. Climb the technical seam and crack to the roof. At the roof move left and launch over the roof. Move back right to finish above the crack line. FA: John Dowd, Ken Nichols, 1975. FFA: Tony Trocchi, Mike Heintz, 1976. *Mordor* variation (5.10+): Easy for some, impossible for others. Climb directly over from the rest stance (head jam helpful). FA: Bruce Dicks, 1977. *GorGo Pass* variation (5.10 PG): After moving left and climbing over the roof, continue straight

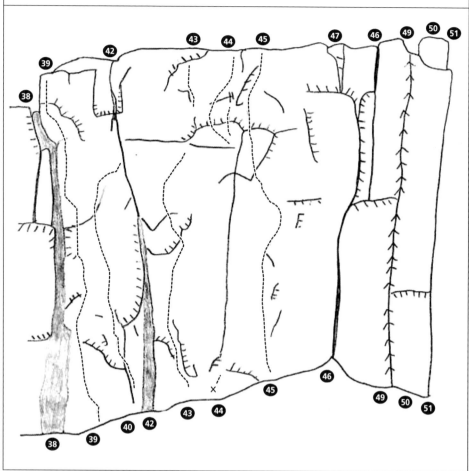

up the face finishing between cedar trees. FA: Ken Nichols, John Clothier, Howard Carney, 1995.

45. In the Presence of God (5.13– TR ★) The impossible-looking face to the right of *Dol Guldor*. Work past a crux down low, up the thin face. Then climb up to a stance to the right of the arch. After the arch climb up and right to another crux and the top. FA: Sam Slater, 1992.

46. Squirrel Cage (5.9 ★) The prominent left-facing corner system. FA: Fritz Wiessner,

William Burling, Percy Olton, 1933. FFA: Sam Streibert, Al Rubin, 1972.

47. Sickle (5.10+ ★) From the ledge on *Squirrel Cage*, ascend the smooth hand crack, undercling left out the arch, and climb the overhang via the crack. A favorite climb for many. FA: Mike Heintz, Frank Tuthill, 1975. FFA: Greg Newth, 1976.

48. Steel Wall (5.11+ TR) Climb the face between *Squirrel Cage* and *Superstructure*. FA: Ken Nichols, 1989.

49. Superstructure (5.11 R) The arête to the right of *Squirrel Cage*. Start on the left side of the arête, then climb up and right to the right side of the arête to the ledge on *Squirrel Cage*. Move left and finish up the left side of the arête. FA: Ken Nichols, Rick Murnane, Bruce Dicks, Rusty Reno, 1987.

50. Black Corner (5.8 ★) The corner system to the right of *Superstructure*. A good 5.8 lead. FA: Sam Streibert, John Reppy, Sam Black, 1964.

51. Stepping Razor (5.9 R) The arête to the right of Black Corner. FA: Ken Nichols, Chad Hussey, 1982.

52. Gully (5.1) On the south-facing wall to the right of *Stepping Razor* is a short chimney. This is commonly used to gain the top of the Amphitheater, especially if you're too tired for another burn on *Dol Guldor*. Dangerous and exposed if not roped.

Fall Wall

If you continue past the Amphitheater area, you will pass a lookout on your right. This is the top of *Reflections of Fall*. Follow the Metacomet Trail to a dip on the right. A faint trail leads to the base. Be forewarned: Birds have been nesting on this crag. Best to check the status of the nests—and bird droppings—prior to climbing at the Fall Wall.

1. Don't Fall (5.8+ R) The left-hand, left-facing corner on the left side of the face. FA: Ken Nichols, Joel Ager, Harold Mullins, 1980.

2. Trial and Triumph (5.11+ PG ★) The steep corner and crack system. Between the aid ascent, toprope ascent, and original and present lead ascents, this is a climb with four

"First Ascents." The climb listed is the most direct line. FA: Ken Nichols, 1984.

3. Silver Meteor (5.12 TR ★) The face climb between *Trial and Triumph* and *Falling Star*. FA: Ken Nichols, 1989.

4. Falling Star (5.11+ TR) The difficult face to the left of *Reflections of Fall*. FA: Ken Nichols, 1989.

5. Reflections of Fall (5.9+ ★) The steep and sustained corner / finger crack—a Connecticut classic. FA: Sam Streibert, Bob Anderson, 1973.

6. Stallion (5.11 R / X; bolt missing 2015) Begin on the west-facing wall and arête just right of *Reflections of Fall*. Climb to a small overhang and horizontal crack. Traverse right and attack the steep face to a small ledge. Continue up the south-facing arête (right side) to the right of *Reflections of Fall*. FA: Ken Nichols, Marco Fedrizzi, 1984.

7. Malmedy Massacre (5.11 PG) The face and right-facing corners that lead to the crack / notch through the overhang. Continue up the left-facing corner system to the top. FA: Bruce Dicks, Ken Nichols, Jim Adair, 1977.

8. Going Begging (5.10– R) Climb the left-facing corner / flake. Trend up and left to the right-facing corner system, then continue up the face to finish. FA: Jim Adair, Mick Avery, 1976.

9. Superpower (5.11+ R / X) Climb up the center of the flake and continue straight up to the small overlap. Follow the crack system and small right-facing corner to the top. FA: Ken Nichols, Sam Slater, 1984. *Direct Finish* (5.11+ R / X): Up the crack, then move left, and up the steep face to the highest portion of the wall. FA: Ken Nichols, Howard Carney, 1997.

East Peak Fall Wall

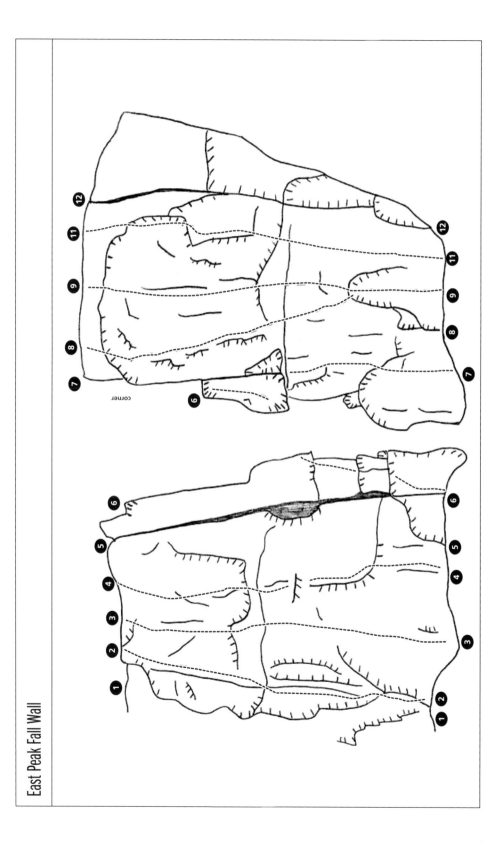

10. Lustration (5.13 TR) The face between *Superpower* and *Hercules Unchained*. FA: John Clothier, 1997.

11. Hercules Unchained (5.11 R) The face to the left of *Crossroads* to the horizontal crack and overlap. Continue up the right-facing corners to the overlap; follow the edge of the overlap to the top. FA: Ken Nichols, Marco Fedrizzi, 1984.

12. Crossroads (5.7) The left-facing corner and crack system. FA: Sam Streibert, Al Rubin, 1976.

To the right of *Crossroads* and before the Alcove Area, there are at least twenty-seven established climbs ranging from 5.3 to 5.11 located among the broken crags, ledges, and gullies.

Alcove Area

If the sun is baking on the Amphitheater, Shakespeare Wall (no topo) is a great place to hang out. Just before you reach the Merimere Face overlook, there is a large ravine / faint trail on the right. The first clean wall on your right is Shakespeare Wall. The Alcove is just beyond it, tucked into a small alcove on the right.

The Alcove

1. Much Ado About Nothing (5.5) As you walk into The Alcove, the shorter corner and crack on the left-hand side.

2. Taming of the Shrew (5.8) As you walk into the alcove, the steep clean hand crack in the right-hand corner. FA: Ken Nichols, Mike Heintz, 1975.

3. Midsummer's Day Dream (5.7 ★) Ascend the steep crack in the alcove, up the center of the west-facing wall. FA: John Reppy, 1964.

4. Coriolanus (5.11– R) A thin crack to the right of the *Midsummer's Day Dream* crack and the arête on the right. FA: Ken Nichols, Bruce Dicks, 1987.

5. Winter's Tale (5.9) The outside, 4-foot-wide wall that separates the east and west sides of the wall. FA: Sam Streibert, Eric White, Peter Welles, 1966. FFA: Ken Nichols, Harold Mullins, 1980.

Shakespeare Wall

Climbs 6 and 7 are located on the clean buttress to the right of The Alcove.

6. As You Like It (5.8+ ★) A great little route. The clean finger crack and face on the left side of the buttress. Ken Nichols, Mike Heintz, Tony Trocchi, 1975.

7. All's Well That Ends Well (5.10+ TR ★) Just right of center of the wall is a thin seam / crack. When the crack ends step right and up to the top. FA: Eric Engberg, 1981. As you continue walking past Shakespeare Wall (west), you will pass a variety of small crags. There are numerous established lines on these short walls—hang a rope and have a ball. Four that are worth the effort include:

8. Gathering Storm (5.6) About 50 feet beyond the Shakespeare Wall is a clean wall with left-slanting cracks and a large left-facing corner. *Gathering Storm* starts up a crack and then follows the left-facing corner. FA: Sam Streibert, Al Rubin, 1976.

9. Out Damned Spot (5.8 R / X) Up the wall 5 feet left of Gathering Storm. FA: Ken Nichols, Al Carilli, 1994.

10. To Be or Not to Be (5.8 R) Starting off a small block, climb up the center of the wall. FA: Sam Slater, Ken Nichols, 1982.

11. Slings and Arrows (5.8+ R) Climb the left side of the wall. FA: Ken Nichols, Bill Sullivan, Jim Ratcliff, 1983.

Merimere Face

This is one of the most dramatic faces in Connecticut, housing one of the best crack systems in the state, *Thor's Hammer*. To find the route, walk along the overlook, drop down to a lower ledge, and look down the wall to spot a huge corner system. The routes are best approached by rappelling from the top, the face to the right of *Thor's Hammer* being your best bet. Finish up one of the routes, or face a terrible bushwhack to the top.

1. Spring Cleaning (5.8 R ★) A great route to toprope. Climb up a broken column to the overhang, to the ramp system. Follow the shallow left-facing corner system above, then trend left to finish close to the arête. FA: Ken Nichols, Bill Sullivan, Mike Lapierre, Chad Hussey, 1981.

2. Thunderbolt (5.11 PG / R ★) One of the most exposed climbs in Connecticut. It has the same start as *Spring Cleaning*, but you follow the ramp system to the right to the left edge of the first roof on *Thor's Hammer* (first pitch belay). Climb to the next ledge system after the second roof, traverse right across the roof, and traverse right again to a steep, clean vertical crack that trends right. Follow the crack to the top. If leading, you may want to preplace a camming unit at the base of the last crack—the moves to the crack are a bit desperate, and you would hate to blow it at

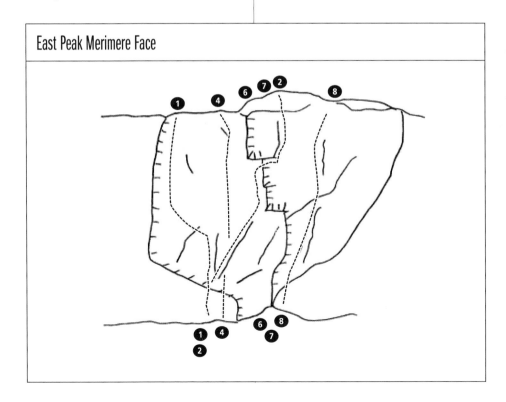

East Peak Merimere Face

the crack. FA Pitch 1: Ken Nichols, Bruce Dicks, 1976. FA Pitch 2: Ken Nichols, 1976.

3. Sledgehammer (5.11 TR) Climb the small overhang just to the left of the *Spring Cleaning* start, up the face to the lower right end of a diagonal overlap high on the face. Undercling up left to a stance and reach straight up to diagonal finger holds above the overlap. Finger-traverse back right about 5 feet, then diagonal steeply up left to good holds and the top. FA: Howard Carney, 1997.

4. Mother Earth (5.11 TR ★) Climb the roof to the right of *Spring Cleaning*. Pass the ramp and continue straight up the face. High-quality climbing and exposure. FA: Ken Nichols, 1984.

5. Rumble of Thunder (5.11 TR) Climb 15 feet up the *Thor's Hammer* corner. Hand traverse 8 feet left, then diagonal up left to the *Thunderbolt* ramp at the point where it suddenly steepens. Finish straight up the face to the right end of a small overlap near the top and finish up a short crack. FA: Ken Nichols, 1997. *Direct Start* (5.12): Starting to the left of a cedar tree, climb straight up the face to join the original route. FA: John Clothier, 1997.

6. Thor's Hammer (5.9 ★) Exciting and exposed wide-crack climbing, underclinging a roof. Ascend the prominent corner and crack system. Bring large camming units for the crux roof and crack afterward. FA: Sam Streibert, John Dowd, 1964. FFA: Mike Heintz, Tony Trocchi, Ken Nichols, 1975.

7. Lightning Strike (5.13 TR ★) The desperate arête system to the right of *Thor's Hammer*. The route follows the arête and the face to the right. Probably the most impressive climb in Connecticut. FA: Sam Slater, 1990.

8. Silmarillion (5.10 PG) Start to the right of *Thor's Hammer*, and get onto the ramp that leads to a vertical crack. Follow the crack to the horizontal crack, move right, and finish up the vertical crack / face and corners. FA: Ken Nichols, 1977.

CATHOLE MOUNTAIN, MERIDEN

As per a city ordinance, there is a regulation concerning rock climbing in Meriden. Please refer to the "Access to Climbing Areas" section in the introduction. Therefore, the information on rock climbing at Washington's Head is for historical purposes only and is not an invitation to trespass. Climbers have visited this crag since the 1970s, and the route information is provided for historical purposes and in the hopes of securing access to this wonderful area in the future.

When viewed from the north, the Pegasus buttress is said to resemble Washington's head—which is the name that locals have used for years to describe this section of Cathole Mountain. The name "Cathole Mountain" refers to the bobcats that once inhabited the territory (Zaborowski, 1997).

Also known by climbers as Cathole Pass, this Traprock crag has been the focus of much debate within the city of Meriden. Over the years the Meriden Land Trust has worked very hard to protect this landmark from development. According to the city, as of 2001, "Washington's Head is part of a 600-acre site which is privately owned. A power plant was approved for 35 acres of the large site. As part of the approval the developer is to transfer the title of the bulk of the site, including the Washington Head area, to the City of Meriden. Therefore, if the Power Plant is built the city will own Washington's Head." However, the power plant was never built and (long story short) the area is now part of Meriden open space.

Directions: From Old Saybrook (Route 9 North): Take exit 15 (Route 66 West) through Middletown. Route 66 joins with I-691. Follow I-691 West to exit 6 (Lewis Avenue / Mall). Turn left off the exit, passing a mall, to Route 71 North. Turn left at the light (after mall). Turn right on Route 71 (Chamberlain Highway) and park at a pullout 0.3 mile farther on the right shoulder of the road. Hike up and left to the obvious crag.

From Waterbury: Take I-84 East to I-691 East. Get off at exit 5. Make a left onto Route 71. Park at the pullout on the right 0.3 mile from the mall.

From Hartford: Take I-91 South to I-691 West. Get off at the mall (exit 6). Make a left at the end of the ramp; turn left at the end of the road at the light. Go up to the end of the road, about 0.5 mile. Make a right onto Route 71 East. See below.

From New Haven / Middletown: Take I-691 West. Get off at the mall (exit 6). Make a left at the end of the ramp. Turn left at the end of the road at the light. Go up to the end of the road, about 0.5 mile. Make a right onto Route 71 East. See below.

Approach: Approximately 0.3 mile up on the right is an entrance to a gravel pit and a paved pull-off area just past it. Park at the paved pull-off; the trail is to the right, where you will see the cliffs. To get to the top of the cliffs, go up to the base and then walk all the way around to the right. You will end up having to go under a large boulder and scramble up a short gully to the top.

Washington's Head

The following climbs begin on the left end of the crag.

1. Catatonia (5.6) The right-facing corner. FA: Eric Engberg, Al Rubin, 1976.

2. Claw Marks (5.6) Climb up the scratches (cracks) to the ledge and continue up the corner. FA: Ken Nichols, 1980.

3. Leopard Spots (5.10 TR) Climb the face between *Claw Marks* and *White Fandango*, starting in the middle corner, move to the right-hand corner, then back to the middle corner, and continue up the face to the top. FA: Ken Nichols, 1990.

4. White Fandango (5.9+ ★) The small overhang and steep left-facing corner. FA: Tony Trocchi, Ken Nichols, Doug Madara, 1975.

5. Fatal Attraction (5.10+ R) From the start of *White Fandango*, climb up and right,

following the steep arête to the ledge. Climb up the middle of the face above, and crack above the upper ledge. FA: Ken Nichols, Jim Ratliff, Rick Orsini, 1989.

6. Phantasmagoria (5.10+ PG ★) The large overhang with a crack. FA: Tony Trocchi, 1975.

7. Friday the 13th (5.11; bolt missing 2015) The roof with the right-facing corner/notch. Climb through the corner/notch, move left into a crack, and finish on the face just to the right of the *Phantasmagoria* corner. FA: Ken Nichols, 1984.

8. Triple Direct (5.12– R/X) A direct line over the small overhangs and difficult face. FA: Marco Fedrizzi, Ken Nichols, 1990.

9. Fool's Mate (5.9 ★) The corner and crack system—intimidating. FA: Ken Nichols, Bruce Dicks, 1976.

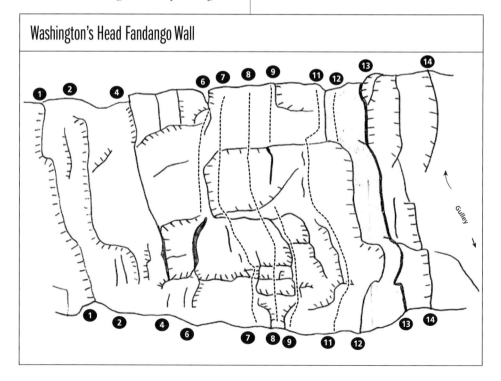

Washington's Head Fandango Wall

10. Rabid Dog (5.11 TR) Climb the corners between *Fool's Mate* and *Killer Cat*. At the top of the corners, traverse right across *Killer Cat* and climb up the steep corner / arête. Finish on *Killer Cat*. FA: Ken Nichols, 1990.

11. Killer Cat (5.10– R) The steep right-facing corner and cracks. FA: Ken Nichols, Topher Brown, Marco Fedrizzi, 1984.

12. Nine Lives (5.9+ R / X) Climb the corner to the steep ramp. Finish up the steep broken face. FA: Ken Nichols, Sam Streibert, Marco Fedrizzi, 1985.

13. Elegant Monkey (5.6 ★) The prominent corner and crack system. FA: Chris Stone, Ken Nichols, 1975.

14. Catwalk (5.2) The large, loose, right-facing corner left of the gully. FA: Chris Stone, 1975.

15. Chimney-Top Corner (5.5) The large corner and chimney to the right of the gully. FA: Ken Nichols, Chris Stone, 1975.

16. Block of Ages (5.5) The crack system with a large chockstone. FA: Bob Poirer, Stewart Sayah, 1973.

17. Satanic Versus (5.9+ R) Start on *Block of Ages* and stem over to the right to a stance on the face above the overhang. Continue up the face above, staying to the right of the arête. At the ledge step over to a short crack and the top. FA: Ken Nichols, Bruce Jelen, 1989.

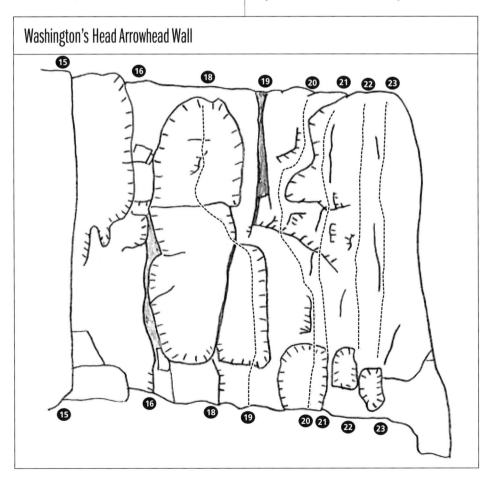

Washington's Head Arrowhead Wall

18. Arrowhead (5.8+ ★ R) Climb the overhang at the notch. Continue up the crack, then move left onto the clean and airy face. FA: Bob Clark, Mike Lapierre, 1981.

19. No Future (5.9+ X) Climb over the roof to the right of *Arrowhead* and up the thin face. The route technically ends at this point. However, you can finish in the chimney or on Arrowhead. FA: Ken Nichols, 1981.

20. Catapult (5.9 R ★) Climb up to the overlap, move left, and launch into a left-facing corner system and steep face. FA: Ken Nichols, Jim Ratcliff, 1989.

21. Realm of the Senses (5.9 PG ★) Climb up to the overlap and continue straight up, following thin cracks. One of the best climbs on the crag. FA: Ken Nichols, Chad Hussey, Mike Heintz, Tony Trocchi, 1981.

22. Millions of Dead Dogs (5.10 TR) The steep face to the left of *Saturday Night Special*. FA: Ken Nichols, 1982.

23. Saturday Night Special (5.9– PG / R ★) Rabbly cracks up the face. FA: Chris Stone, Ken Nichols, Dusty Nelson, 1975.

24. Pink Elephants (5.5) The large corner / crack system. FA: Bob Poirer, Stewart Sayah, 1974.

25. Imperial Wizard (5.11+ TR ★) Climb the blank-looking face to the left of *Danzig*. Finish on the small corner / overlap / roof and face above. One extremely hard move on an otherwise superb 5.10 face. FA: Ken Nichols, 1986.

26. Danzig (5.12 TR ★) Work up the center of the steep, sustained face, past shallow corners, to the overlap and corner. Climb over the small roof, step left, and continue up the face. FA: Mike Heintz, 1988.

27. Jaguar (5.10+ R / X ★) The outside corner and face. A very technical move, or tricky lunge, brings you past the crux. Then finish up the strenuous overlap and face above. FA: Ken Nichols, Marco Fedrizzi, 1985.

28. Pegasus (5.8+ ★) One of the best climbs in Connecticut. Follow the steep corner / crack system that ends with a traverse, out right, under the roof. FA: Casey Newman, 1975. A variation, *Palomino* (5.4), traverses left, around the corner, and onto the face, instead of the final traverse right under the roof. FA: Mike Lapierre, Phil Costello, Roger Rahn, Franco Ghiggeri, Bob Clark, 1981.

29. Cat-o-Nine-Tails (5.9+ R ★) Follow the face and outside corner to the right of *Pegasus*. FA: Al Long, Sam Streibert, 1976.

30. Bobcat Arête (5.10+ TR ★) Climb the arête and overlaps to the left of *Mind Bender Direct*. FA: Bob Clark, 1988.

31. Mind Bender Direct (5.9+ / 10- PG ★) One of the best climbs in Connecticut. The fixed pitons have been stolen, so placing gear is tricky. A large camming unit, placed horizontally, and RPs, placed at the lip, protect the final roof. Climb up the slab and move left into the corner system. From the top of the corner, move right onto the steep face, then trend back left under the roof system. Reach high over the lip of the final roof for a great finish. FRA: Ken Nichols, Garry Waltman, 1983.

32. Golden Book (5.6) The large open corner—somewhat loose. FA: Ken Nichols, Chris Stone, Dusty Nelson, 1975.

Washington's Head

LAMENTATION MOUNTAIN, MERIDEN

As per a city ordinance, there is a regulation concerning rock climbing in Meriden. Please refer to the "Access to Climbing Areas" section in the introduction. Therefore, the information on rock climbing at Lamentation Mountain is for historical purposes only and not an invitation to trespass.

For many years the Evening Wall was a favorite for many climbers. The crag is nicely secluded and offered a variety of difficult climbs, lower-angle face climbs, and a couple of graceful corners.

The Evening Wall is located on Lamentation Mountain and is best approached from the Dr. Francis Giuffrida Park in Meriden. Next to the parking area at Giuffrida Park, you will find a kiosk that contains a map of the area and park regulations. One of the regulations, as of 2001, states that rock climbing and rappelling are prohibited. The Evening Wall is located off of Giuffrida Park property; however, it is located on City of Meriden property—refer to page xiii of the "Access to Climbing Areas" section.

Because of the climbing restriction in Giuffrida Park, the climbing on Chauncy Peak (the aesthetic ridge above the east side of Crescent Lake) is not listed in this guide. The premier crag on Chauncy Peak—Looking Glass—overlooks Crescent Lake and has many fine climbs. This wonderful area will, it is hoped, be open to climbers in the future.

Directions: From I-91 North: Take exit 20, Country Club Road / Middle Street. Take a left off the exit and proceed to the stop sign. Continue straight on Country Club Road for 2.6 miles until you see the Dr. Francis Giuffrida Park entrance on your right. Continue to the parking area next to Crescent Lake.

From I-91 South: Take exit 20. Make a left on Middle Street and then a right on Country Club Road. Continue on Country Club Road for 2.6 miles until you see the Dr. Francis Giuffrida Park entrance on your right. Continue to the parking area next to Crescent Lake.

From I-691: Take exit 8 (Route 5 North). Follow Route 5 North for 0.4 mile to the light. Take a right on Westfield Road. Follow Westfield Road to the intersection with Bee Street (0.9 mile). Take a left (continues as Westfield Road) and continue for 0.1 mile to the Dr. Francis Giuffrida Park entrance on your left.

Approach: From the kiosk on the north end of the parking lot, follow the white-blazed trail (on the west side of Crescent Lake). Hike for about 12 minutes and the trail will come to an intersection. Continue hiking north for another 4 minutes to where the trail splits; veer left (northwest). After another 3 minutes the trail comes to an intersection (south = hard left; west = left; north = straight). Take a left, heading west, and the trail becomes blue-blazed. After another 3 minutes you will pass a gazebo (good landmark).

From the gazebo another 6 minutes on the blue-blazed trail will bring you to the top of a cliff. Hike the ridge for a couple of minutes, and you will come to a view of a blue water tower, power lines to the left, and a field to the right. You are now on top of the "Wailing Wall." To reach the bottom of the Wailing Wall, continue along the blue-blazed trail for 1 minute and take a left down a gully. There are approximately twenty-five routes on this cliff.

From the Wailing Wall continue on the blue-blazed trail for another 2 minutes. There is a faint descent trail on the left, which brings you to the southern end of the Evening Wall.

Wailing Wall

Not the best climbing in Connecticut but not a bad area for a beginner during early spring or late fall—before the vegetation grows in. Twenty-nine routes, not listed, are found on this small crag. Have an adventure.

Evening Wall

A secluded area that will, eventually, open up because of the diseased hemlock trees that are destined to fall in the future.

1. Downspout (5.3) The low-angle chimney on the left side of the crag. FA: Ken Nichols, 1980.

2. Dry Mouth (5.5 R / X) The face between *Downspout* and *Wrinkled Face*. FA: Al Carilli,

Ken Nichols, Howard Carney, 1993.

3. Wrinkled Face (5.4) The low-angle, juggy face to the right of *Downspout* and up the center of the face. FA: Ken Nichols, Bill Sullivan, 1980.

4. Commonplace (5.5 PG / R) Left of the *Five o'clock Shadow* corner, climb up the crack into a right-facing corner. Continue up the blocky corner to the top. FA: Ken Nichols, Franco Ghiggeri, 1980.

5. Five o'clock Shadow (5.6) The awkward left-facing corner and crack system. FA: Ken Nichols, Franco Ghiggeri, 1980.

6. Shaggy Beard (5.3 PG / R) A nice beginners' climb. Up the face just right of the arête into the crack / fissure. FA: Ken Nichols, Franco Ghiggeri, 1980.

7. Drizzle (5.5 R) The face just right of *Shaggy Beard*. FA: Ken Nichols, Mike Barker, 1987.

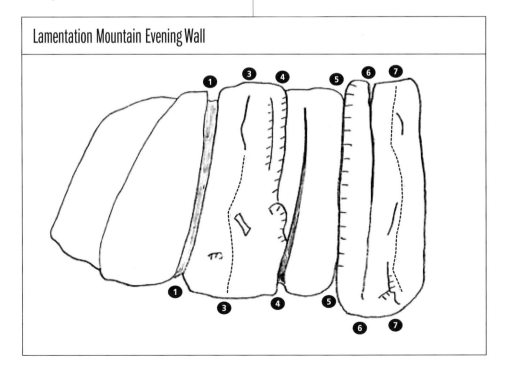

Lamentation Mountain Evening Wall

8. Mad Scramble (5.3) The unattractive face and steep crack to the right of the corner / gully. FA: Ken Nichols, Bill Sullivan, 1980.

9. Drifter (5.5 R) The face between *Mad Scramble* and *Pitch Dark*. FA: Ken Nichols, Mike Barker, 1987.

10. Pitch Dark (5.4) On the right side of the loose-looking wall; follow cracks and corners. FA: Ken Nichols, Franco Ghiggeri, 1980.

11. Kick the Bucket (5.8– R) The steep corner on the left side of the main buttress. Climb up the corner, left over the overlap, then back right through the roof. Finish by following a shallow crack. FA: Ken Nichols, 1980.

12. Cows on the Run (5.9+ R) Climb the corner / arête just to the right of *Kick the Bucket*. When you reach the *Kick the Bucket* upper crack, step left and climb the face to the top. FA: Sam Slater, Ken Nichols, 1982.

13. Spanish Inquisition (5.11+ / 5.12–TR ★) Just to the right of the arête, muscle up the steep orange face / right diagonaling seam to the overlap on *No Rest for the Weary*. (**Alternate start:** Climb up *No Rest for the Weary* to the overlap.) Climb over the overlap, trending right to the second overlap. Continue over the second overlap and up the sustained face to the top. FA: Ken Nichols, 1985.

14. No Rest for the Weary (5.10+ TR ★) Climb over the small overhang to the overlap. Work left, then up to a stance just to the right of the arête. Continue up the face to the right of the arête. FA: Ken Nichols, 1980.

15. Crime and Punishment (5.11+ R / X ★) Start up *Climb Wave*; at the second (larger) overlap, traverse left and desperately work over the overlap to a stance at the base of a right-facing corner. Climb up the corner, traverse left at the arête a couple of feet, and continue up the face. Traverse a few feet left into a short corner and continue the struggle to the top. FA: Ken Nichols, Sam Slater, 1982.

16. Climb Wave (5.10+ PG ★) Probably the most reasonable of the desperates on the main wall. Start up the right edge of the lower overlap to a bucket. Layback and struggle up the thin cracks and open corner to a stance below the square roof. Layback again and struggle up the crack, past a protruding block, to the top. FA: Ken Nichols, 1980.

17. TNT (5.9 ★) Go up the large right-facing corner to a roof. Squirm over the roof, following the crack to the top. FA: Mike Lapierre, Bob Clark, 1980.

18. Blasting Cap (5.8+ ★) A good variation—awkward crack climbing. At the roof on *TNT*, move right and follow the crack to the top. FA: Bob Clark, Mike Lapierre, 1980.

19. Bottleneck (5.3) The large chimney with chockstones. FA: Ken Nichols, 1980.

The following climbs ascend the buttress to the right of the *Bottleneck* chimney.

20. Tactician (5.10 TR ★) Follow the thin face just right of the arête. FA: TR Ken Nichols, 1987.

Lamentation Mountain Evening Wall

21. Smear Tactics (5.10 R ★) Climb up the left-facing corner to a small ledge. Go over the overlap and aim for a small right-facing corner system just right of *Tactician*. FA: Ken Nichols, 1980.

22. Fear Tactics (5.10 R ★; bolt missing 2015) Climb up the face to the right of *Smear Tactics* to the right edge of the small ledge. Continue up the face, aiming for the small right-facing corner just right of *Smear Tactics*. FA: Sam Slater, Ken Nichols, Mike Guravage, 1982.

23. April Fools (5.8 PG ★) Climb up the center of the buttress, aiming for an open corner that diagonals to the right. Continue up the corner to a small ledge. Step left and finish up the face just right of the crack. FA: Mike Heintz, Ken Nichols, 1980.

24. Archangel (5.7 ★) A very nice route. On the right side of the buttress is a clean right-facing corner. Climb up the face and follow the beautiful corner. FA: Mike Lapierre, Micky Walsh, 1978.

25. Indiscipline (5.8 R) Wander up the arête to the right of Archangel. FA: Stewart Sayah, Bill Ferrucci, 1982.

There are three routes, 5.5, 5.4, 5.3, on the low-angle face to the right.

PINNACLE RIDGE, PLAINVILLE

Pinnacle Rock is located on private property and climbing is not officially allowed. Please refer to the access section in regard to Pinnacle Rock. During the days of the first ascents of *Emerald City* and *Zambezi Hatchet Head,* there were no houses. The approach was through pastures and past cows. While to the author's knowledge, climbers have never been asked to leave, overtime parking has become more restricted. Throughout the 1980s and early 1990s, there was a parking lot at the trailhead. This lot has been closed. If choosing to explore this area, do your part to foster good relations by being polite to residents of the neighborhood, keeping the noise to a minimum, and picking up trash left by people who are too ignorant to pack it out. Carpooling is highly recommended (Starbucks is popular as of 2015). The following information on climbing at Pinnacle is presented for historical purposes and is not an invitation to trespass.

Pinnacle Rock is the epitome of suburban climbing: The cliffs brood over the backyards of Middle America below. The ubiquitous lawnmower and the sounds of children playing on swing sets constantly serenade the climber. Unfortunately, the cliffs here are not immune to suburban blight: broken bottles, graffiti, and trash. Climbers have done their best to keep the area as clean as possible, but it's an uphill battle. Although not quite in the class of an out-of-towner's "destination crag," such as Ragged Mountain, this is a favorite spot for many local climbers in central Connecticut and has its own charms that grow on you.

There are some interesting artifacts located near Pinnacle Rock. One of these is Hospital Rock. Found within a short hike from the top of Pinnacle Rock, Hospital Rock contains the names of more than one hundred patients who were quarantined in a smallpox clinic during the 1700s. As an experiment, the patients were purposely exposed to the smallpox disease. Once infected, they were quarantined and then cared for. The hope was that the patients would become immune from potential deadly outbreaks of the disease, which were common during this time.

Another interesting artifact of this area, dating from the 1950s, is the remnants of a Nike Missile System Base, located behind the ridge to the south of Pinnacle Rock. These facilities were constructed during the Cold War in response to the perceived threat of a nuclear attack. If you walk down the ridge, you can see the tops of the bunkers where military personnel and missile systems were once located. For detailed information on these sites, located throughout New England, a search of the Internet will provide detailed information.

Directions: From Waterbury: Take I-84 east to exit 34, Crooked Street. Make a left at the end of the ramp. Go to the end of the road, about 0.25 mile, and make a left at the light—Route 372. Go about 0.7 mile to a VW car dealer on the right corner. Make a right at the light onto Metacomet Road. See below.

From Hartford: Take I-84 west to exit 33 (Route 72 West). Take exit 2 (Route 372) and make a right at the end of the exit onto Route 372 East. Travel 0.1 mile to the light and take a left onto Metacomet Road. See below.

Veronica Sassu on *Locomotive Face*
PHOTO DAVID FASULO

Approach from Metacomet Road: Go another 0.5 mile and pass a small pond on the left at a curve in the road. The main cliff complex is above on the right. Park in the area, but avoid parking in the vicinity of the "No Parking" signs to nurture the fragile relationship that exists between climbers and the neighbors. The obvious old semipaved road (impassable to vehicular traffic) into the woods leads to a climber's trail up to the base of the cliffs. If you follow the road in its entirety, it will deposit you on top of Pinnacle Rock. A trail branches off to the right to access the base of the wall.

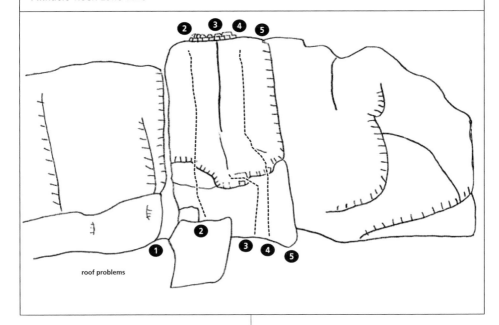

roof problems

Pinnacle Rock

Lone Pine

When facing the cliff complex from the road below, Lone Pine is located at the left, separated from the main cliffs of Pinnacle by a large gully and featuring predominately unappealing and poorly protected roof problems, with two notable exceptions: *Superslab* and *Supermantel*, two of the area's minor classic 5.10s.

To the left of the obvious *Superslab* face, just beyond the 5.2 corner, is the continuous overhanging buttress that is home to the aforementioned collection of roof problems, all in the range of 5.10 to 5.12. Take your pick and have fun. Be prepared to have holds pull off in your hands.

1. Pine Line (5.3) The corner and crack with the pine tree on top. FA: Sam Streibert, 1971.

2. Superslab (5.10 R; bolt missing 2015) Start on top of the big block and climb the short, awkward, left-facing corner. Climb up the face above (crux), avoiding holds on *Supermantel*, its neighbor to the right. FA: Ken Nichols, Bob Clark, Jim Wilcox, Bruce Jelen, Rich Murnane, Chad Hussey, 1986.

3. Supermantel (5.10+ ★) Easier for shorter climbers but still a befuddling crux for all. Climb the low face just to the right of the *Superslab* block, then reach up to and traverse across the lip of the roof on good holds. Then meet "Mr. Crux." Continue up the 5.9 crack to finish. FA: Harry Brielman, 1980.

4. Superfacial (5.11 TR) The small roof and face between *Supermantel* and *Cardiac Arête*. FA: Ken Nichols, 1986.

5. Cardiac Arête (5.5 X) The arête to the right of *Supermantel*. Avoid the initial roof by moving right, and then back left to the main face. FA: Ken Nichols, Bob Clark, 1980.

To the right of the Superslab block, the quality of the routes is low. Routes range from easy to 5.11 roof pulls.

Emerald City Slab

Across the dirt gully to the right of Lone Pine, the first attraction is a low-angle face of pretty rock with a stellar 5.8 finger crack and seam splitting it in the middle.

6. Wizard of Oz (5.7 R) The thin crack on the left side of the face. Move a little left when it ends, and continue up on interesting moves. FA: Ken Nichols, Warren Wooley, 1980.

7. Emerald City (5.8 G ★) A Pinnacle classic. A great thin crack and face climb up the center of the slab and, for once, good protection make this an area must-do. FA: Mike Heintz, Kim Smith, 1974.

8. Cowardly Lion (5.8+ R) The face between *Emerald City* and *Scarecrow*. FA: Ken Nichols, Jim Ratcliff, 1989.

9. Scarecrow (5.7 R) The left-facing corners and face. Dubious protection in the expanding flake / corner. FA: Ken Nichols, Warren Wooley, 1980.

10. Tin Man (5.7 R) The arête to the right of *Scarecrow*. FA: Sam Slater, 1985.

Pinnacle Rock Emerald City Slab

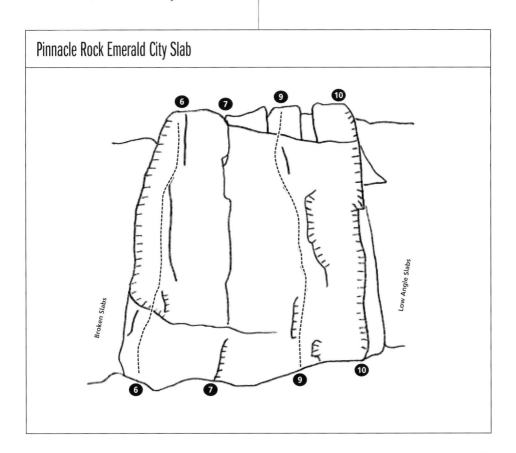

A-Frame Wall

To the right of the Emerald City face is a broken, low-angle face with a few low-quality routes. The following routes begin on the left side of the steep main buttress, farther to the right.

11. Wild and Woolly (5.7) Climb the overhang and left-facing corner system, passing a ledge with a tree. FA: Ken Nichols, Warren Wooley, 1980.

12. Mossad (5.9+ PG / R ★; bolt missing 2015) Another Pinnacle classic at the left end of the main buttress, this entertaining route starts up a small but awkward overlap. Continue up to a larger overlap, over this (crux), and up a beautiful face (bolt) to the top. FA: Bob Clark, Ken Nichols, 1986. The route can also be climbed by starting up *Wild and Wooley* (5.8+) for about 15 feet and then moving right to the overlap and joining the route. FA: Ken Nichols, Mike Heintz, 1981.

13. Lil' Roofs (5.11– TR) The roof and face system between *Mossad* and *Star of David*. Starting about 10 feet right of *Mossad*, climb straight up the cliff over two small overhangs.

14. Star of David (5.9+ R / X) A body length left of an ugly-looking crack, head up into a small A-shaped arch, step left, and pull over the overlap. Go up a dirty left-facing corner to the next overlap, then climb the face to a crack at the top. FA: Ken Nichols, Bob Clark, Steve Willard, 1985.

15. Badlands (5.4) The crack to the left of *A-Frame*. FA: Mike and Fred Heintz, 1980.

16. Superstitions (5.4 R) The arête to the left of *A-Frame*. FA: Mike Heintz, Ken Nichols, 1981.

17. A-Frame (5.6 ★) Climb the impressive A-shaped alcove using either corner. Exit out the overhanging chimney at the top. FA: Ken Nichols, Mike Heintz, 1980.

18. Brave New World (5.11– R ★) From the ledge on *A-Frame*, work up the right wall to the horizontal crack and get established on the arête. Follow the arête (right side) to the top. FA: Ken Nichols, Marco Fedrizzi, 1984. *Age of Dinosaurs* variation (5.12 TR): Once established on the arête, traverse left and climb up the center of the steep wall on the right of the A-Frame arch. FA: Ken Nichols, 1990.

19. Wild Kingdom (5.11– PG ★; bolts and pitons missing 2015) Tackle the giant overhanging buttress to the right of the *A-Frame* arch. From the ledge on *A-Frame*, work right under the overhang. Move up, then slightly right (piton missing), then up the right-facing corner system to a two-bolt belay on the left. Move left and follow the clean corner system to the top. FA: Mike Heintz, Ken Nichols, 1981. Second pitch variations: The face above just left of the belay stance (5.6) and the face just right of the belay stance (5.5).

Pinnacle Rock A–Frame Wall

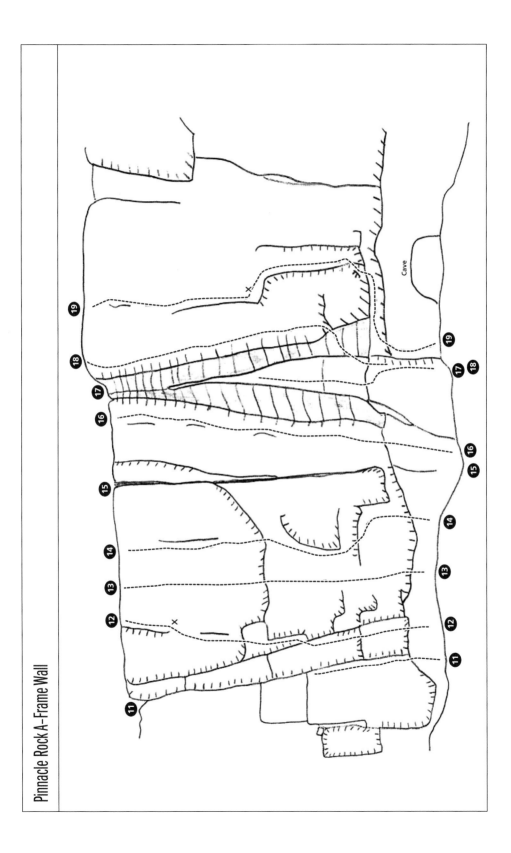

Dream Weaver Wall

This is the large buttress of rock that extends from the right edge of the cave—*Wild Kingdom*—to the prominent right-facing corner forming *Herbarium*.

20. Dream Weaver (5.9+ PG ★) A classic Pinnacle expedition. Climb the face right of the cave-like recess to the overlap, then climb up through the notch. Continue up the crack and move right at the triangle roof. Traverse right under the lip of the roof system to a belay under the left end of the third roof. Traverse right under the roof for 15 feet, pull the roof (awkward 5.9++) and up the crack to the top and the end of a great route. FA: Tom Egan, 1970s. FFA: Mike Heintz, Ken Nichols, 1980. *Straight Up* variation 5.5: At the triangle roof continue straight up the main corner / crack system. FA: Ken Nichols, Harry Brielman, 1980. *Leaders Choice* variation 5.5: At the triangle roof traverse left 35 feet and climb the second pitch crack and corner on *Wild Kingdom*. FA: Ken Nichols, Franco Ghiggeri, 1980.

21. Edge of Darkness (5.9+ R) Climb up the right side of the *Dream Weaver* edge / arête, move right, and continue up the arête to the ledge. Climb up the crack above the roof, move left, and finish on the face above. FA: Ken Nichols, Joe Vitti, 1986.

22. Woolly Bear (5.9– R) Climb the face just to the right of *Edge of Darkness*, traverse a few feet right at the overlap, clear the overlap, and climb the face above to the ledge. Continue up the left-facing corner system and face. FA: Ken Nichols, Joe Vitti, 1986.

23. Psycho Path (5.9 PG / R ★; bolt missing 2015) Another classic Pinnacle expedition. Start 25 feet right of *Dream Weaver* and climb

the column face to a stance (bolt). Crank over the roof; move left and over the second roof to a ledge. Move right, launch over the final roof at a shallow right-facing corner, and finish up the exposed face. FA: Ken Nichols, Mike Heintz, 1981.

24. Flying Squirrel (5.10– PG) On the right end of the overhanging buttress is an intimidating right-facing corner. Climb up the corner / overhang to a stance on the left. Continue up the right-facing corner to the ledge. Continue straight over the roof at the corner and crack system. Finish on the face above. Ken Nichols, Mike Heintz, 1980.

25. Dungeons and Dragons (5.10 PG ★; bolt missing 2015) Climb *Flying Squirrel* to the stance above the overhang. Work right across the face to an overlap and up the face to the ledge, past a bolt. Climb the roof 6 feet left of Dream Weaver at the right-facing corner (hidden gear placement). Finish up the face. FA: Ken Nichols, Joe Vitti, 1986.

26. Great Expectations (5.8 PG / R ★) A great route, but protection can be difficult—double ropes recommended. Otherwise, a "breathtaking" lead. Head 10 to 12 feet up the *Herbarium* corner, then traverse all the way out left to a large inside corner-and-ramp system that leads back up right. Belay at the base of the corner. Go up the corner and ramp to the roof, then up and left (crux, marginal pro with tiny wires) to the top. FA: Rocky Keeler, Al Rubin, 1973.

27. Steam Engine (5.10– TR) Work past the overhanging start of *Tiptoe*, traverse left, climb the arête and face just right of *Great Expectations*, and finish over the middle of the roof. A harder variation (5.10) is to climb the face right of the arête and finish on the right end of the roof. FA: Joe Vitti, 1987.

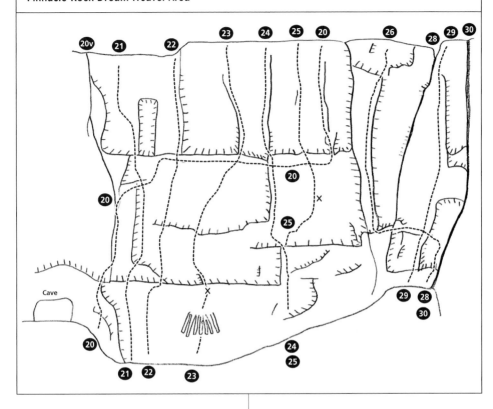

28. Locomotive Breath (5.7 PG ★) Another Pinnacle classic. Climb up the *Herbarium* corner for 10 to 12 feet, then left to the base of the right-leaning crack. Continue up the crack to the top. This is excellent climbing with nice exposure—a fine lead for experienced leaders solid in the grade. FA: Tom Egan, 1970s.

29. Tiptoe (5.9– R) Struggle over the overhang (can be loose) to the left of the *Herbarium* corner at a small left-facing corner. Continue up the left-facing corner system and face. FA: Ken Nichols, Mike Heintz, 1980. *Locomotive Face* variation (5.9–; TR): Midway up the *Tiptoe* corner wander up the face just right of *Locomotive Breath* to the top.

30. Herbarium (5.5 ★) The large inside corner is a benchmark for finding nearby routes. FA: Adrian Juncosa, Bob Harding, 1970s. *Don't Touch* variation (5.6): After the start climb the crack on the right face and then trend right near the top to finish on *Lost World*. FA: Bill Sullivan, Mike Lapierre, 1981.

Right Wing Wall

This is the clean, open face extending from the prominent right-facing corner, *Herbarium*, to the right end of the wall.

31. Lost World (5.9– R ★; bolt missing 2015) A classic low-angle face climb, 10 feet to the right of the *Herbarium* corner. Climb up the smooth face to the bolt, then tiptoe up the delicate face and head up, aiming for small corners and some protection. There is very little protection. Placements that look solid on the cruxy middle section are in suspect rock. The crux on the lower face is protected by a bolt. FA: Ken Nichols, Chad Hussey, Mike Heintz, 1981.

32. WWC Memorial Route (5.9+ X) A harder version of its neighbor to the left. Named as a tribute to the father of Bob

Lauren Humphrey finishing *Zambezi Hatchet Head* PHOTO DAVID FASULO

Clark. One of the first Connecticut climbers to be certified as a AMGA guide, Bob has been one of the area's most prolific pioneers and icons since the 1970s. Climb up to the overlap on *Right Wing*; step left and up to a ledge. Continue straight up the face. FA: Bob Clark, Franco Ghiggeri, 1985.

33. Right Wing (5.5 PG ★) A good route and another minor classic at Pinnacle. Climb up the giant right-leaning flake/corner system until it ends. Move up and right, following the right-facing corners. Protection is well spaced; it's not a lead for 5.5 leaders.

34. Deep Knee Bend (5.5 X) Start left of *Yucca Flats* and aim for a ledge above the *Right Wing* flake/corner. Continue up the corners and face to the right of *Right Wing*. Be careful of glass. FA: Ken Nichols, Kathy Clark, 1981.

35. Yucca Flats (5.7 R) Start a few feet to the right of *Deep Knee Bend* and climb up the wall, aiming for a large fissure and then the top. FA: Ken Nichols, Mike Heintz, 1981.

36. Suffocation (5.6 R ★) Climb the short wall and over the overhang at a right-facing corner. Continue up shallow right-facing corners and the face to the top. FA: Mike Heintz, Ken Nichols, 1981.

37. Zambezi Hatchet Head (5.8 PG ★) Another classic at Pinnacle; a great route. Climb the short wall to a ledge, up the thin crack, and over the small roof at a right-facing corner. Continue up the crack, corner, and face above. Some run-outs but otherwise solid pro. Being John's first first ascent, he was given the honor of naming the route. FA: Mike Heintz, John Sahi, 1974.

38. Zumwot Brittle (5.6 R) Starting a body length right of *Zambezi Hatchet Head*, climb past the overlap and up the face. FA: Mike Heintz, Harry Brielman, 1981.

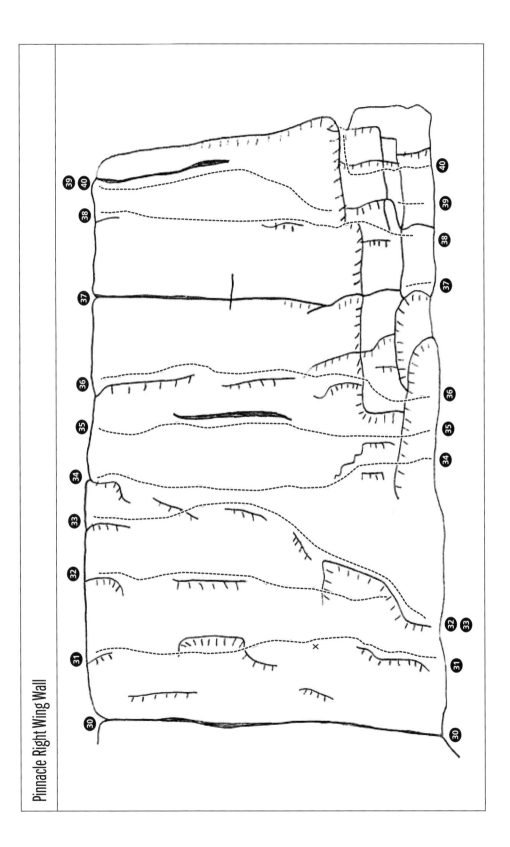

Pinnacle Right Wing Wall

39. Xanadu (5.6 R ★) Go through the break in the overhang a few feet right of *Zumwot Brittle*. Trend right, aiming for a crack and the summit. FA: Mike Heintz, 1980.

40. Wild Weasel (5.10 R) Climb the right-facing corner to the right of *Xanadu*, traverse to the right end of the roof, and reach over the roof to a bucket. Over the roof then up the second *Casual Corner* ledge. Move left and finish up the blunt arête. FA: Sam Slater, Ken Nichols, 1982.

41. Russian Tea Room (5.9+ R) Start 8 feet right of the *Xanadu* corner, climb past a low overlap, and continue up the face just left of a network of small right-facing corners to the main overlap. Pull over the main overlap 4 to 5 feet from its left end. Finish up the vertical crack on *Xanadu*. FA: Ken Nichols, Boris Itin, 2005.

Entertainer Wall

A steep, south-facing wall to the left of the crack and corner system *Narrowing Experience*. The following climbs are located on a south-facing wall around the corner from *Xanadu*.

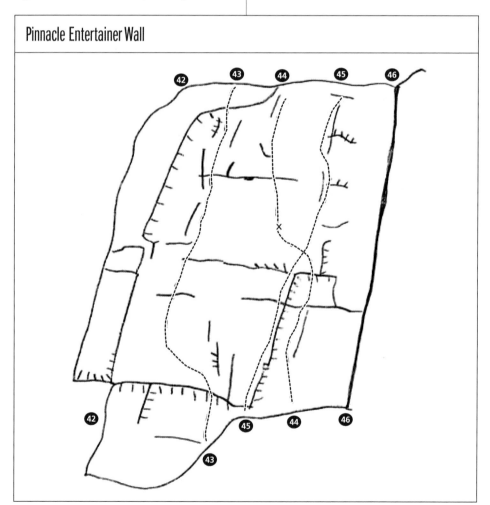

Pinnacle Entertainer Wall

Bob Clark on *The Entertainer* PHOTO CHAD HUSSEY

42. Casual Corner (5.5) Short but nice. Follow the ledge to the base of the steep crack. Climb up the crack to the base of a ramp that leads up right. Continue up the ramp to the top. Mike Heintz, 1980. *Casual Arête* variation (5.6 R): Climb up the first corner on *Casual Corner*, then traverse left over the blunt arête to join *Xanadu*.

43. The Entertainer (5.10 R ★) Fingery, and an exciting lead for climbers solid in the grade. Climb up the lower face, then follow the thin crack / face just right of *Casual Corner*. FA: Ken Nichols, Sam Slater, 1982.

44. Funshine (5.11– PG; bolt missing 2015) Start just right of *Sunshine*, climb up the short face to a stance, then diagonal up and left to the blunt arête (bolt) and straight up to the finish. FA: Joe Vitti, Ken Nichols, David Fasulo, 1987.

45. Sunshine (5.9– X ★) Start at the left-facing corner. Climb up the corner to a stance, and continue up the right side of the face. FA: Chad Hussey, Sam Slater, Ken Nichols, 1982.

46. Narrowing Experience (5.6 R) The huge corner with the crack is difficult to protect. FA: Ken Nichols, 1980.

Cracked Wall

This is the last major buttress on the right end of Pinnacle Rock. It contains a selection of obvious crack climbs.

47. Quasar (5.7+ R) The face just right of the corner. It has poor protection but makes for fun climbing. FA: Mike Heintz, Chad Hussey, Ken Nichols, 1981.

48. First Crack (5.4 ★) A Pinnacle classic, great for beginners as a toprope or lead. Climb the prominent crack—well protected for a change.

49. Zzyzx Road (5.7 R / X) The face between *First Crack* and *Montana Wildhack*. FA: Ken Nichols, Bob Clark, 1984.

50. Montana Wildhack (5.5 X) The face between the first and second cracks, starting just left of a short crack. Nice climbing and another good beginner's route, but toprope this one. FA: Kim Smith, Eric Butterfield, 1976. *Wildhack Direct* variation 5.4 (50v): Ascend the middle of the face to join *Montana Wildhack*.

51. Second Crack (5.7 PG ★) The second prominent crack on the wall.

52. Tasmanian Devil (5.10+ R ★) A finger-cranker over the small overhang and the face between the second and third cracks. Start about 4 feet to the right of *Second Crack*, crank over the roof, then trend right to a short right-facing corner and up to the top. FA: Ken Nichols, 1982.

53. Third Crack (5.7+ PG) The third prominent crack on the wall. FA: Al Long, Al Rubin, 1980.

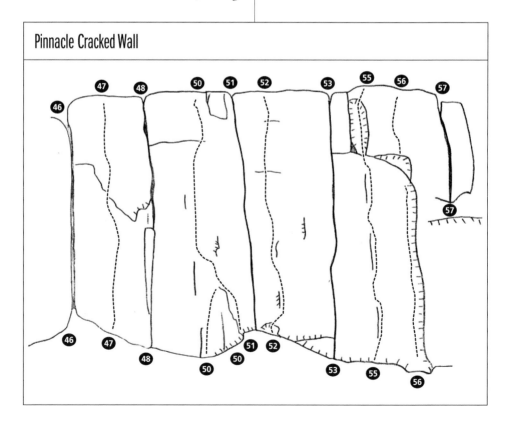

Pinnacle Cracked Wall

54. Scalped (5.9 R / X) The face between *Third Crack* and *Tomahawk*. FA: Ken Nichols, Al Carilli, 1993.

55. Tomahawk (5.9+ R) The face 10 feet to the right of *Third Crack*. Steep and pumpy face climbing. FA: Ken Nichols, Sam Slater, Chad Hussey, 1982.

56. Beans and Franks (5.6 X) The arête on the right end of the face. FA: Bob Clark, Don Pelletier, Gary Martin, 1980.

There are several short routes located to the right of the main part of the cliff, above a short step.

57. Sixth Sense (5.6) A first lead for many, this is the short, awkward crack off the ledge. Climb the gully or approach from the right. FA: Ken Nichols, Bob Clark, 1980.

58. Kiddy Slab (5.1–5.7) The right end of the cliff has a low-angle slab and a nice arête to play on.

RATTLESNAKE MOUNTAIN, FARMINGTON

While lacking the sweeping faces of many crags, the charms of Rattlesnake Rock are the complex crack and corner systems that abound on this wall. The main wall gets plenty of sun and is a good place to climb in the late fall and early spring. Rattlesnake Mountain also contains a good selection of boulders and a cave that form Will Warren's Den. According to legend, Will Warren was flogged for drinking and not attending church. In response to the flogging, Will attempted to burn down the town in the 1600s. A little upset, the townspeople chased him into the hills, and he was hidden by an Indian squaw and never found. The cave is marked with a plaque and is a historical marker. Rattlesnake Rock is located on Town of Farmington property. The crags close to Rattlesnake Rock (Porcupine Hole, Nautilus, and Green Wall) are on private property and as far as the author knows, rock climbing is not permitted. A few climbs are listed on these crags for historical purposes only in the hopes of gaining access to these crags in the future. Although the Metacomet Trail passes over these cliffs, the routes listed for Porcupine Hole, Nautilus, and Green Wall are not an invitation to climb or trespass on these three small crags.

Pinnacle Parking and Approach

Directions: From Waterbury: Take I-84 east to exit 34 (Crooked Street). Make a left at the end of the ramp. Go to the end of the road, about 0.25 mile, and make a left at the light—Route 372. Go about 0.7 mile and make a right at the light onto Metacomet Road. See below.

From Hartford: Take I-84 west to exit 33 (Route 72 West). Take exit 2 (Route 372) and make a right at the end of the exit onto Route 372 East. Travel 0.1 mile to the light and take a left onto Metacomet Road.

Travel on Metacomet Road 0.5 mile and pass a small pond on the left at a curve in the road. The main Pinnacle cliff complex is above on the right. Park in the area, but avoid parking in the vicinity of the "No Parking" signs in order to nurture the fragile relationship that exists between climbers and neighbors.

Pinnacle Rock approach: The trail is across from the pond behind the dirt parking area (same approach as Pinnacle Ridge). Hike up the old dirt road, past cement blocks, to the ridgeline. Turn left (north-northeast) onto the blue-blazed Metacomet Trail and hike for 25 minutes to the base of Rattlesnake Rock. *Note:* In the summer the last section of the trail crosses power lines and can be overgrown with weeds / poison ivy. The trail is also more strenuous than the Route 6 approach. From the left end of Rattlesnake Rock, continue on the trail for 5 minutes to Will Warren's Den; another 5 minutes from the den will bring you to the Green Wall; another 5 minutes will bring you to Porcupine Hole.

Route 6 Parking and Approach

From the Pinnacle approach, continue on Route 372 and take a right on Route 10 North. Veer right onto Route 6 (heading East). If coming from Hartford, take exit 38 (Colt Highway US 6 West).

Parking 1: Eighty feet past Pinnacle Road in Farmington (heading east from Pinnacle Rock), there is a small parking area on the right (known as Settlement Road). This area adds 0.1 mile to the approach but has much better parking. The trail intersects with the trailhead for parking option number 2.

Parking 2: At the top of the hill, near the TV towers, is a "Metacomet Trail" sign. On the opposite side of the road is a small pullout with very limited parking, just off the main road. From this parking area head up the road for the TV towers and immediately take a right onto the blue-blazed Metacomet Trail. From this point the top of the Green Wall is a 25-minute hike, and the top of Rattlesnake Rock (1.2 miles) is a 30-minute hike.

There are three small crags you will pass on the way to Rattlesnake Rock if approaching from Route 6 in Farmington. These crags lie on private property (2015) and are not open to climbing to the author's knowledge. Porcupine Hole is a short cliff. *Jean* (5.10–; FA 1980) ascends the face (leaving the arête alone) to the right of the chimney with a boulder lodged in it. The next is the Nautilus Wall, the short, steep wall on the very left end of the Green Wall. There are four 5.9 climbs on this wall, which follow the thin seam / cracks. The seam / crack on the right is *Nautilus* (5.9+; FA 1980). The Green Wall is the secluded 40-foot crag. A few routes are listed for historical purposes only; it is not an invitation or excuse to trespass. Obvious routes (if opened to climbers in the future) include: *Green Goddess* (5.8+): The thin crack to the right of the chimney that finishes up the face, just right of the crack / slot (FA 1980); *Jimnasium* (5.9+ R): The thin line between *Green Goddess* and *Bleu Cheese* (FA 1985); *Bleu Cheese* (5.9+): The face climb that ascends the face, passing a bolt (missing) and the horizontal crack (FA 1981); *Tangled Up in Green* (5.5): The second chimney system (FA 1980); *Top Heavy* (5.9 R / X): The steep face between the chimney and *Lightheaded* (FA 1985); *Lightheaded* (5.4): The crack / fissure to the left of *Top Heavy* (FA 1980).

Rattlesnake Rock

While lacking the sweeping faces of many crags, the charms of Rattlesnake Rock are the complex crack and corner systems that abound on this wall. The main wall gets plenty of sun and is a good place to climb in the late fall and early spring. The cliff is located on Town of Farmington open-space property. Climbs are described from left to right.

1. Near Miss (5.7 R) Follow your nose up the arête, traverse left at the roof, and finish on the short face above. FA: Ken Nichols, Bob Clark, Bill Sullivan, 1981.

2. Roller Coaster (5.11– R ★) Probably the best section of rock on the crag. Climb up the center of the face to the overlap and follow it up to the right. Then climb left and up the shallow corner. Traverse back right to the middle of the roof and launch over the center. FA: Sam Slater, 1983.

3. Achilles Heel (5.10 R / X) Climb the face 6 to 7 feet left of the start of *Down-to-Earth*. Join *Roller Coaster* where it jogs right, then up the face to the roof. Over the roof at the small left-facing corner left of *Slip Knot*. FA: Ken Nichols, Chad Hussey, 1984.

4. Down-to-Earth (5.10) Climb up the left-facing corner to the roof. Traverse left under the imposing roof to the arête. Continue traversing left around the arête, move down and across the short wall, and finish on the low-angle wall at a stance. FA: Ken Nichols, Bruce Dicks, 1980. *High Rocker Finish* (5.9–): At the left end of the roof, climb directly over the roof instead of bailing left. FA: Ken Nichols, Bob Clark, 1980.

5. Slip Knot (5.9– ★) Climb up the left-facing corner, just as you do on *Down-to-Earth*. Instead of traversing left, move out to the right and finish up the short face. FA: Ken Nichols, Al Rubin, 1980.

6. Darkness at Noon (5.11 TR) Climb up the face and crack to the small roof to the right of *Darkness at Noon*. Continue over the roof on the right side. Then traverse back left and continue up the center of the buttress. FA: Ken Nichols, 1984.

7. Night Shift (5.7) Start up the rabbly cracks, move right, and finish up the crack / right-facing corner system. FA: Ken Nichols, Francis Gledhill, 1980.

8. Juddgement Seat (5.10– R / X; fixed gear missing) The broken face 9 feet to the right of *Night Shift*. FA: Ken Nichols, Chet Judd, 1983.

9. Antivenin (5.9+ R / X) The face 4 to 5 feet left of *Snakebite*. FA: Ken Nichols, Jim Wilcox, 1986.

10. Snakebite (5.8) The left-hand line of small cracks and the short corner. FA: Ken Nichols, Al Rubin, 1980.

11. Hard Nut to Crack (5.9+ PG / R ★) The centerline of thin cracks, overlap, and airy face. A good climb with somewhat intimidating protection. FA: Ken Nichols, Al Rubin, 1980.

Rattlesnake Rock

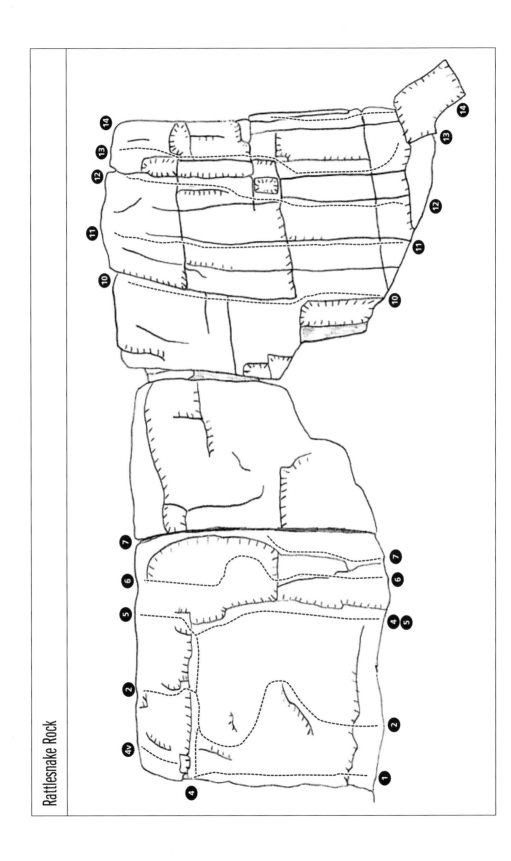

Anne Parmenter starting *Down-to-Earth* PHOTO BOB CLARK

12. Solidarity (5.5 ★) Enjoyable crack and face climbing at a moderate grade. Climb up the right-hand crack and corner system. FA: Mikey Walsh, 1970s.

13. Cahoots (5.4) Start on the boulder and follow your nose up the cracks, corners,

and small ledges. FA: Harold Mullins, Mark Meany, 1978.

14. Moondog Delight (5.7+) Start on the boulder and climb the arête and crack on the left to the top of the thin needle. Step right and finish up the arête and face. FA: Ken Nichols, Al Rubin, 1980.

Rattlesnake Rock Southeast Wall

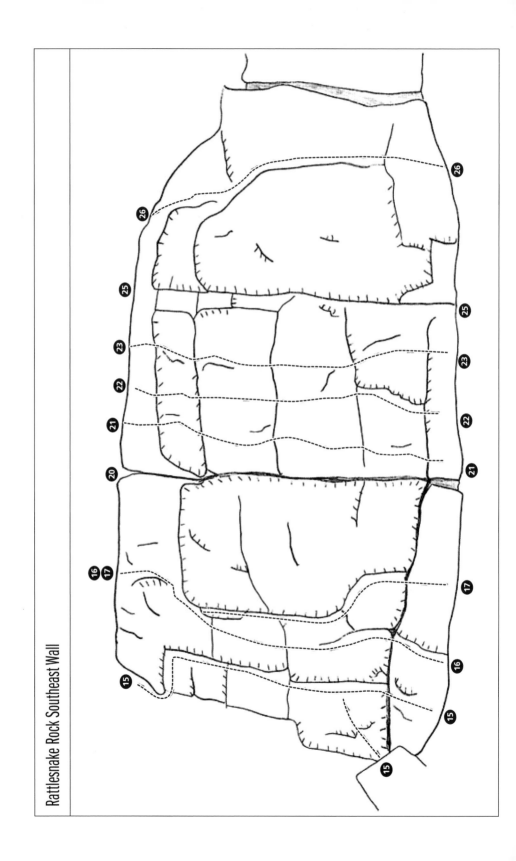

15. Duck Over (5.7 PG ★) From the boulder, traverse right to gain the prominent corner. Follow it to the overhang, traverse left, and finish up the arête. FA: Ken Nichols, Bill Sullivan, 1980. *Direct Start* variation (5.10+ R): Attack the overhang to gain the corner system. FA: Ken Nichols, Chad Hussey, 1984.

16. Pieces of Eight (5.8) Climb up the left-facing corner to the large horizontal crack. Continue up the crack and left-facing corners to the top of the buttress. Climb up the short face to the top. FA: Ken Nichols, Pat McDermott, 1994.

17. Pit Viper (5.10) The left-facing corner and arch system to the top of the buttress. Finish up the short face. FA: Ken Nichols, 1980.

18. Rocky Road (5.10 R / X) The face and horizontal cracks just to the right of *Pit Viper*. FA: Ken Nichols, Bob Clark, Mike Lapierre, 1985.

19. Serpent (5.10+ R / X; fixed gear missing) The face and horizontal cracks to the right of *Rocky Road* and 7 feet left of *Climbing Bind*. FA: Ken Nichols, Marco Fedrizzi, 1985.

20. Climbing Bind (5.8) The prominent crack and corner system. FA: Ken Nichols, 1980.

21. Ivy League (5.8 R) The steep face just to the right of *Climbing Bind*. FA: Ken Nichols, Mike Guravage, Bill Sullivan, Mike Lapierre, 1983.

22. Rattler (5.11 R / X ★) The steep face above the left-facing corner of *Stooges*. FA: Ken Nichols, 1986.

23. Diamondback (5.11 R / X ★) The steep and sustained face to the left of *Franny and Zooey*. The face just to the right is 5.12. FA: Ken Nichols, 1983.

24. Crotalus Horridus (5.12– TR) Follow *Diamondback* to the first ledge, then climb the brown face a few feet left of *Franny and Zooey*. FA: Ken Nichols, 1992.

25. Franny and Zooey (5.7–) The left-facing corner and crack system. FA: Gavin Grover, Francis Gledhill, 1980. *Three Stooges* variation (5.4): Approach the corner system by ascending the left-facing corner system in the middle of the open face. Traverse right on the narrow ledge and up *Franny and Zooey*. FA: Bill Sullivan, Harold Mullins, Ken Nichols, 1980.

Note: There are two low-quality and poorly protected routes between *Franny and Zooey* and *Verdant*. The left side of the face is 5.9+ and the right side 5.7+.

26. Verdant (5.5) The crack and corner left of *Squeezed Out*. FA: Harold Mullins, Bill Sullivan, Ken Nichols, 1980.

27. Squeezed Out (5.6) The short chimney. FA: Ken Nichols, 1980.

The cliff continues to the right and has many established climbs. Most of these climbs are short or dirty, but a couple of good hand cracks can be found near the right end.

SLEEPING GIANT STATE PARK, HAMDEN

When viewed from the New Haven area, the skyline resembles a sleeping giant lying on his back. According to a trail map provided by the Sleeping Giant Park Association, "One local Indian legend relates how the spirit Hobbamock diverted the Connecticut River from its original course in the Quinnipiac County and moved it far to the east. The benevolent spirit Kiehtan then cast a spell upon Hobbamock, causing him to sleep eternally in repose as the 'Sleeping Giant.'"

Sleeping Giant is located in northern Hamden and operated by the Connecticut Department of Energy & Environmental Protection (DEEP). A parking fee is charged on weekends April through November. The Mill River, which flows through the park, is stocked with trout. Aside from the DEEP, the park's advocate is the Sleeping Giant Park Association (SGPA), a nonprofit organization that works to maintain the trail system and acquire additional property for the park. The SGPA has been acquiring land on Sleeping Giant since 1924. The park currently consists of approximately 1,500 acres.

Technical rock climbers have been exploring Sleeping Giant for almost one hundred years. One of the earliest explorers was Hassler Whitney, who was a sophomore at Yale University in 1925 when he discovered the climbing at Sleeping Giant. According to Waterman (1993), "When later Yale climbers resumed exploration of the Sleeping Giant cliffs, they could never be sure when they were on new ground, so thoroughly had Whitney probed the possibilities." Whitney is best known in New England for the 1929 first ascent of the Whitney-Gilman Ridge on Cannon Cliff, New Hampshire, with

Bradley Gilman. Hassler Whitney, along with his brother Roger Whitney, Tom Rawles, and Steve Hart, formed the first group of the Yale Mountaineering Club. From 1933 to 1935 the prolific Fritz Wiessner climbed at Sleeping Giant along with Hassler and Roger Whitney, Henry Beers, William Burling, Betty Woolsey, and Bill House (Waterman, 1993).

In addition to first ascents at Ragged Mountain, during this time period Fritz Wiessner ascended one of the most prominent features at Sleeping Giant, *Wiessner's Rib* (5.6). Wilson Ware and William House added *The Warehouse Run* (5.7), a girdle traverse of The Chin, in 1934. This was the first route of its kind in the country.

From the late 1930s to the early 1950s, Sleeping Giant was explored and enjoyed by climbers. Unfortunately, an accident in 1953 closed the area to climbers for years. Due to this closure, climbers began to explore other Connecticut areas more extensively. Climbing at Sleeping Giant didn't really regain popularity until the late 1970s. The lack of popularity can be attributed to the Giant's often loose rock, the poison ivy that abounds in this area, and the better climbing found elsewhere. However, this is a fun area to explore in the late fall and early spring. Area classics include: *Vineland* (aka *Rhadamanthus*), *Wiessner's Rib* (two-pitch version), *Eric's Arête*, *Defender*, and *Yvette*. Please note that there are many other routes and variations that are more than likely squeezed between these routes, and some of the route names and lines probably differ from the first ascents.

Throughout the 1980s and 1990s, climbing activity has been sporadic, mostly concentrated on the classics on The Chin as well as the Left Hip. It is hard to say who made many of the first ascents, but during the 1980s Alex Catlin and William Ivanoff scoured the outlying crags. According to

Kevin Sweeney on the *Wiessner's Rib* PHOTO DAVID FASULO

Ivanoff's 1986 guidebook for The Right Knee, at least forty-four documented climbs exist; and his guide for The Tower / Left Hip Area (1986) contains twenty-seven routes plus many variations. This edition of *Rock Climbing Connecticut* only focuses on The Chin. To enjoy Sleeping Giant, wear a helmet, lower and belay from the top if rock or gear is suspect, and be courteous to onlookers and folks hiking along the top of the ridge. If you would like to lead, beware of poison ivy at the base and the loose rock.

Directions: From Route 10: Follow Route 10 through Cheshire to Hamden. Turn left onto Mount Carmel Avenue. Sleeping Giant State Park is opposite Quinnipiac University. Park at the main parking lot across from Quinnipiac.

From I-91: Take I-91 to exit 10. Stay on Route 40 North (the Connector) until the expressway ends. Turn right onto Route 10 North. At approximately 1.4 miles turn right onto Mount Carmel Avenue. Sleeping Giant State Park is opposite Quinnipiac University. Park at the main parking lot across from Quinnipiac.

The Chin

Sleeping Giant's main climbing area, The Chin, is located on—you guessed it, his chin. The Chin is about 90 feet high and contains many loose sections. The northern end of the cliff is described here. The southern section of the cliff is very broken and loose. To reach The Chin from the parking lot, follow either the Tower Trail for 15 minutes or the White Trail (shorter) to a point where the two meet under The Chin. At this junction you are beneath *Wiessner's Rib*. Scramble up the talus and poison ivy

to the base of the cliff. To reach the top of the cliff, continue from the junction up the Tower Trail for 2 minutes to a junction with the blue (Quinnipiac) trail on the left. Follow the blue trail to the ridge.

The following route descriptions and line drawing for The Chin have been compiled via an online guide and a rough copy of a guidebook for Sleeping Giant that was in progress. Since climbers have frequented The Chin as early as the 1930s, some of the information regarding route names and lines of ascent is probably not accurate.

1. Rhadamanthus Corner (5.5 PG) To the right of the monkey face (the profile on the left) is a corner system that finishes on an overhang. The lower-angle face, leading to the upper corner system, can be slick.

2. Vineland (aka *Rhadamanthus*) (5.10+ R ★) This is one of the best lines on The Chin. Pitch 1: Begin on the initial hand crack of *Wiessner's Rib* and climb up to a stance. Instead of moving up the corner system to the right, step up and left and follow the arête to the large belay ledge. (The first pitch, as described, is added for variety. It is much simpler to scramble up the left side of the buttress to the ledge.) Pitch 2: From the ledge follow the steep finger crack / left-facing corner to the top. Be careful of poison ivy in the crack and poor protection at the start. FRA: Sam Streibert, Bob Crawford, 1966. FFA: Jim Adair, 1970s.

3. Mountaineers Route (aka *Bolted*) (5.9 PG / R) Follow *Wiessner's Rib* past the crux layback, then follow the crack on the left face to the belay ledge. From the ledge a bolt (in very poor condition, 2015) moves into the steep dihedral and airy finish on the arête to the right.

Sleeping Giant

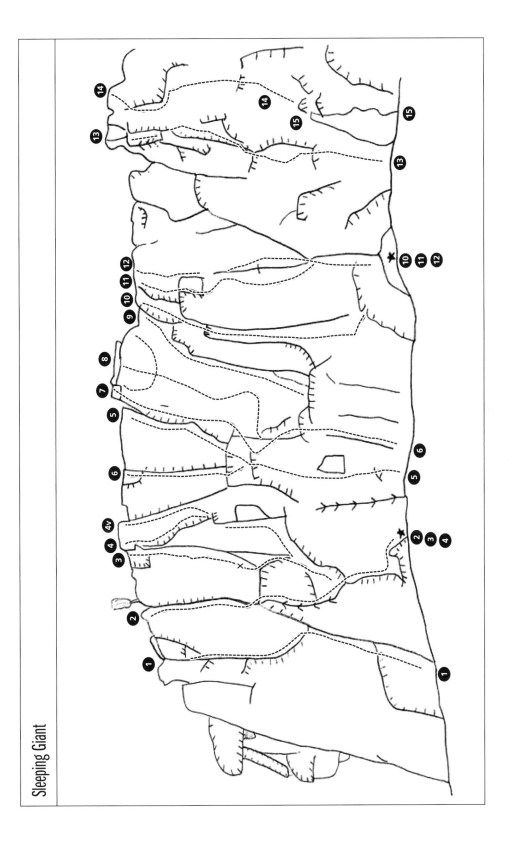

4. Wiessner's Rib (5.6 PG ★) From the base of the buttress, climb up and left on a blocky ledge to a wide hand crack in a corner. Climb up the crack / corner to a small ledge, and continue up and right to a clean, low-angle dihedral. Layback up the dihedral (crux) and follow cracks to a stance below the exposed arête at a small triangular ledge. Follow cracks up the left wall; step left and up to the top. FA: Fritz Wiessner, 1930s. *Two Pitch* variation—probably the nicest way to enjoy the route: After the crux dihedral, climb up and left to a large ledge on the arête (Mountaineers Route) and belay. Pitch 2. Place a piece of gear low and then traverse right, then up the right side of the arête. *Study Hall* variation 5.6: About a third of the way up the final headwall on *Wiessner's Rib*, traverse right a bit to a tree-covered ledge. Climb up the exposed inside corner, just to the right of the *Wiessner's Rib* finish, to the top.

5. Open Book (5.8 TR) To the right of the start of *Wiessner's Rib* is a corner (often wet). Just to the right of that corner is a poorly protected face that leads to a loose block. Climb up the center of the gray lichen face to the block. Climb / layback past the block. (The block is very dangerous. Who knows when it will fall?) Wander up the face to the open, left-facing corner. Layback up the left side of a short steep corner and continue up the larger corner to the top.

6. Old School (5.6 PG) Start on a broken corner just to the right of *Open Book*. Climb up the corner and crack system (past old pitons) to a ledge. Move left and up the ugly corner between *Study Hall* variation and *Open Book*.

7. The Edge (5.9 TR ★) A great short route. Ascend *Open Book* or *Old School* to the ledge beneath a short, steep corner. Step right over the corner onto the blunt arête. Layback up the exposed arête on great rock. A good winter route.

8. Micron (5.10 TR ★) Ascend *Open Book* or *Old School* to the ledge beneath a short, steep corner. Move right onto the open face, then back left, and ascend the center of the face on small, sharp holds. Two-thirds of the way up the face, you have three choices: *Left Finish* (5.10): Traverse up and left to a finish on *The Edge*. *Center Finish* (5.11): Work up the center of the desperate face. *Right Finish* (5.10): Move right, close to the corner, and up the face.

9. Hassler (5.6) Start up *Old School* and move right, or scramble up the right side of the buttress to a ledge beneath *Scorcher*. From *Scorcher* climb up and left to a large ledge. Follow the crack and corner system to the right of the *Micron* face, to the top.

10. Bruiser (5.9 X) This line ascends the parallel crack system, on the left side of the *Scorcher* buttress, to the small ledge, and finishes up a short corner system. Although many of the loose blocks have already fallen on the author, this route should be avoided due to loose rock.

11. Scorcher (aka *Tourist Treat*) (5.9 TR ★) Scramble up the gully to the right of the broken buttress to a ledge. Climb up the right side of the arête for 20 feet to a stance. Move left and ascend the left side of the arête, eventually moving back right to a stance on the arête. Move back left and finish up the steep left side.

12. Eric's Arête (5.9 TR ★) Scramble up the gully to the right of the broken buttress to a ledge. Climb up the right side of the arête for 20 feet to a stance. Continue up the center of the arête, ascending corners, for 10 feet to a stance. Step right and follow great cracks and textured rock up the right side of the arête.

Michael Kodas on *Vineland* (aka *Rhadamanthus*) PHOTO DAVID FASULO

The next two climbs should be toproped.

13. Defender (5.11) / Defender Direct (5.11+ / 5.12– R ★) Follow your nose to a ledge with a steep / overhanging corner. Climb up the corner and move right passing old pitons, fighting your way up the steep wall on excellent rock. According to an older guide, the route finishes 3 feet left of the sharp arête at 5.11 (and may jog left earlier than the direct line). FA: Bruce Dicks, George Mandes. FFA: Bruce Dicks, Henry Lester. *Defender Direct*: The natural line continues just to the right of the sharp arête at the desperate, overhanging, off-finger crack (crux). If belaying from the top, which is highly recommended, a quarter-inch bolt marks the top of the route. The rating is not confirmed.

14. Frenchman's Cap (5.9 R) From the top of *Yvette*, or to the right of *Defender*, move right across the steep face. Follow cracks, a small roof, and corners to the arching overlap, then follow the corner to the top. FA: John Reppy, Sam Streibert.

15. Yvette (5.9+) To the right of the gully is a beautiful finger crack that ascends a clean 30-foot slab. FA: John Reppy, Sam Streibert.

16. Hassler's Hangout (5.4–5.7) To the right of *Yvette* is a section of low-angle face and corner systems. A steep orange wall marks the right side of this area.

The following route description is referenced from John Peterson's Connecticut Climbing web page, Sleeping Giant Online Guide.

The Warehouse Run (5.7) This north-to-south girdle traverse was the first of its kind in the country. **First pitch:** The climb starts on a ledge about 15 feet below an overhang accessed by scrambling up a fourth-class ramp. Climb left past an old pin and up to a good ledge about 30 feet away. **Second pitch:** Step down, cross a groove (*Frenchman's Cap*) with two pins, then climb up and left around corners. Cross the overhanging, left-leaning buttress of *Defender* on a downsloping ramp. Step across the chimney. Angle up and left to a vine-infested belay ledge about 15 feet from the top. **Third pitch:** Continue left and up almost to the top of the cliff. Climb around the corner and step down on large blocks to a ramp. Hand-traverse around another corner, step left and down, and climb on nice layback holds to a niche. This downclimbed section was formerly rappelled. **Fourth pitch:** Climb down and left. Step across a wide groove at a pin. Climb up past the belay stance on *Wiessner's Rib*, continuing on to the prominent south-sloping platform by the start of *Rhadamanthus*. **Fifth pitch:** A short descent is made from the far side of the platform. The route continues at this level, eventually crossing an easy gully and on to a belay at a large pillar. This 130-foot pitch may be broken at the gully into two pitches to avoid rope drag. **Sixth pitch:** From the pillar step up and around a corner and on to another corner with an old ring pin. Step up and around this corner and walk across a wide broken gully to the base of the low-angle buttress. **Seventh pitch:** Ascend the low-angle buttress to the top. The total length of the traverse is about 600 feet. FA: William House, Wilson Ware, 1934. First recorded free ascent: Bill Ivanoff, Bob Schrader.

CHATFIELD HOLLOW STATE PARK, KILLINGWORTH

Chatfield Hollow is home to some of the best, and hardest, routes in Connecticut and is definitely worth a visit. The climbing at Chatfield Hollow is located adjacent to the 355-acre main park. The main park has nature trails, a loop road (closed in the winter), and a small lake for swimming. Schreeder Pond, at the northern section of the loop road, was built in the 1930s by the Civilian Conservation Corps (CCC) and is one of the eleven bodies of water in Connecticut designated as a trout park. These trout parks are stocked weekly during fishing season from the state's fish hatcheries. With all the park amenities located close to the climbing, Chatfield Hollow is a good destination for climbers trying to balance climbing with other family activities. Aside from the Main Wall at Chatfield Hollow, two smaller crags are included. Feather Ledge is a pleasant small crag located to the south of Route 80 that is relatively warm on cold days when the sun is shining. Schreeder Ridge is a small crag located within the main park close to the beach facilities and parking.

The rock at Chatfield Hollow is a type of metamorphic rock called Monson gneiss. The rock was lifted due to collisions between North America and the European and African continents, creating north–south hills and valleys running throughout Connecticut. Millions of years of erosion and glacial ice have exposed the ledges, and the melting of glacial ice 17,000 years ago deposited several glacial erratics in the surrounding area. The abundance of boulders provides many fine boulder problems in the vicinity.

While not the highest cliffs in Connecticut, ranging from 20 to 50 feet high, Chatfield Hollow does offer some fine crack and face climbs. The north end of Chatfield Hollow's Main Wall and a south-facing slab in the center are good places for young climbers and beginners. Chatfield Hollow's Main Wall also has one of the best traditional routes in Connecticut, *Forearm Frenzy Direct*, and more recently one of the best hard sport climbs, *Shapeshifter*.

Climbers have been ascending the walls at Chatfield on a regular basis since at least the early 1970s. These climbers ascended many of the obvious lines, but who actually made the first ascent can be difficult to determine. Furthermore, ancient pitons have been found in the vicinity of the Indian Council Caves located at the main park entrance. From 2011 to 2013, glue-in bolts and anchors were positioned on previously toproped climbs as well as new routes—creating sport climbs of extreme difficulty. It should be noted that the fixed bolts were not always installed by the person listed for the FA (first ascent). Along with anchors for new routes, bolted anchors have recently (2015) appeared on the top of climbs in an attempt to increase safety and protect the environment. Also note that climbers should stick the first bolt on most of the sport routes.

Directions: From Route 9: Take exit 5 (Route 80 East). Continue to the intersection (John Winthrop Middle School) and turn right on Route 80. Continue straight through the rotary and Chatfield Hollow State park is about 2 miles on your right.

I-95 to Route 79: Take exit 61. Follow Route 79 North to Route 80. Take Route 80 East. Chatfield Hollow State Park is on your left.

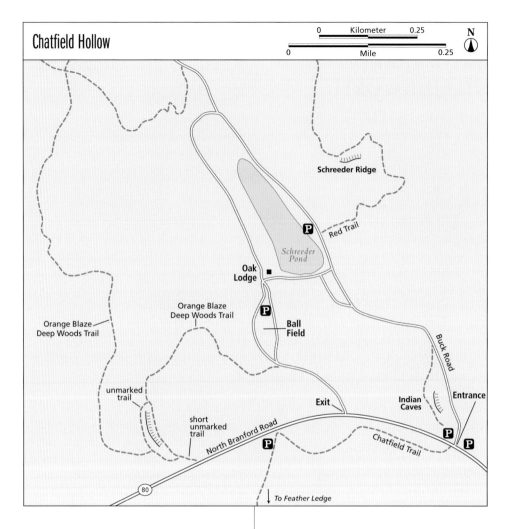

You can park just outside the gate for Chatfield Hollow State Park or in a small pull-off on Route 80 just west of the park on the south side of the road.

Approach: From the main parking area: Walk west on Route 80. You will pass a dirt parking lot (Chatfield Trail—and alternative parking) on your left at 0.3 mile. Farther up the road (0.1 mile), you will reach a guardrail on your right. There is a narrow path on either side of the guardrail. Follow the path to the crag by taking your first right off the main (lower) trail (there is another trail that will take you to the top of the crag).

This will lead you to the prominent Forearm Frenzy wall—the steep clean wall with a prominent zigzagging hand crack.

The top of the cliff is part of the Deep Woods Trail. This trail forms a loop trail that is part of Chatfield Hollow. From the top of the cliff, it is approximately a 0.25-mile hike to the park, where you'll find a baseball field and a swimming area. If you take the trail from the bottom of the cliff, it is about a 1.5-mile hike to the northern end of the park, which has a scenic millpond and picnic area.

From inside the park: This is a good spot to park if you would like to enjoy the

Greg Shyloski on *The Cold Vein* PHOTO DAVID FASULO

park as well as climb. It is also a nicer walk than that up the main road. If the loop road is open (entrance fee), follow it past the beach / swimming area on your left. Follow the loop road to the other (west) side of the beach to a pine grove and a small nature center. Park here or near the ball field just past the pine grove. Walk south past the ball field and you will reach the orange-blazed Deep Woods Trail on your right. Follow the trail for 10 minutes to the top-left section of the cliff.

Warning: The Deep Woods Trail skirts the top of the cliff. If you are using toprope anchors, please mark them so a hiker does not trip on your webbing or anchor rope. You can hang a pack or webbing as a warning to hikers. If using the fixed anchors, it is prudent to use a safety rope to set up some of the fixed anchors.

Main Wall

1. Left Side (5.7) The short corner and crack on the left side of the cliff.

2. Boulder Blast (5.11+ TR) The short, steep face / boulder problem through the roof.

3. The Coven (5.9 R ★) The slanting finger crack. Move right at the small overhang, then back left. A higher-difficulty finish climbs directly over the small overhang. FA: Jim Wilcox, Rick Palm, 1986.

4. Chris Crack (5.10+ PG ★) The overhanging finger crack and face. You may want to tape up. FA: Ken Nichols, 2000.

5. Time Wounds all Heels (5.8+ PG ★) The steep face and nose with the horizontal cracks—short but fun—to fixed anchors. FA: Chad Hussey, Chris Hyson, Mike Heintz, Mike Lapierre, Jim Wilcox, 1988.

6. Kiddy Crack (5.3) The crack on the left side of the low-angle slab.

7. Kiddy Slab (5.4) The face to the left of the corner.

8. Kiddy Corner (5.4) The easy corner.

9. Mudskipper (5.10 TR) The short arête and face to the right of *Kiddy Corner*. FA: Greg Shyloski, 2012. *Caped Crusader* (5.8+ TR): Climb up the right side of the arête. FA: Gregg Doster, 1970s.

Chatfield Hollow Main Wall

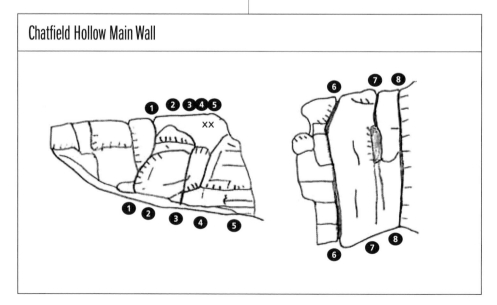

10. Fear the Wolf (5.11; sport / mixed) Up the arching corner (gear placement) or straight up the steep face (no gear) until under the roof at the first bolt. Climb under the roof to the corner (bolt), then hand-traverse out right (bolt) and gymnastic moves lead over the roof left of the arête to fixed anchors. FSA: Greg Shyloski, 2014. *Tiptoe* variation (5.9–; sport / mixed): Instead of hand-traversing across the roof, climb up the corner and foot-traverse over the lip then to the top. *Knee Jerk* variation (5.10; sport / mixed): Hand-traverse a couple feet right after the corner and over the roof directly over the third bolt.

11. Don't Do It Hank's Way (5.5) The steep crack / corner on the right side of the over-hang. FA: Hank Folsom, 1974. FFA: Rick Marin, Joel Anderson, 1970s.

12. To Jolt or Not to Jolt (5.10 R ★) The pocketed wall to the right of *Trad Crack* to fixed anchors. FA: Bob Clark, 1983.

13. Clark Bar Crack (5.5 G ★) The enjoyable crack system. Well protected.

Climbs 14 through 19 climb the short steep wall between *Clark Bar Crack* and *Kyle's Corner*.

14. Gregarious (5.10 / 5.10+ R; height dependent) Work up the face just left of *Jungle Face*, making a long reach to gain a good hold. Make another long reach to the left edge of a shelf, step left, then con-tinue a few more reaches to a finish up the crack. *Sullivator* variation (5.8–): If you can-not make the initial reaches, head up *Clark Bar Crack* to the first small ledge, then step right onto the face. FA: Gregg Doster, Tom

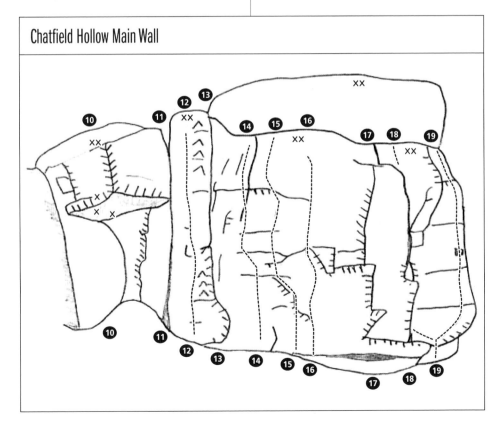

Chatfield Hollow Main Wall

Saunders, 1970s. FFA: Jim Wilcox, Chad Hussey, Bill Sullivan, Rick Murnane, Mike Lapierre, 1988.

15. Jungle Face (5.10– R ★) Start just left of a small right-facing corner. A reachy move gains a good horizontal. Then meander left toward the small shelf. Climb up right then back left for a cleaner finish. Shared fixed anchors can be reached from above the climb.

16. Gneiss Face (5.10+ R) Start at the small right-facing corner. Work past the technical face, reaching for a good hold on the left-slanting edge. Finish up the face on good holds. Shared fixed anchors can be reached from above the climb.

17. P&H (5.7+ ★) Paddle over the rock spikes and up a corner to the top. Leaders should beware of the sloping, and sometimes dirty, top-out. Fixed anchors above the ledge.

18. Wall of Light (5.9–) A good steep line with a tricky top-out. Follow the crack as it veers left. Shared fixed anchors. FA (aid): Tom Saunders, Chuck Macbeth, Hank Folsom, 1970s.

19. Steep Steps (5.9 TR) Follow the ledge to the arête on the right side of the wall. Work up the arête to a good hold / small block just left of the arête. Continue the struggle to the top. Shared fixed anchors.

20. Exposed (5.8+ / 5.9+ TR) The face climb on the wall left of *Kyle's Corner*. Step up to the arête and follow the arête and face to the top (5.8+). Step onto the arête, then work up the middle of the face (5.9+).

21. Kyle's Corner (5.6 ★) Use large camming units on this large corner system. Can be toproped from a large tree, or use fixed anchors.

22. Spider (5.8+ R) Start just left of the arête and climb up large holds to the ledge.

23. Kevin's Romp (5.7 R) Follow the awkward corner to the ramp, romp up, and continue left to finish on *Kyle's Corner*.

Climbs 24 through 28 ascend the steep wall above the ledge system. These climbs are bolted and mixed climbs with fixed anchors.

24. Captain Moonlight (5.12–; sport and gear) Climb *Spider*, starting just left of the arête and up large holds using gear, then veer right climbing past a bolt to gain the ledge. Starting at a good pocket, place gear and then climb past two bolts up the steep wall to the fixed anchor. FA: Morgan Patterson, 2012.

25. The Anarchist (5.13; sport and gear) Extreme face climbing up the *Psycho Jap* wall. Follow the corner (*Kevin's Romp*) to the sloping ledge. A small camming unit protects the start, and then follow four bolts past tiny edges up the overhanging wall to the shared anchor on *Psycho Jap*. FA: Ryan Richetelli, 2012.

26. Psycho Jap (5.12; sport) Originally climbed in the 1980s by Bill Lutkus, it was a neglected toprope climb for many years afterwards. In 2011 the route was cleaned by Greg Shyloski and is now a frequently climbed (or attempted) route at Chatfield. Solo up the corner in the middle of the *Psycho Jap* wall to a stance and stick clip the first bolt. Pass two bolts aiming for a large hold under the low roof. Up the steep face, passing bolts to a fixed anchor. The finish is awkward. From the big holds in the middle, go to the last bolt (some climbers opt for an easier finish to the right) and commit to a difficult top-out boulder problem right near the anchor. First Sport Ascent: Greg Shyloski, 2011.

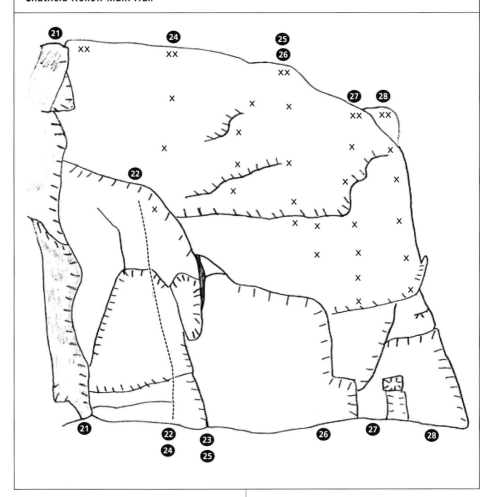

27. The Cold Vein (5.12+ ★; sport) Steep and technical climbing up clean rock to the right of *Pyscho Jap* and left of *Bloody Beetroots*. From a small ledge climb past bolts to a fixed anchor left of the *Bloody Beetroots* arête. FA: Nate Labieniec, 2011.

28. Bloody Beetroots (5.11− ★; sport) Very cool route. Stick-clip the first bolt and position yourself under the roof and arête on the right end of the *Psycho Jap* wall. Up and left over the roof and onto the arête. Continue up the arête passing bolts, and then reach right at the top to a fixed anchor on the right. A variation to this route goes left after the fourth bolt to clip the final bolt and anchor on *The Cold Vein*. FA: Ken Nichols R / X finishing up the right side of the arête, 2000. FSA: Greg Shyloski, 2011.

Climbs 29 and 30 ascend the large low-angle slab to the left of *Lisa's Layback.*

29. Edgy (5.4 R ★) Ascends the left side of the clean slab, passing a small overhang.

30. Super Slab (5.5 ★) A great beginner climb. Climb up the slab and small overhang to the left of *Lisa's Layback.* Bolt anchors on top.

31. Lisa's Layback (5.4 ★) The large left-facing corner.

Climbs 32 through 40 ascend the clean, overhanging wall with the prominent crack system.

32. Shapeshifter (5.12 ★; sport) Probably the best of the new hard sport routes at Chatfield. Originally toproped by John MacLean in 1990. Start on *Forearm Frenzy* and reach left to clip the first bolt. Climb back down to the stance and move left to the starting holds left of the start of *Forearm Frenzy.* Trend up left, then back right up the steep face, passing bolts to a small right-facing corner. Continue up and slightly right, passing bolts and the intimidating roof to fixed anchors. *Caution:* There are some loose holds / flakes under the roof. FSA: Greg Shyloski, 2010.

33. Silver Wings (5.12; sport) An alternate and airy finish to *Shapeshifter.* Climb past the first five bolts on *Shapeshifter,* then head left past two bolts through the roof and a fixed anchor. FA: Greg Shyloski, 2012.

34. Forearm Frenzy (aka *Feel Flows*) (5.11 PG ★) The free ascent was originally climbed in two pitches. Chuck led up to the horizontal crack below the crux and set up a hanging belay, and then Ken led through. The obvious hand crack diagonals up right to a horizontal crack. Traverses right at a horizontal, then follow the left-slanting crack to good

holds. Follow the horizontal crack left and finish on the right edge of the roof. *Note:* The left-hand finish is rarely done. Most people finish on the *Direct Finish* at the anchors. FA: Gregg Doster, Tom Saunders, 1970s. FFA: Chuck Boyd, Ken Nichols, 1984. *Feel Flows* is the name of the original aid ascent.

35. Forearm Frenzy Direct (5.11 PG ★) One of the best climbs in Connecticut. More popular than *Forearm Frenzy* (aka *Feel Flows*) because it is easier to toprope and lead—especially with the more recent addition of fixed anchors. Instead of moving left at the horizontal after the crux left-slanting crack, continue straight up the face at a shallow crack left of the arête to fixed anchors.

36. Zeitgeist (5.12+; sport and gear) Climb *Forearm Frenzy* to the horizontal crack where the crack makes a Y. Climb the face just left of the two bolts to the large horizontal crack. Place gear and finish on the fixed anchor above. FA: Nate Labieniec, 2012. A variation to this route, *Its Own Spirit* (FA: Greg Shyloski, 2012), starts on *Hollowhead Crew* and then finishes on *Zeitgeist.*

37. Modern Collective (5.13–; sport) A difficult link-up of sport routes on the *Forearm Frenzy* wall. Start on *Hollowhead Crew* and climb to the large horizontal. Traverse left and clip the first bolt on *Zeitgeist,* then traverse left to the shallow corner and fifth bolt on *Shapeshifter.* Finish on *Shapeshifter* or *Silver Wings.* FA: Ryan Richetelli, 2012.

38. Hollowhead Crew (5.11+ / 12–; sport and gear) About 10 feet to the right of *Forearm Frenzy,* start is a thin face leading to a handhold about 10 feet off the ground. Stick-clip the first bolt and work up to the jutting handhold. Continue up the face to the left of two more bolts to finish on *Forearm Frenzy Direct.* First toproped by Chuck Boyd in the 1980s and called the

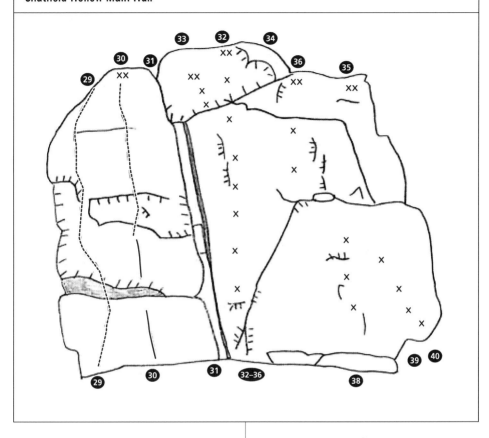

Boyd Void. FA: Ryan Richetelli (gear only), 2009. FSA: Ryan Richetelli, 2009. A variation to this route, *Pisces* (5.12–), heads up and right after the jutting handhold past a shared bolt for *Magic Central* (fourth bolt on right) to finish below the left-slanting crack of *Forearm Frenzy*. FA: Greg Shyloski, 2012.

39. Blinded by Puss (5.11; sport and gear) Start a couple feet left of the arête, or just around the corner below the low roof for more adventure. Climb past three bolts, then head up and right, climbing just left of the arête. A piece of gear placed in a horizontal crack protects moves to the bottom of the left-slanting crux crack on *Forearm Frenzy*. FA: Nate Labieniec, 2013.

40. Magic Central (5.13–; sport, gear optional) A sustained link up of hard climbing. Start on *Blinded by Puss*, but after the third bolt move up and left past a fourth bolt (*Pisces* variation) to the top of *Hollowhead Crew* at the horizontal crack midway up the cliff. Continue left onto *Zeitgeist* and traverse left to the fifth bolt on *Shapeshifter*, and finish on *Silver Wings*. FA: Nate Labieniec, 2012.

41. Boulder Up (5.6) Just around from the *Forearm Frenzy* wall and to the left of the descent gully is a corner with a pleasant low angle slab above. Climb up the corner, then move left onto ledges 15 feet up. Continue up the face above trending left close to the arête and straight up to the top. FA: Greg Doster, 1970s.

To the right of the *Forearm Frenzy* wall are a couple of low-angle slabs and gully descents. The following climbs begin to the right of these dirty slabs.

42. Ramp (5.8+) Climb up and left on the ramp, then up the short face. Trend right to finish.

43. Short Stuff (5.7) Climb up the ramp and head straight up the cracks and face.

44. Red Point (5.10 R) The technical face to the left of *Marmalade*. FA: Ken Nichols, 2000.

45. Marmalade (5.10+ ★) The short but sweet finger crack. After Mike and Bill made the first free ascent, they looked at their fingers and decided *Marmalade* was an appropriate name for the route. FA: Mike Lapierreand, Bill Sullivan, 1973.

46. Jim's Jem (5.10–) The face and arête to the right of *Marmalade*. The original route started on the left side of the arête. You can also start up the right side of the arête. Named for Jim Wilcox, a well-liked Connecticut climber who wrote a guide to Chatfield in the 1990s, and passed away much too soon. FA: Jim Wilcox, Mike Heintz, Chad Hussy, Rick Murnane, 1988. Two bolts added 2015.

47. Low Bridge (5.6) The short corner system. FA: Gregg Doster, Tom Saunders, 1970s.

48. Keystone (5.11– PG / R) The crack, corner, and roof system. FA: Jim Wilcox, Rick Palm, 1988.

49. Wallow in the Hollow (aka *Deadman's Curve*) (5.12+ ★) Extreme, steep, fingertip climbing up the short clean wall. First toproped in 1988 by John MacLean, who named this route after the many falls low

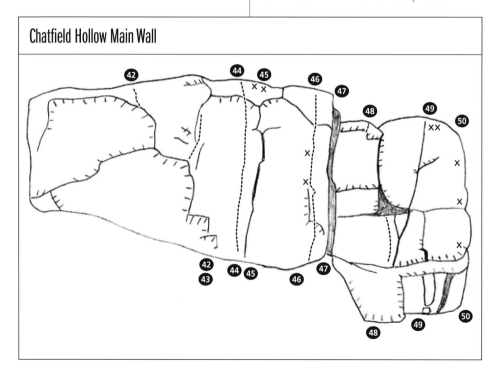

Chatfield Hollow Main Wall

on the route, which resulted in long swings into the "hollow." Fixed anchors have been placed at the top of the route.

50. Sleep Walker Arête (5.11–; sport) Climb up the arête and the face to the left past three bolts. After the third bolt, move left to finish at the top of the *Wallow in the Hallow* crack. FSA 2014.

51. Charmer (5.9+ R) Up the crack under the *Sleep Walker Arête* to the ledge. Up the arête to a second ledge, and finish up the face between the arête and small left-facing corner. FA: Ken Nichols, Glenn Gello, Steve Batt, 2000.

Feather Ledge

Feather Ledge is a small but pleasant crag located south of Route 80 and the main portion of Chatfield Hollow State Park. When the leaves are down and the sun is shining, it is a good cold-weather climbing area. The addition of fixed protection and anchors has increased the popularity of this area. However, climbers have more than likely established first ascents on this cliff several years beforehand.

Approach: Start from the climbers' parking lot up the road (west) from the main parking area for Chatfield Hollow. Follow the unmarked fire road, which narrows to a well-worn trail, for about 11 minutes to a junction with the blue-blazed trail marked by a sign ("RTE 80 .5 mi" with an arrow

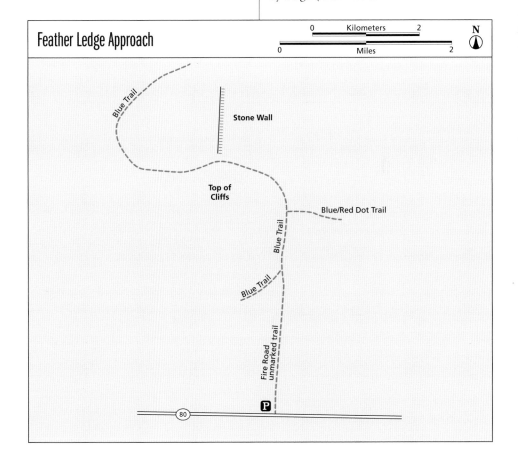

Feather Ledge Approach

pointing down the fire road; and "2 mi" with an arrow pointing toward the Blue Trail). Continue straight / south on the blue-blazed trail for 1 minute and you will arrive at the junction of an alternate trail (blue-blazed with orange dot) on your right. Continue straight / south on the blue-blazed trail for 5 minutes and you will be at the top of Feather Ledge. The trail continues east and meanders to the base of the cliff. Leave the Blue Trail just before a stone wall leading to the central buttress. From the base of the main buttress, near the stone wall, the Slab Wall is left of the buttress and the 9-Wall is to the right.

Slab Wall: The 35-foot west-facing wall to the left of the buttress and stone wall.

The climbs and two walls are listed from left to right.

1. One Step Forward (5.9- PG) Past horizontal cracks to a bolt about midway up the wall. Continue straight up the smooth slab to the fixed anchor. Traditional gear required to supplement the bolt.

2. Pipe Dreams (5.7 to 5.9 PG) Begin at the right side of the slab on the crack that diagonals up and left. Follow the crack to the first bolt, trend up and left to the next bolt. You can head left and finish on *One Step Forward* (5.7) or head right then back left (somewhat contrived) to the fixed anchor (5.9).

3. Glad I'm Not High (5.9 PG) Start on *Pipe Dreams*, but continue straight up the left side of the short arête / buttress.

9-Wall: The steep 40- to 50-foot wall to the right of the buttress and stone wall.

4. TR (5.10+ TR) Work your way up the right side of the short arête / buttress.

5. Rad Trad (5.7 PG) Follow the corner and cracks up the left side of the 9-Wall to the shared fixed anchor.

6. Rusty Old-Timer (5.9+; sport) The original route had a single old ¼ bolt protecting the climb. Climb past three bolts left / center of the 9-Wall to the fixed anchor.

7. Just Say Yes (5.9+; sport and gear) Start on *Rusty Old-Timer* (first bolt) then move right and climb past two bolts on the right / center of the 9-Wall. At the overlap (camming unit protects finish), move left to the fixed anchor. Alternate start: Climb the slanting finger crack to the right (gear) to the second bolt.

8. Bandana (5.8+) The prominent crack / corner to the right of *Just Say Yes*. About 10 feet from the top, traverse left, following the crack / overlap to the fixed anchor.

9. Butt-Hurt Yankee (5.9) Fifteen feet right of *Bandana*, climb up the clean face, then continue up the flakes and overlaps to finish up the middle of the triangle face.

Note: There are scattered boulder problems and ledges west of Feather Ledge that are accessed from the Blue Blaze / Orange Dot Trail that is passed on the way to Feather Ledge.

Schreeder Ridge

Schreeder Ridge, also known as Pad Crag for its sparsely protected starts, is a small, 35-foot crag located within the main park area. To reach Schreeder Ridge, drive or park outside the gate and walk to the main beach area in Chatfield Hollow State Park. Across from the changing rooms for the Schreeder Pond beach, follow the Red-Blazed Ridge Trail that starts up a wood stairway. After 10 minutes you will be at the top of the south-facing cliff. There are approximately six routes, some with fixed anchors and fixed gear, ranging from 5.8 to 5.11 on this small crag. Best climbed in the early spring or on a warm winter day.

COCKAPONSET STATE FOREST, DEEP RIVER

Located in the Cockaponset State Forest, Pine Ledge is a 75-foot crag at its highest point and contains several roofs and blocky corners. The rock is similar to that of nearby Chatfield Hollow (Monson gneiss), and while not displaying sweeping faces, the steep climbs contain abundant large holds and formations unique for Connecticut climbing. Pine Ledge faces southwest and is best climbed when the sun is out during the late fall or early spring.

For many years this was a "junk" crag, but it has been cleaned up by local and visiting climbers. The cleanups involved the removal of many TVs and several bags of garbage. Please help to improve and maintain this area by removing trash each time you climb. Most of the routes listed have been cleaned and equipped with bolts and fixed anchors—creating a true sport-climbing area. However, unlike some "fall-anywhere" sport-climbing areas, due to the ledgy nature of Pine Ledge, an attentive belayer is required. If the ledges make you nervous, most of the climbs are easily toproped due to the fixed anchors.

Climbers have been visiting (infrequently) Pine Ledge since at least the 1970s. Many of the now established lines have been aid-climbed, led, or toproped prior to 2009. However, from 2009 to 2014, local and visiting climbers added fixed protection and anchors to this once neglected area. Since their efforts, the area has received a significant face-lift and has become a sort of destination crag for climbers—especially from Rhode Island. For this edition, the FSAs (first sport ascents) are listed.

DIRECTIONS AND APPROACH

From Route 9 south: Take exit 5 and make a right off the exit. There is a small parking area across from the exit behind the "Welcome to Deep River" sign, or travel 0.3 mile west on Route 80 to a parking area on the left side of Route 80 next to a pond.

From Route 9 north: Take exit 5 and turn left. There is a small parking area across from the exit behind the "Welcome to Deep River" sign, or travel 0.5 mile to a parking area on the left side of Route 80 next to a pond.

Approach 1: This is a pleasant approach following an old fire road, except for the very end where you need to cross a couple streams. From the parking area on the side of Route 80 next to the pond, continue west on Route 80 0.1 mile to an unmarked fire road on the right (north) side of the road marked with an orange "Connecticut State Land" sign (if you reach the ambulance station, you have gone too far). There is parking for one car at this spot. Follow the road / trail, passing close by a house on your left, to a split after 2 minutes. Veer right at the split and continue on the trail for 10 minutes to a junction. Take a left at the junction and cross a river (the trail floods on this section). Continue on the trail for another minute and you will see the main access road and cliff on your right—use the path of least resistance (due to drainage) to get to the road. The climbs are easily accessed from the road at this point. If you continue down the road (right), you will gain the trail leading to the top of Pine Ledge on the left. Continue on the road a little farther and you will reach the Roadside Crag on your right.

Approach 2: This approach takes about the same time as approach 1, but the trail is

Mary Stevenson on *Sideways Glances* PHOTO DAVID FASULO

less muddy at the end and therefore more popular. However, the first couple minutes of the trail pass through private property, and is therefore included for historical purposes since it has been the standard approach (without known restrictions) for many years. From the parking area on the side of Route 80 next to the pond, follow Route 80 east about 0.1 mile to a unmarked dirt road just before West Bridge Lane on the left (north). Follow the dirt road for about 8 minutes to a split. Veer left at the split and in 3 more minutes you will arrive at a large dirt road. Walk left on the road (1 minute) to the base of Pine Ledge. To reach the top of Pine Ledge, walk right on the road to gain the trail leading to the top of the cliff on your left. If you continue a little farther down the road you will reach the Roadside Crag.

Driving to base of Pine Ledge: For this approach a high-clearance vehicle, and possibly four-wheel drive, is required. The condition of the state-forest (dirt) road varies from year to year. Do not use this approach after a heavy rain or if there is snow on the road. Furthermore, the gate is typically closed in the winter and reopened late in the spring depending on the amount of rain and condition of the road. Although it is convenient to drive to the base with a high-clearance vehicle, it is best to walk in to reduce impact on the road and not become intertwined with the very limited parking at the base of

the cliff. Also, be careful not to back off the bridge if parking in this area. Walking to the cliff takes about the same time as the bumpy drive on the dirt road.

From Route 9 in Deep River, take exit 5 onto Route 80 west. Route 80 will come to a light, where you'll go right (still Route 80), and after 3.2 miles from the exit you will reach a stoplight. At the light go right onto Cedar Swamp Road until it turns to a dirt road. Travel on the dirt state-forest road for 0.3 mile and take the first right-hand turn on Pine Ledge Road (unmarked dirt road). After 2.7 miles (from the beginning of Pine Ledge Road) you will encounter a huge boulder and small pullout on your left. The road is typically blocked off just beyond this point with large boulders.

From I-95 take Route 79 north (exit 6) to Route 80 (rotary in Madison) and follow Route 80 east for 2.9 miles to Chatfield Hollow. From Chatfield Hollow follow Route 80 east for 5.2 miles to a traffic light. Take a left on Cedar Swamp Road and continue as described above.

Base of Pine Ledge and top: From the parking area at the base of the cliff, a very short walk leads to the start of *Kinky Women*—the tallest and cleanest portion of the cliff facing the two-car parking area. On the right edge of the crag, just after rounding the corner on the dirt road, is a trail leading to the top of *Kinky Women* and *Park & Play*.

Pine Ledge

1. Sideways Glances (5.6 ★; sport) This route starts on the ledge about 25 feet left of *Kinky Women*. To reach the belay ledge, climb the start of *Triple Lindy*, or *Kinky Women* (if *Triple Lindy* is wet), past two bolts and traverse left on the slabby ledge to a belay at a tree below the start. If switching leads, clipping the first bolt at the base of *Sideways Glances*, and then downclimbing to the belay tree will simplify the transition. From the belay tree climb up the black face, passing bolts, then traverse right (feet low on clean slab), clipping the final bolt on *Triple*

Lindy to a fixed anchor. FSA: David Fasulo, Ron Gautreau, 2013.

2. Park & Play (5.11– ★; sport) The climb can be led in one pitch from the ground, but it is more enjoyable to have your belayer positioned to better see you, and to reduce rope drag, while at the crux by belaying from the ledge above. To reach the belay ledge, climb the start of *Triple Lindy* past two bolts and traverse left on the slabby ledge to a belay at a tree left of the start. If switching leads, clipping the first bolt at the base of *Park & Play* and then downclimbing to the belay tree will simplify the transition. Right

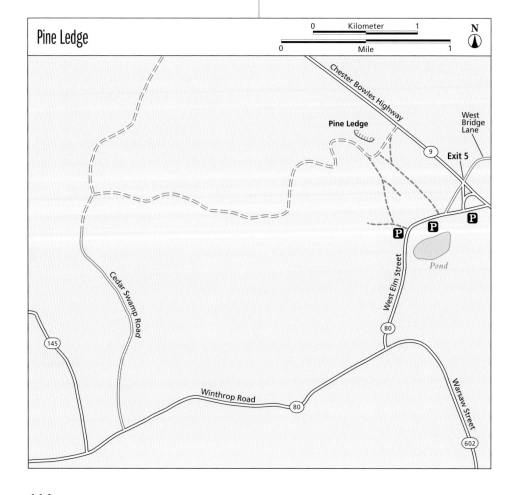

Pine Ledge

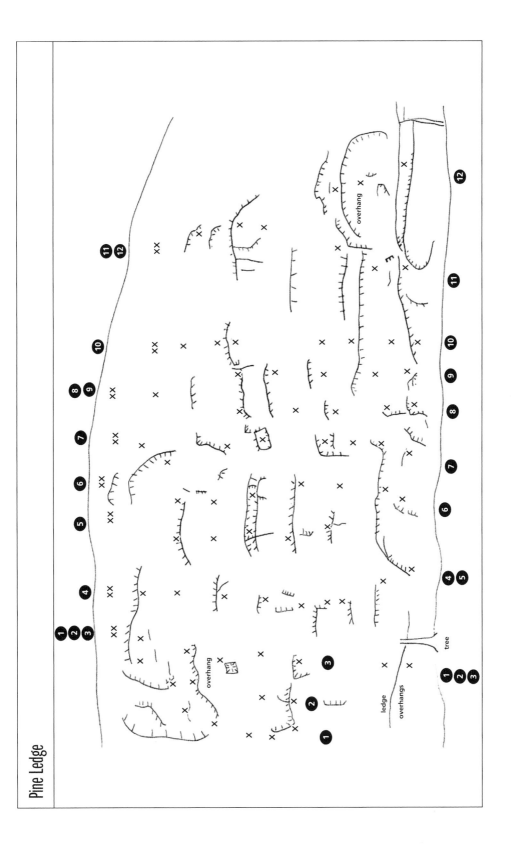

of *Sideways Glances* and left of *Triple Lindy*, climb over the first roof at a flake. Wander up to the next roof and the crux bolt. Move right and use a hold on the lip of the roof to gain a stance, and then move back left and up the technical face over the roof. Finish on *Sideways Glances*. The original route finished left of the shared anchors for *Sideways Glances*, but adding another anchor would be excessive. FSA: David Fasulo, 2013.

3. Triple Lindy (5.11; sport) Just left of a large tree close to the cliff, climb past two bolts to a ledge. Continue past blocky corners to a steep and technical roof, then a shared anchor with *Sideways Glances* and *Park & Play*. FSA: Christopher Beauchamp, 2010.

4. Kinky Women (5.7+ ★; sport) Excellent climbing at the grade. Meander up the steep clean face to a tricky mantel above the final overhang and then anchors. The first bolt is a bit low (placed after the first ascent), but the lower section is wet / slippery in the spring and scary without it. FSA: Brian Phillips, 2010.

5. Jaimie (5.11– ★; sport) Start on *Kinky Women* (skipping the first bolt and placing a long runner on the second reduces rope drag), then move right and follow the line of bolts through roofs to anchors. The final large roof requires an awkward maneuver. FSA: Christopher Beauchamp, 2009.

6. Champ's Channel (5.10–; sport) Much better climbing than it appears from the ground, as is true with the entire crag. To the right of *Jaimie* and left of *Syndication* follow bolts to the ledge. Meander through steep corners and overhangs to a fixed anchor. FSA: Christopher Beauchamp, 2012.

7. Syndication (5.9 ★; sport) Start up the steep corner to the right edge of the ledge. Continue up the uniquely featured rock to a fixed anchor. FSA: Christopher Beauchamp, 2010.

8. TV Party (5.10 ★; sport) Start up the deceptively difficult overhanging crack system to a rest after two bolts (best to stick-clip the first bolt). After a rest, follow bolts to a shared anchor with *Change of Heart*. FSA: Christopher Beauchamp, 2009.

9. Change of Heart (5.10–; sport) Just right of *TV Party*, steep climbing past two bolts leads to easier climbing and then the shared anchor with *TV Party*. FSA: Christopher Beauchamp, 2010.

10. War of the Privileged (5.10+; sport) A steep start leads to moderate climbing and the large clean roof above; over the roof to fixed anchors. FSA: Christopher Beauchamp, 2014.

11. Kickapoo Joy Juice (5.11– ★; sport) Very cool climbing. Start at the left edge of a clean overhang at a flake. Up the overhanging flake past the roof and two bolts. Easier climbing continues up the face to a tricky steep / blocky overhang and anchors. FSA: Christopher Beauchamp, 2010.

12. Shabbat Elevator (5.11; sport) The difficulty is somewhat height dependent. On the right end of the clean overhang, work up over the lip of the roof to a stance below a steep overhang. Launch over the roof at a bolt to good hold at the lip; another gymnastic move past a bolt gains a ledge. Finish on *Kickapoo Joy Juice*. A variation to the route works out the right edge / lip of the second overhang to the good holds in the center. FSA: Christopher Beauchamp, 2009.

Danny Howard on *Shabbat Elevator* PHOTO DAVID FASULO

Dark Arts Boulder

Left of the two-car parking area in front of Pine Ledge is a large featured boulder. Two sport climbs ascend each side. *Kill Your Television* 5.9 (sport) is the bolted route on the left (5.10 if starting from the ground and not off the boulder), and *Audible* 5.9+ (sport) is the sport climb on the right. The top of the boulder can also be accessed by the slab on the opposite side. FSA: Christopher Beauchamp, 2009 and 2010.

Roadside Crag

Follow the dirt road (typically blocked with boulders) past the two-car parking area around the corner from the right end of Pine Ledge. On the right side of the road is a small crag that has a clean section at its left end. *Road Warrior* (5.10; sport; FSA: Christopher Beauchamp, 2010) passes three bolts to a slung tree.

Pine Ledge South

From the two car parking area at the base of the cliff, head up the road and hike on the Approach 2 trail for five minutes to a cairn on the right. Follow the climber trail for a minute to the left edge of a cliff at the base of a swamp. The climbs are described from left to right

Ocean State (5.11-; sport) The steep, featured arête on the left side of the cliff past bolts to a fixed anchor. Difficult to toprope due to rope drag near the anchors. FSA: Brian Phillips, 2014.

Left Edge. The left edge of the arête on the left end of the large overhanging wall, has been climbed and is being developed as of 2015.

Rocky Point (5.9; sport) Just past the large overhang is a left facing corner/roof system. Up the corner, trend left to left facing corner, to finish on an overhang. Six bolts to a fixed anchor. FSA: Brian Phillips, 2014.

Road to Rhode Island (5.10; sport) On the right edge of the cliff start five feet left of the bolt line. Work up to the first bolt, then continue past six bolts and steep roofs to a fixed anchor. FSA: David Curry, 2014.

COCKAPONSET STATE FOREST, DURHAM

Located off the Mattabesett Trail in the Cockaponset State Forest, Bear Rock Ridge is an overhanging crag of gneiss-quartz conglomerate that is approximately 70 feet high. This crag is one of a few "sport crags" in Connecticut—meaning a majority of the routes are protected by rappel-placed bolts and contain fixed anchors to descend from. Sharp quartz edges, and steep climbing, combine for routes that are both technical and pumpy. Stick clipping is highly recommended for most of the routes. Please note climbers *must* carpool due to the *very* limited parking; otherwise access will become a problem. There is a good coffee shop in downtown Durham that is convenient.

Climbers have been exploring Bear Rock Ridge for decades. According to author and climbing guide Freddie Wilkinson, "When I got my first pair of rock shoes (circa 1991) I started going out there and bouldering / scrambling around, it was the first 'mountain' in my life I ever got to explore on my own. I remember finding that wall and thinking it was pretty cool and someday would be a developed crag. In 1992 I took Bob Clark out there and we set up a TR on the central 5.10ish line, which Bob generously let my younger sister Posie name 'Posie's Porpoise.' We had just been to Maine for summer vacation and she had seen a porpoise." A sport route was established a few years later, but it wasn't until 2014 that the crag was fully developed. The cliff is very difficult to toprope, and there is virtually no protection on most of the climbs. The

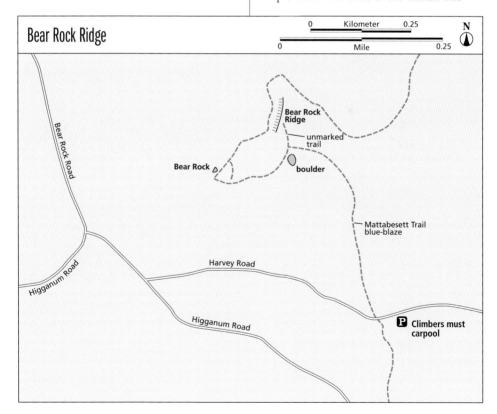

Bear Rock Ridge

Brian Phillips on *Devil's Lettuce* PHOTO DAVID FASULO

routes were cleaned and equipped, mostly by Chris Beauchamp, creating a popular sport-climbing crag.

Directions: From I-91 take exit 15 to Route 68 east to Route 17 south. From downtown Durham continue south on Route 17. Veer left onto Route 79 and take the immediate left onto Higganum Road. At the junction with Bear Rock Road, go right and take the first left (0.1 mile) on Harvey Road. Travel 0.4 mile to a small parking lot on the right.

From Route 9 take exit 9 to Route 81 north and go west (left) on Route 154. Take the immediate left on Candlewood Hill Road, which becomes Higganum Road. After 6.4 miles make right on Harvey Road. Travel 0.4 mile to a *small* parking lot on the right.

Approach: From the parking area walk back down the road (west) about 60 feet, and the blue-blazed trail is on the right (north). Follow the trail for about 8 minutes and you will come upon a large boulder on your left. Follow the unmarked trail on your right for a few minutes to the base of the cliff. If you continue up the blue-blazed trail from the unmarked trail, after another 3 minutes you will come to a Y junction. Veer right at the junction and the blue-blazed trail will converge after 2 minutes. (If you veer left at the junction, you will come to a large overhanging buttress / boulder—Bear Rock.) Continue hiking on the blue-blazed trail (north), and after 5 minutes you will come to a ridge of white rock that drops off on your right (top of climbs). Continue along

Bear Rock Left

the blue-blazed trail, which drops down to the base of the ridge. This trail continues down and left. Take the unmarked trail that skirts along the base of the overhanging wall.

1. Symbiotic Seven (5.7; sport) The only moderate climb on the cliff and a good warm-up. FSA: Michelle Chappel, 2011.

2. Memories (5.11; sport) Long sling on the first bolt (stick clip) to mitigate rope drag. Steep climbing up the left side of the crag. FSA: Chris Beauchamp, 2011.

3. Recollections (5.12; sport) Steep, and technical, climbing on the left end of the crag. FSA: Chris Beauchamp, 2011.

4. Rainbows and Unicorns (5.10+) Good climbing, but the upper crux (left at last bolt) is somewhat loose and intimidating. FSA: Chris Beauchamp, 2011.

5. S-Ticket (5.11e; sport) Originally bolted in 1993, the bolts were tampered with. Excellent route with dynamic moves on the upper roof. *Note:* Clipping the second bolt (2015) is exposed to a long fall. Reequipped by Chris Beauchamp, 2008.

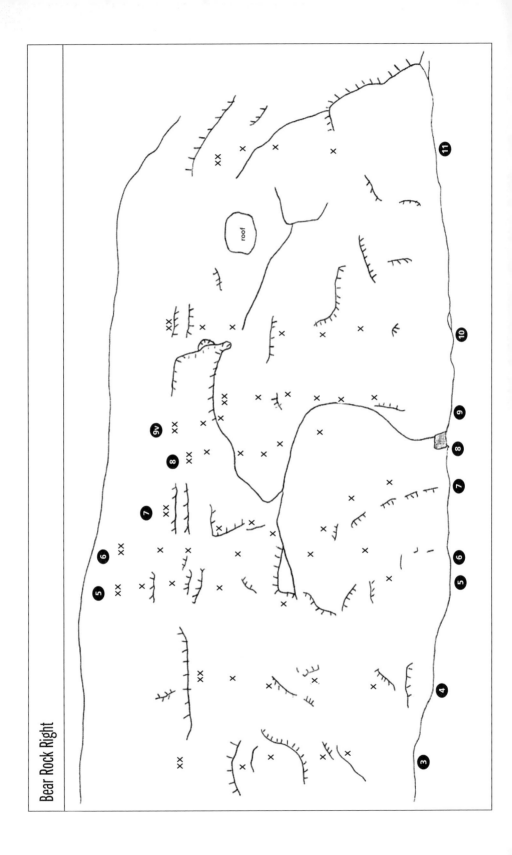

Jeff Laggis on *Garbajistan* PHOTO CHRISTOPHER BEAUCHAMP

6. Chossmosis (5.11+; sport) A steep route that shares its start with *Shit Ticket*. After the first bolt, trend right and straight up the face to anchors. *Note:* The route is also climbed (better climbing) by starting on *Chosstacular* and joining the route after the third bolt. FSA: Chris Beauchamp, 2012.

7. Chosstacular (5.10 ★; sport) Good climbing up the steep central portion of the crag. FSA: Chris Beauchamp, 2009.

8. Double Check Your Nuts (5.12+) Start up the crack left of *Garbajistan* sharing the first two bolts to the right on *Garbajistan*. Follow the crack out through underclings before punching straight up steep and technical terrain. Up to a big roof and easier climbing to fixed anchors. FSA: Chris Bridge, 2014.

9. Garbajistan (5.11+ ★; sport) Technical climbing to the anchors below the roof.

FA: Chris Beauchamp, 2011. 9v *My Ovaries are Killing Me!* variation (5.12 e; sport): An extension to *Garbajistan*. More and more difficult technical climbing up and left of the anchors. Be aware that quickdraws on the *Garbajistan* anchor can get in the way of a key heel hook. FSA: Chris Bridge, 2013.

10. Posie's Porpoise (aka *Morozyvo*) (5.10 ★; sport) A popular route on steep rock—biggest holds you'll ever fall off of. A key chockstone / hold up high seems to be solidly in place. FA: TR Bob Clark and Freddie Wilkinson, 1992. FSA: Chris Beauchamp, 2008.

11. Finger Flight (5.12; sport) A difficult route tackling the right end of the overhanging wall. Can stay wet in the spring. FSA: Chris Bridge, 2014.

WEST ROCK RIDGE STATE PARK, HAMDEN AND NEW HAVEN

At 627 feet above sea level, West Rock Ridge has fantastic views of New Haven Harbor and Long Island Sound. For several years West Rock was the property of the City of New Haven and was off-limits to climbers. However, West Rock is now a Connecticut state park and is open for climber access. Access could change; do your part by being courteous, clean, and careful. West Rock, especially the Main BD (Barker-Daniel) Wall (300 feet), has the potential for the longest routes in Connecticut. It also has the most potential for taking the ride of your life (or the end of it) on loose blocks the size of refrigerators! Aside from the loose rock and the blocks that can be found on many of the routes, beware of huge patches of poison ivy in the summer. West Rock is really best climbed during a mild winter or early spring day, wearing a helmet and perhaps shoulder pads.

Considering that Hassler Whitney was a student at Yale in the 1920s and one of the climbers on the first ascent of the Whitney Gilman Ridge in New Hampshire in 1929, it is likely that climbers have been exploring West Rock since the 1920s and 1930s. The area seemed to get renewed attention in 2002, and then again in 2012–14, with the addition of several mixed and sport routes.

East Rock, which is just east of West Rock and has a stone tower for a landmark, is a town park and is currently off-limits to climbers.

There are four main climbing sections for West Rock Ridge: Barker-Daniel (BD) Wall, South Buttress (aka Ball Field Slabs), Old Quarry Wall, and Wintergreen buttresses.

Please note that all areas on West Rock contain loose rock. The BD Wall is the largest of the cliffs and is located north along the ridgeline from the South Buttress / Ball Field Slabs. Access to the BD Wall is via the paved road, and there are established routes. However, the BD Wall is just too loose and dangerous to mess with and is not included in this guide. The South Buttress and Old Quarry Wall have become increasingly popular. The Wintergreen area is so named because it utilizes the Lake Wintergreen parking and approach in Hamden.

Directions to Amhryn Field for the South Buttress and Old Quarry Wall: From Route 15: Take exit 59 to Route 69 South (converges into Whalley Avenue). Continue on Whalley Avenue for 1.2 miles to Blake Street. Take a left onto Blake Street. Take a left on Austin Street and then a left onto Hard Street. Take a right into the town park / Amhryn Field. To exit the park, follow Stone Street to Blake Street. It should be noted that many people also park in the Blake Street Center located next to the park and use a short bridge to access the ball fields.

Approach for the South Buttress and Old Quarry: Walk toward the baseball field, and behind the third-base dugout is a trailhead. Follow the blue / white-blazed trail for 2 minutes to an intersection, then take a right on the Green Trail for 1 minute to an unmarked trail on the left. Continue up the unmarked trail for less than a minute to a junction with an unmarked trail on the left (HB junction). To reach the Old Quarry Wall, continue straight on the unmarked trail, through poison ivy, to the base of a large corner system. To reach the South Buttress (Ball Field Slabs), take a left at HB junction and continue on this trail for 2 minutes. You will reach an unmarked trail on the right. Continue up this trail, then fourth-class

Silas Finch on the second pitch of *Nickel and Dime* PHOTO CHRIS BEAUCHAMP

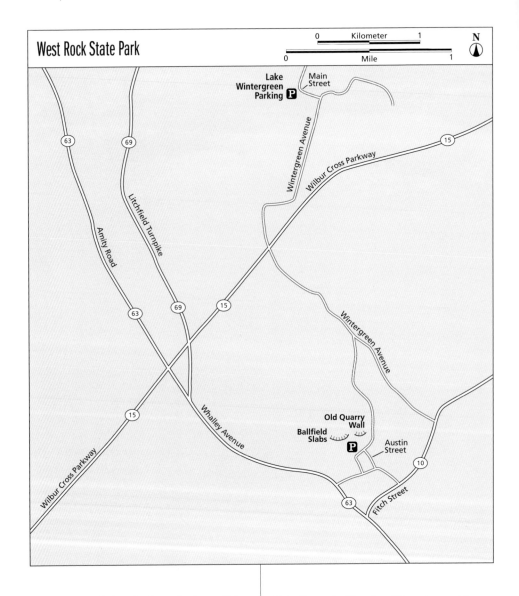

West Rock State Park

0 Kilometer 1

0 Mile 1

N

Lake Wintergreen Parking **P**

Main Street

Wintergreen Avenue

Wilbur Cross Parkway

63

69

15

Litchfield Turnpike

Amity Road

63

69

15

Wintergreen Avenue

15

Whalley Avenue

Wilbur Cross Parkway

Old Quarry Wall

Ballfield Slabs

P

Austin Street

10

63

Fitch Street

scrambling up ledges leads to the base of the routes. You can also reach the top by taking a right on the trail after the dugout (not well marked) and continuing up and left, joining the Red Trail to the top and the parking lot / overlook.

Directions to Wintergreen crags:
From Fitch Street (Route 10), head north on Wintergreen (next to Southern Connecticut State University). Follow Wintergreen to

Main Street in Hamden. There is a parking lot for the hike and Wintergreen Lake access.

Approach to Wintergreen crags:
From the West Rock State Park Lake Wintergreen parking lot, hike up the dirt road past the intersection with the White Trail and continue straight on the road / Yellow Trail for 8 minutes to the water tower. Veer left at the water tower, continuing on the Yellow Trail for about 5 minutes

to a road. Cross the road and you will intersect the Blue Trail. Take a right (north) on
the Blue Trail for about 20 feet, then follow
an unmarked trail west and then south for
about 5 minutes (top of Gold Glitter buttress). Continue another few minutes to the
Break-Through buttresses. A good marker
is the clean buttress on the left with a thin
crack start to a slab with a bolt on the right
(*Emergency Break-Through*).

South Buttress

Ball Field Slabs

While much of this area is loose, some dramatic climbs have been established in this
area. While lines were climbed decades ago,
Dan Griffiths had the vision to first add the
mixed / sport routes. Note that loose rock
still abounds, and that some of the sport
routes tend to wander a bit (at least the easiest line) from the path of the bolts. This area
is very warm in the summer. Also, close
your systems (climbers tied into both ends
of the rope) due to the long lowers that may
result in lowering someone off the end of a
rope. Seventy-meter rope for descents.

Historical note: The left end reaches
183 feet in height and for a long time was
marked by a huge white streak of paint.
Apparently, a fifty-five-gallon drum of white
road paint was stolen from the Department
of Environmental Protection (DEP) depot
and poured from the top of the cliff.
Admirers of the ridge complained that the
white paint detracted from the orange rock.
Eventually, climber Martin Torresquintero
was asked by state officials to paint over the
white streak with brown paint to match the
color of the cliff. As a result, the climb *White
Streak* (5.10+), which used to ascend this
prominent landmark, is a little more difficult

to locate. The finishing holds on the upper
face are also more difficult owing to the layers of paint—forget about friction. From the
western lookout of the parking lot, hop the
wall and walk to a lookout. If you can make
out the section of the cliff (steep face just
after an overhang) with brown paint, you
have found *White Streak* (two-bolt anchor on
top). However, due to massive loose rock, this
route should not be climbed.

Ball Field Routes

These routes are approached by scrambling
up fourth-class ledges.

1. Nickel and Dime (5.9+ ★; sport) One of
the most spectacular settings in Connecticut.
A two-pitch sport route on the sweeping
walls. Work your way up fourth-class ledges
to the *Kinesthesia* ledge. Up the arête on the
left past four bolts to a fixed anchor. Pitch
two climbs past six bolts to fixed anchors.
The difficulty of the route varies depending
on the line of ascent. Staying left and right of
the bolts on the second pitch follows the path
of least resistance. FSA: Mike Mobley, Dan
Griffiths, 2011. *Trad Start* variation (5.8+ R):
From the *Kinesthesia* ledge, climb the crack
corner on the left to the top of the first pitch
of *Nickel and Dime* to fixed anchors.

2. Big Al's Supercrack Crack (5.9) Starting
from the ground below the *Kinesthesia* ledge,
climb the crack to the start of *Nickel and
Dime* and the *Kinesthesia* ledge. Much loose
rock was dislodged to uncover the route.
FRA: Mike Mobley, 2011.

3. Kinesthesia (5.11; sport) Scramble up
to the ledge to the right of *Big Al's Crack*.
Follow the line of seven bolts, past loose
blocks midway, to a fixed anchor near a
tree (careful of loose blocks). FSA: Morgan
Patterson, 2013.

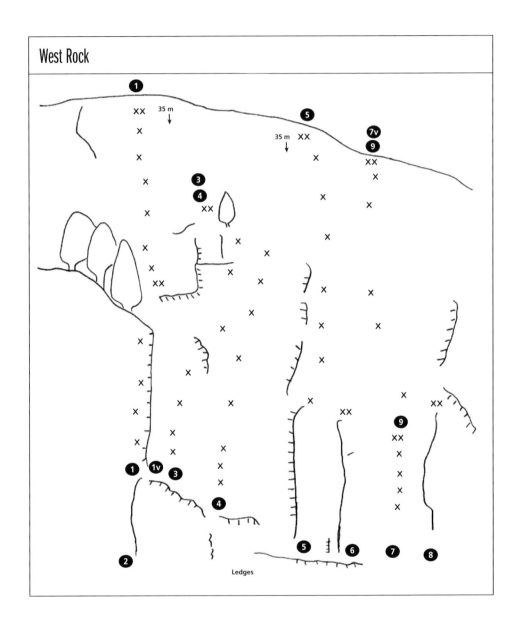

West Rock

4. 30 Second to All Night (5.10; sport) Start on the ledge below and right of the *Kinesthesia* ledge. Work up the face and arête, passing eight bolts, then traverse left at the ledge to the anchors on *Kinesthesia*. FSA: Mike Mobley, 2013.

5. That '70s Show (5.9+ ★; mixed / sport) Starting on a ledge (fourth-class scramble on exposed terrain) up the 5.8+ crack and corner (gear) to a bolt on the face to the right. Staying to the right of the second bolt keeps the rating at 5.9. Straight up at the second bolt is about 5.10+ and staying left of the upper bolts keeps the rating in the 5.9 range. Seven bolts to fixed anchor. Descend with 70-meter rope and a closed system (both climbers tied-in) to prevent lowering off the end of the rope. Knot the end of the ropes for a rappel. FSA: Dan Griffiths, Mike Mobley, 2011. *Drill Wavin' Extension* variation: The line of bolts on the right can be reached after the second bolt on *That '70s Show* (using gear recommended). The route is loose and not high quality.

6. West Rock Crack (5.11 ★ PG) The beautiful low-angle finger crack that is ascended via a variety of methods. There is ample gear, but very strenuous to place. Start up the shallow right-facing corner on the left, then work right into the crack. Up the crack (optional jog right and then back into the crack two-thirds up) to fixed anchors. Direct start: Start straight up the tips crack (5.11+).

7. Drill Wavin' New Haven (5.11+; sport) The blank-looking bolted face to the right of West Rock Crack. Four bolts to a fixed anchor. FSA: Dan Griffiths, 2007.

8. Sheets of Wrath (5.9 TR) To the right of *Drill Wavin' New Haven* is a set of fixed anchors. Apparently this route contains loose plates of rock (not climbed by the author).

Fixed anchors at the top of the pitch for toproping. FRA: Dan Griffiths, 2011.

9. Drill Wavin' New Haven Extension (5.9; sport). Not a high-quality route but sometimes used to access the top of *Drill Wavin' New Haven* or *Sheets of Wrath* for toproping via *That '70s Show*.

Old Quarry Wall

These routes are found to the right of the Ball Field slabs. From the approach mentioned, continue straight at HB junction for about 20 feet and then left over a small berm into a clearing. Head toward the back of the clearing (careful of poison ivy) and follow a small trail to the base of a large open corner (Crackrock Corner). You can also follow the trail to the top of the climbs and set up topropes.

Much of the route information for the Old Quarry Wall was provided by Morgan Patterson, 2014 as well as mountain project.com, 2015.

1. Tasmanian Pain Coaster (5.12; sport) Up the face to the right of a left facing corner, past three bolts, to fixed anchors. FA: Greg Shyloski, 2015.

2. The Golden Ghetto (5.12; sport) Start to the right of the diagonal crack and left of *The Tree of Life*. Climb past bolts then move left at the top to a shared anchor with *Tasmanian Pain Coaster*. Five bolts to a fixed anchor. FA: Greg Shyloski, 2015.

3. The Tree of Life (5.11; sport) Starts on the left end of the cliff, about ten feet right of a right diagonal crack. Climb past four bolts to a fixed anchor. FA: Greg Shyloski, 2014.

4. Scifentology (5.12; sport) Start twenty feet left of Run for Cover, up a corner and arête past five bolts to a fixed anchor. FA: Greg Shyloski, 2014.

Will McNeill on the *Devil's Cut* PHOTO DAVID FASULO

5. Run for Cover (5.12b; sport) Located on the small wall on the left side of the quarry, this route ascends the small overhanging roof section. Start up the obvious ramp, then climb left under the overhang to a crack out left. Continue straight up the wall on pinches and crimps to a fixed anchor. FSA: Elliot Ashe, Greg Shyloski, 2014.

6. Traxamillion (5.11; sport) Start on *Run For Cover*, but head right following five bolts to a fixed anchor. FA: Greg Shyloski, 2015.

7. A B-Boy's Alpha (5.11; sport) The sport route between *Traxamillion* and *The People's Rock*. Five bolts to a fixed anchor. FA: Greg Shyloski, 2015.

8. The People's Rock (5.10+; sport) Nice climbing on a clean face and good holds. Four bolts to a fixed anchor. FA: Elliot Ashe, 2014.

9. Slightly Removed (5.11; sport) Work up the steep face and broken corner system fifteen feet left of *Desparéte*. The upper section climbs a clean crack and beautiful face (trend right then back left). Seven bolt to anchors, but the lower section is not well protected. FA: Hunter Pedane, 2014.

10. Desparête (5.13; sport) This exposed route climbs out to and up the large orange serrated arête on impeccable stone. Start on *Devil's Cut*, ascending the corner. At the seventh bolt, launch out left using powerful, technical moves to the arête. Desperate climbing up the arête leads to an anchor. FSA: Elliot Ashe, 2014.

11. Devil's Cut (5.10–; sport) Climb the large corner below *Desparête* past a small overhang and past six bolts to a ledge. From the ledge move up and left to an undercling and pass three more bolts to a fixed anchor. FSA: Doug Kern, Morgan Patterson, 2014.

12. Evil Beauty (5.11+; sport) This route starts under the large roof 10 feet right of *Devil's Cut* and climbs features up a slightly overhanging face past four bolts on the left side of the roof. At the roof step left and climb up the corner past one more bolt to a fixed anchor. FSA: Morgan Patterson, 2014.

13. Crackrock Corner (5.9+; sport) This route climbs the large dihedral in the center of the quarry. Climb past three bolts to the large overlap. Continue past three more bolts following the corner up and right, to a three-bolt anchor on the arête. FSA: Morgan Patterson, 2014.

14. Fiendish Following (5.10; sport) Follow *Crackrock Corner* to the second bolt and traverse left out the overlap to a bolt. Climb past a small overhang and two bolts to a rest at the large overlap. Climb left, smearing along the overlap past two bolts back to the corner. Traverse left onto the left wall of the corner following good holds to an anchor. FSA: Morgan Patterson, 2014.

15. Tax Evasion Haven (5.9; sport) Climb the dihedral to the second bolt, then traverse right at the small overlap and follow five bolts trending up and left to the arête. Shares anchors with *Crackrock Corner*. FSA: Mike Mobley, 2014.

Wintergreen Area

The Glitter Buttress is the buttress on the left (north) from the unmarked approach trail.

1. Trapp Chute (5.6) The chimney on the left end of the buttress. Head right after the chockstone to finish on *Load of Trapp*. The most pleasant of the "Trapp" routes.

2. Load of Trapp (5.4) The left side of the blocky buttress and central dihedral. Follow a wide crack 3 feet right of the arête to the top of the buttress.

3. Pile of Trapp (5.8+) Up the dirty central dihedral. Finish on the face to the left to avoid loose rock.

4. All That's Gold Doesn't Glitter (5.11– ★; sport / mixed) Stick-clip the first bolt just right of the *Pile of Trapp*, then ascend the ramp on the left to the ledge. Pass the bolt

to a ledge, then three bolts lead up the arête and face. An optional gear placement protects a move out left to fixed anchors. FSA: Chris Beauchamp, 2013.

5. Thunderballs (5.11–) To the right of *All That's Gold Doesn't Glitter*, climb the roof on the right using the crack on the left side (tape helpful). Follow the crack on the left to the top. FRA: Rick Kraft, 2013.

6. Pick'm Lick'm Roll'm Flick'm (5.9) The crack on the right of the roof system. Starts in the open book and breaks left to the slab before tackling the crack. After clearing the roof, follow the crack on the right side of the buttress. Good climbing, unique route name. FRA: Chris Beauchamp, 2013.

7. Trappy (5.9; mixed; PG / R) Start on the right edge of the buttress. Climb to a bolt about 15 feet up. Climb to the right of the

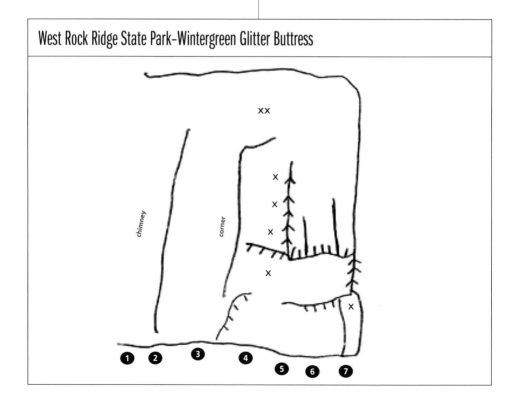

West Rock Ridge State Park-Wintergreen Glitter Buttress

nose (marginal gear placement) then onto the arête. Pass the overlap and finish on *Pick'm.* FRA: Chris Beauchamp, 2013.

8. Path in the Woods (5.10– or 5.7+) Start on the right end of the buttress / south-facing wall. Climb up the arête just right of the left-facing corner. Move past the low horizontal crack to the roof (using a hold out right). (5.10–) Move up and left at the arête to the roof and then left into the left-facing corner. (5.7+) Keep your feet low in the horizontal and move left into the left-facing corner. Finish up the wide crack to the top. FRA: Chris Beauchamp, 2013.

Break-Through Buttresses

These are a series of relatively solid buttresses about 50 feet south of the Glitter Buttress. It is probably easiest to find the route *Emergency Break-Through* (see below), and then orient yourself from that point. This section is not well suited for toproping from above.

9. First Rodeo (5.6) This route ascends the buttress left of *Emergency Break-Through* up a left-facing corner and hand crack, that changes to a right-facing corner, then left-facing corner. After reaching the ledge, "ride" the pillar / buttress to fixed anchors. Medium to large camming units helpful.

10. Blocky Chimney—more of a landmark. The loose chimney between *First Rodeo* and *Emergency Break-Through.*

11. Party Line (5.8) Follow the left side of the *Emergency Break-Through* buttress (thin cracks) past a left-facing corner and finish on the left-facing corner / crack to shared fixed anchors.

12. Emergency Break-Through (5.9 ★; mixed) This route is located on a 12- to 15-foot-wide buttress with a thin crack up the center leading to a slab with a bolt on the right arête. Up the right side of the buttress to a stance below a bolt. Up the arête and through a blocky area. Finish on the

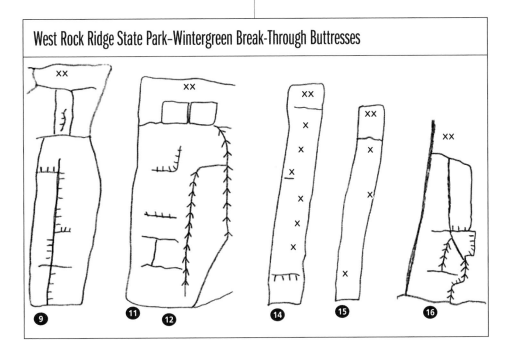

West Rock Ridge State Park-Wintergreen Break-Through Buttresses

wide crack on the right (large camming units) side of the buttress to fixed anchors. Seventy feet. FRA: Chris Beauchamp, 2013.

13. Ugly routes. There are routes just to the right of *Emergency Break-Through*. They include the broken corner and the loose buttress to the right.

14. Obelisk (5.11 ★; sport) Just past some loose buttresses is a clean and solid slab / pillar. A line of six bolts leads up the pillar to fixed anchors. FSA: Rick Craft 2103.

15. Minor Contrivances (5.7; mixed) A short walk south / right from *Obelisk* is a slender pillar. Starts on the lower right side and goes up the middle—the line is contrived by fixed gear. A bolt marks the start and two more bolts, separated by poorly protected stretches of easier climbing, lead to fixed anchors.

16. Rough Ryder (5.9 ★) A great route—too bad it is short. Climb up the right edge of the right-facing corner. Follow the left-slanting crack for 30 feet to fixed anchors. FRA: Jeff Laggis, 2013.

17. Old and New (5.5) Forty feet right of *Rough Ryder* is a low-angle 40-foot buttress. Up the center of the buttress (piton on right halfway up 2015) to fixed anchors.

ROSS POND STATE PARK, KILLINGLY

A long cliff band that reaches 85 feet at its highest point. While not a destination crag for the climber on a cross-country climbing trip, this cliff has routes for beginners and experts alike. Connecticut and Rhode Island climbers have frequented this area for many years. In recent years some excellent sport routes have been established, but check to see if they are intact before launching into the unknown as fixed gear seems to come and go.

Directions: From I-395 North: Take exit 90 (Route 6 East) to the first exit on the right (not numbered). At the end of the ramp, take a left. Travel 0.8 mile on Ross Road and take a left onto the dirt road marked with a boat launch sign. Follow the road for 0.5 mile to a large parking area.

To return to I-395 going south, reverse the way you came. To go north, reverse the directions given below.

From I-395 South: Take exit 91 east (Route 6 East). Soon after the exit, take a right at the blinking light (sign for Old Furnace State Park and a boat launch sign). After 0.5 mile make a right on Ross Road (another boat launch sign). Stay right at the fork in the road. After 0.3 mile turn right onto a dirt road marked by a boat launch sign. Follow the road for 0.5 mile to a large parking area.

To return to I-395 going north, reverse the way you came. To go south, reverse the directions given above.

To access the cliff, walk up the trail leading from the parking lot to the left edge of the cliff system—about 1 minute. A well-worn trail leads across the top of the cliff. A trail also skirts the top of the cliff. If climbing on the right end of the crag, a trail

Brian Phillips on *Chosstacular* PHOTO DAVID FASULO

leaves the parking lot (large boulder) and skirts a pond and the lower end of the cliffs. Hike about 5 minutes to the junction of an unmarked trail on the left that leads to the final three climbs listed.

Parking Lot Wall

The short wall on the left end of the crag is quickly accessed up the hill from the parking lot.

1. Quick Step (5.5) A good beginner lead. Start at the right side of the boulder and follow the crack and corner on left side of wall. Pass the small roof on the right and then pass the large flake to the top.

2. Fancy Footwork (5.10 R) The face just to the right of the *Quick Step* crack.

3. Fancy Fingers (5.12– TR) Up the face left of the *Slippery When Wet* crack.

4. Slippery When Wet (5.8 ⋆) The aesthetic crack in the middle of the Parking Lot Wall. Best appreciated by not using the horizontal crack or any face holds.

5. Tincture of Benzoin (5.9 PG / R ⋆) Start at the base of the right-facing corner and climb straight up the face passing two horizontal cracks.

6. Laughing Man (5.9+ TR) The face climb between *Tincture of Benzoin* and *Double Mantle*. Aim for a hairline crack near the top.

7. Double Mantle (5.7 R) Start on the right side of the wall under a small overhang. Mantels and thin moves gain the top.

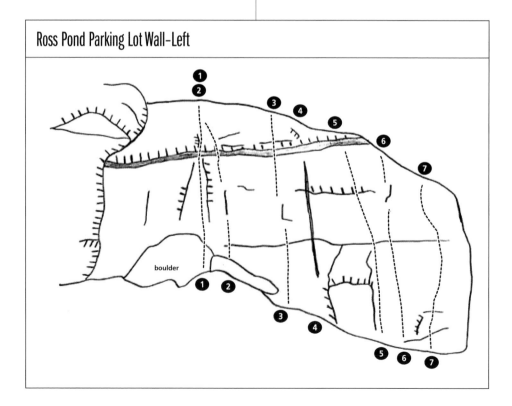

Ross Pond Parking Lot Wall–Left

Ross Pond Geometric Wall

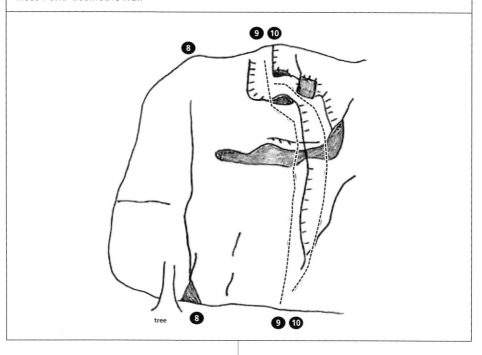

Around the corner (right) from the Parking Lot Wall is the Geometric Wall.

8. Crack of Despair (5.10+ ★ PG) The crack and face climb starting behind a tree on the left side of the wall—trickier than it looks.

9. Crucible (5.11+ PG) The technical corner and roof system on the right-hand section of the Geometric Wall. FA: Ken Nichols.

Neutron variation (5.11– TR): Climb up to the second roof on *Crucible* and traverse left, but instead of heading up the crux inside corner, traverse left to the arête and finish up a short crack.

10. Good Book (5.9 PG) Layback and underling up the blocky corner and roof system. After the upper square roof, traverse left to join *Metron* to the top.

The next major buttress to the right is the Party Wall. A trail to the left of *La Losa* leads to the top of the cliff, or approach from the trail skirting the top of the cliff.

11. La Losa (5.8 ★; sport) Ascend the slab on the left end of the buttress passing five bolts (missing 2015) and finishing right of the arête at fixed anchors. FSA: Brian Phillips 2012.

12. Bed Spins (5.5) The ugly corner separating *La Losa* from the steep wall.

13. Devil's Lettuce (5.8+ PG ★) A great climb that has remnants of pitons from decades past. Follow blocky right-facing corners to a small roof, pass the roof into the large inside corner, and exit left under the large roof at the top. Leader's note: The climb ascends the short arête on the left past the first roof into the corner. However, if

leading, climb up the corner and place gear high, then downclimb and up the short arête. *Orange Matter* variation (5.8+ TR ★); Start just right of the *Bed Spins* corner, and climb up corners and ledges leading up to a shallow corner and the right side of the large roof. Join *Devil's Lettuce* to the top.

14. Panty Raid (5.9 TR) Start on *Devil's Lettuce*, then traverse up and right on a corner / ramp, then up the face to a ledge. Climb past a scary block, then up the steep face and left-facing corner to the top. A crack at the top edge of the cliff marks the route when setting up.

15. Thumper (5.6 R) There are a pair of cracks on the right end of the wall. Thumper is the crack on the left. More difficult to protect than it looks. Finish at a fixed anchor.

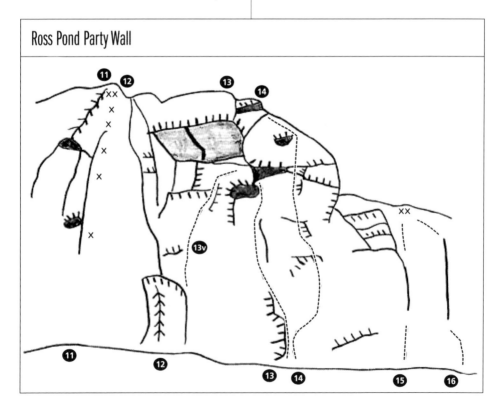

Ross Pond Party Wall

16. Topside (5.7 R) The crack system on the right end of the wall. When it ends, traverse left to the fixed anchor.

Table Rock is the unique buttress / spire 100 feet to the right of the Party Wall

17. Invitation to Dinner (5.9+ R ★; aka *La Mesa* 5.9) Climb the left edge of the spire to a short vertical crack and stance. Traverse out right a few feet, then over the overlap to the top. Variation 5.10 R. Climb the first 20 feet and traverse right. Climb the face just to left of the right-hand arête. Up to the horizontal and finish up the right side of arête. Description for *La Mesa* (5.9 ★; sport): A unique climb. Climb the narrow buttress past five bolts (bolts missing 2015) to a ledge on the left side of the spire. Traverse right around the corner under the overhang, passing a bolt to the ledge on the right. Pass one more bolt up to the fixed anchor.

The next two climbs ascend the 85-foot orange wall just to the right of La Mesa.

18. Slacker (5.7 TR) Wander up the face (left / center) to an overhang. Crank over the overhang and up to the top. Finishes at the notch on the left. Often wet.

19. Specter (5.6 TR ★) Climb up the right / center of the orange face. Finish at a small right-facing corner. Good climbing and exposure at a moderate grade.

The next three climbs are on the far end of the crag. To reach this crag from the parking area, follow the trail that skirts the pond below the crag (huge boulder near parking lot). Shortly after reaching the second pond, a trail will lead up to the far north end of the crags. Otherwise follow the trail that skirts the bottom of the cliff.

20. Gneiss Jugs (5.8; mixed—two bolts and gear) About 30 feet to the left of the *Disneyworld* platform, look for a blocky overhanging right-facing corner. Stick-clip the first bolt. Make deceptively easy moves up the overhang to turn the corner on the left. Up a short face then scramble to another face that wanders up the arête to the top.

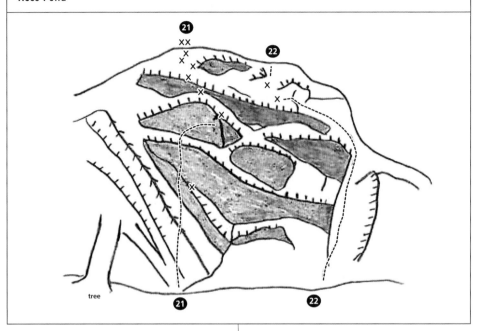

The next two climbs begin on a platform under a clean face and roof.

21. Don't Bleed on Me (5.11 ★; sport) Multiple cruxes on great rock. Stick-clip the first bolt then work up the left side of the face to gain a handhold left of the arête at the large overhang. Clip and traverse right toward a positive flake on the right. Surmount the overhang and go left to surmount another overhang just right of a bolt. Up easier moves to an overhanging face and desperate layback (don't get cut on the last hold) to the anchor. Seven bolts to anchor.

22. Disneyworld (5.7 ★; mixed—two bolts and gear) A wonderful creation. Climb the dihedral on the right, passing the blocky roof. Continue up the right side of the crag, passing two bolts, following the arête and crack on the left. Finish up the steep arête (small camming unit helpful). Descend on the trail to the right or rappel *Don't Bleed on Me*.

23. Something Dirty (5.9–; sport) Start on the northernmost section of the crag 50 feet to the right of *Disneyworld*. Follow bolts to a break in the overhang. Pull through the intimidating overhang and on to fixed anchors. Six bolts to anchor.

LANTERN HILL, NORTH STONINGTON

Dating back to the 1870s, the Lantern Hill was part of a silica mine. Fortunately, it was purchased by the Mashantucket Pequot Tribal Nation in 1994—thereby preserving this wonderful area. Lantern Hill derives its name from its ability to be seen from the Long Island Sound when the sun strikes the walls of white and milky quartz.

Rock climbers have been frequenting Lantern Hill on a regular basis since the 1970s, and several popular climbs can be found on the steep and clean quartz faces. Lantern Hill is currently (2015) open to the public, and Foxwoods has provided trail markers for various loops from the casino. With regard to rock climbing on Lantern Hill, the Mashantucket Pequot Tribal Nation does not explicitly permit or deny rock climbing on Lantern Hill. The MPTN has been generous with regard to access to

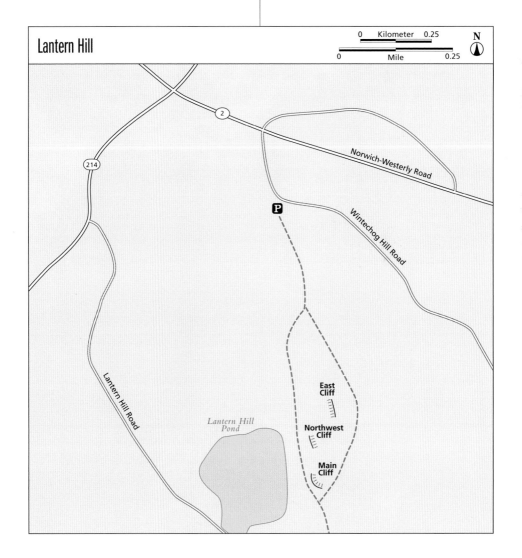

Mary Stevenson on *Porcelain Arête* PHOTO DAVID FASULO

Lantern Hill for many years, so do your part by helping to keep this area pristine.

Directions: Take I-95N to exit 92. Go left off of the exit ramp to get on Route 2 west. After 6.7 miles and just before the casino take a right on Milltown Road, which will take you around and under the Route 2 overpass to get on Wintechog Hill Road. After 0.6 mile there is a pullout on the right. There is not an abundance of parking, so carpooling is recommended. Up the hill a sign marks the start of the Lantern Hill Trail. Follow the trail for 5 minutes to a split. Take a right on the red-blazed trail and after 12 minutes you will reach the base of the main wall—the prominent clean quartzite cliff about 50 feet high. A trail on the right end of the cliff leads to the top.

Main Cliff

1. Starting Point (5.3) Up the large left-facing corner / crack system to a ledge. Move right and up the large left-facing corner to the top.

2. Sharper Image (5.6 R) Nice rock and climbing. A few feet right of *Starting Point*, climb up the right-facing corner and straight up the face to the base of the left-facing corner. Up the corner to the top.

3. Blackbeard (5.7 ★ PG) A couple feet right of *Sharper Image*, climb up steep bulges aiming for a small / sharp left-facing corner that turns to a thin crack. Up the crack and face to the base of the arête. Up the right side of the arête (gear placements left of the arête).

4. Swan Dive (5.9 R) Up *Blackbeard* to the right-diagonaling flake and crack system to the top.

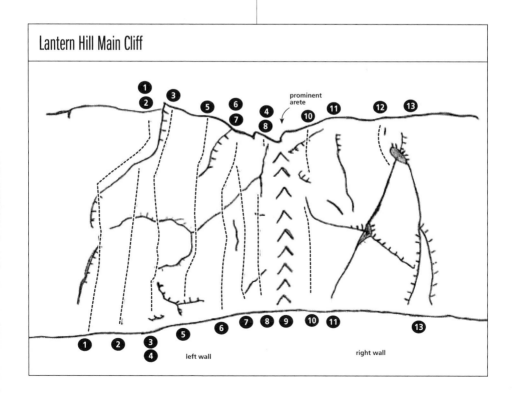

Lantern Hill Main Cliff

5. Jolly Roger (5.8 R) Enjoyable moves on good rock. Climb the blocky face and cracks right of *Blackbeard*, then up left-facing corners to the base of the large left-facing corner and the face on the left to the top.

6. Quartz Master (5.10+ TR) Climb the steep face left of *Zen Master* and the thin crack. Finish on the outside corner / arête leading to the top.

7. Zen Master (5.10+ ★ X) About 10 feet left of the *Porcelain Arête*, at a small left-facing corner, up the face passing to the right of a hairline crack.

8. Unnamed (5.10+ ★ TR) About 6 feet left of the *Porcelain Arête*, up the face to a bulge, move left a bit, then up the technical lower-angle rock to the base of the crack. Up the crack to the top.

9. Porcelain Arête (5.9 ★ R) A beautiful climb up the prominent arête on sharp holds. Finishes left of the arête. Variation (5.9 R): Midway up the arête move left to the base of a crack and finish up *Unnamed*.

10. Alabaster (5.9+ R ★) A few feet right of the arête, climb up to a large, rounded hold. Up the headwall to a left-slanting crack, then up the short arête at a quartz jug to the middle of the overhang. Over the overhang to the top.

11. Milky Way (5.10+ PG / R) Follow the steep crack on the left side of the wall to the V notch. Climb up and left following the left-leaning crack to the top.

12. Black Jack Crack (5.9) Up the crack on the left (same as *Milky Way*) past the V notch to the left side of the chimney. Follow the left-slanting crack about 10 feet, then up the face to the top.

13. Skunk Dog (5.8+) Layback up the chimney / corner on the right, then chimney to the top.

Upper West Side

The wall up and right of the main wall has a few routes. The middle of the face, trending left to a horizontal then back right, is *Hard Wall* (5.10 TR). Straight up the center is 5.11. The arête to the right is *Layback Corner* (5.9+ TR). Other routes can be found on scattered crags and the northwest ridges in the area.

Northwest Side

On the approach to the Main Wall, there is a set of crags (about 6 minutes before reaching the Main Wall) up the ridge on the left known as the Northwest Side. This area has at least thirteen established routes. Of these, one of the better crags, *Crystal Heights*, has a steep clean wall with thin cracks running up it. *Foxbite* (5.11+) is the clean / thin crack system on the right end of the wall, and the arête to the right is *Borderline* (5.10–).

MATTATUCK STATE FOREST, PLYMOUTH

Located in the Mattatuck State Forest, Whitestone is a southwest-facing cliff of gneiss with good views of the Naugatuck River valley. The top of the cliff is located along blue-blazed Whitestone Cliff Trail. The rock varies in color from white to gray to black and ranges in height from 25 to 60 feet. The cliff has a pleasant low-angle slab for beginners, as well as a few steep, difficult cracks and corners for the experts. Whitestone is a good place to climb when the temperature drops but the sun is shining. A couple of rusty pitons hearken back to the early climbing that went on here several decades ago. Considering that there are several moderate climbs, and unknown climbers have frequented this area for many years, first ascents are not listed.

Directions: From I-84 East or West, take Route 8 North to exit 37 (Route 262). At the end of the ramp, take a right onto Route 262 East, crossing the river on Frost Bridge. (If coming from Route 8 South, take a left at the end of the ramp.) At the far side of the bridge, turn right onto Waterbury Road. After 0.5 mile turn left onto Spruce Brook Road. Pass Greystone Road on the right. A short distance farther (0.3 mile) is a small (four-car) parking area on the left, by a gated forest road. Park here.

Approach: Follow the forest road/Whitestone Cliff Trail uphill. The road levels out and splits. Bear right following the blue blazes—there is an old pavilion on the left (if you reach the pavilion, you have gone too far). About 2 minutes past the junction, the road intersects the blue-blazed trail. Turn right on the blue-blazed trail/Whitestone Cliff Trail, cross a brook, and follow the trail uphill 0.3 mile to the cliff. The blue-blazed trail goes to the summit of the cliffs, and an unmarked trail leads left along the base of the cliff.

To approach the base of the climbs, hike downhill and to the left on the unmarked trail for 1 minute. A fourth-class move gains the base of the *Prime Climb* slab. Continue along the trail to the left end of the cliff. From here a trail leads to the top of the cliff, where the climbs from the left end of the cliff to *Hollywood* can be easily accessed.

Robert Dest on *Smokehouse* PHOTO DAVID FASULO

Whitestone Cliff

1. Super Stout (5.9 R) Starting slightly left of *Baldy*, climb straight up, crossing a series of diagonal cracks and overlaps.

2. Baldy (5.10 X ★) Begin as for *Tree Skirt*. Move left onto the blank face above a small tree. Continue over the bulge to the top.

3. Tree Skirt (5.7 R ★) Scramble up the ramp and duck behind the pine tree into a V groove with a finger crack. When the finger crack fades into a seam, step right and mantle onto the top of the flake. Continue up the thin seam and face to the right. A natural and aesthetic line.

4. Nectar of the Gods (5.9+ TR ★) Start between *Smokehouse* and *Tree Skirt*. Climb dark rock to a ledge, then continue up the blank-looking white face to the top. High-quality rock and climbing.

5. Smokehouse (5.7+ PG / R ★) Five feet to the left of *Bushwhack* is a small ledge (looks as much like a boulder as a ledge). From the ledge climb to the crack / corner to a small ledge halfway up the cliff. Layback (shaky gear and committing move) up the left side of the overhanging bulge. From the ledge on top of the bulge, follow a thin crack up great rock and a crack to the top. A medium camming unit helps to protect the route after the overhang.

6. Belly Roll (5.10– R ★) Boulder up the overhanging corner just left of *Bushwhack*, or start on *Smokehouse*. Continue up the face to the right of *Smokehouse*, aiming for the parallel cracks just above the ledge. Climb between the two cracks to the steep face above and the final bucket holds at the top.

7. Bushwhack (5.7– PG) Climb the right-facing corner to a short crack. Follow this to a small ledge, then move left and finish on the clean white face on good holds. The top section (best part) can be avoided by continuing along the ledge / ramp off to the right, keeping the route at 5.5 and better protected.

8. Romancing the Stone (5.6) Climb the right-leaning crack that ends just below a tree-covered ledge. Scramble up from the ledge. Great climbing—too bad it is so short.

9. Lichen It Hot (5.9+ TR) Climb the black face between *Olden Way* and *Vertical Limit* to the ledge system. Lower, or scramble to the top.

10. Olden Way (5.5 PG) Start just to the right of *Romancing the Stone*. Climb up and right to the horizontal crack; then continue up the right diagonal crack to the ledge. Scramble to the top.

11. Vertical Limit (5.6 R) Start at a short right-facing corner 6 feet left of *Going Vertical*. After an awkward start, diagonal right to the arête forming the *Going Vertical* corner. Continue up the left side of the arête and continue up the gray low-angle rock to the top. Variation (5.7 TR): From the top of the block, climb straight up the face to join *Vertical Limit*.

12. Central Rock (5.6 ★ PG) Climb the right-facing corner on the left end of the *Prime Climb* slab. Two-thirds up the corner, traverse left over the corner and up the *Vertical Limit* face. Easier than it looks.

Whitestone Left

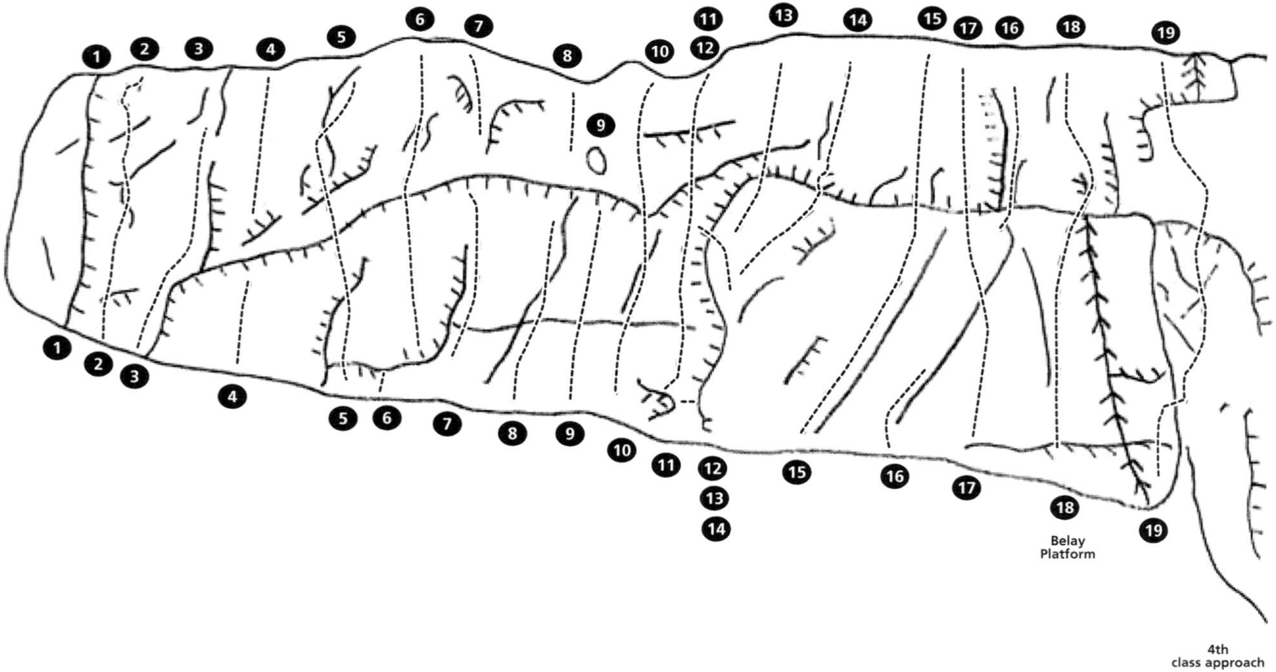

Belay Platform

4th class approach

13. Dead Vertical (5.6) Climb the right-facing corner on the left end of the *Prime Climb* slab. Move a couple feet to the right at the roof and climb over the roof and continue up the face to the top. Variation (5.7+ TR): Climb the black face just right of the corner to the roof to join *Dead Vertical*.

14. Going Vertical (5.5 PG ★) Climb the right-facing corner on the left end of the *Prime Climb* slab. Halfway up, follow the right-leaning cracks up to and through the lip at the black rock / crack.

15. A Prime Climb (5.7– R ★) Follow the central crack up, then right, to the overlap. Traverse left a couple of feet, and climb over the overlap at an awkward crack. There is poor protection past the overlap.

16. Stone Age (5.4 ★) Start 3 feet to the right of the central crack system that splits the face. Follow the black flake up to a crack and through the overlap and up the corner system.

17. Carabiners (5.8+ R / X) Start a few feet right of the *Stone Age* crack. Up the face crossing the crack then over the roof and the small corner / crack just right of the *Prime Climb* roof and up the face.

18. Simpler Times (5.4 R ★) Climb the low-angle face on the right edge of the slab. Continue over the right end of the overlap, and finish right of *Stone Age*.

19. Batman (5.5) Start to the right of the arête and work up to the overlap and the Y crack. Past the crack to the ledge and finish up the right-facing corner and roof.

The remaining climbs are located down and to the right of the belay platform for the *Prime Climb* slab.

20. Palm Pilot (5.9 R) Starting 3 feet left of *Brigit*, climb the black face and over a 12-inch overlap to the base of an overhanging dihedral with two thin cracks on its right wall. Climb the dihedral and make a long reach up and left. Mantle up onto the ledge, joining *Structures* to finish.

21. Structures (5.9+ ★ PG) Starting in the mossy open book, follow a crack to the base of an overhang. Hand-traverse left under a roof to gain a small ledge and then finish straight up a short face with two vertical cracks.

22. Brigit (5.11– ★) Follow *Structures* to the overhang; traverse right into the base of the dihedral. Technical bridging leads to a strenuous finish.

23. Dreadlock (5.8 ★) Follow a crack at the right side of the right ramp up and onto the face. Continue to the top on either of two cracks (the left side is easier).

24. Hollywood (5.9 R) Begin 3 feet downhill (left) of *AMCer*. Follow the steep vertical crack on the left to a good hold. Continue up the shallow corner system to the right of the arête to a ledge. From the ledge, either work up the thin face to the right of the arête, or step left around the corner and continue up the short face and arête. *Conor's* variation (5.9 R): Begin as for *Hollywood*. Fifteen feet up reach left for the edge / fin and gain the small ledge. Finish as for *Hollywood*.

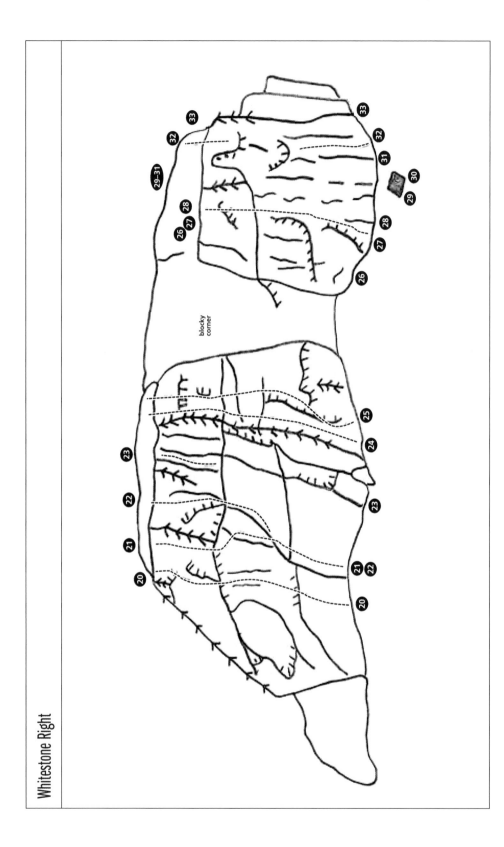

25. AMCer (5.8– R) Start in a short dihedral left of the blocky corners. Up the middle corner and follow a vertical crack on the right, then move right onto the face. Continue straight up on positive holds past two large horizontal cracks to a small left-facing flake in the center of the face. A thin, poorly protected move leads to the ledge.

The next eight climbs are located on a small buttress on the right end of the cliff.

26. Stoked (5.11 PG / R ★) Climb the overhanging face and thin vertical seam on the left end of the crag. From a small ledge halfway up, follow a hand crack 3 feet right of the arête to the top. Steep and technical moves on great rock.

27. Super Kitty (5.11+ / 12– TR) A few feet to the right of *Stoked* is a thin crack / seam / right-facing corner on clean white rock. Thin moves for hands and feet lead to a ledge. Continue up *Stoked* from the ledge.

28. Throwing Stones (5.9+ R) Start just right of a left-facing corner, and follow a crack / right-facing corner to the top of the cliff.

29. Side Steppen (5.8 R) Start as for *Searchlight*, but follow the crack on the left past the steep face to the top of the cliff.

30. Searchlight (5.8 PG / R) Start at a right-leaning fissure / crack system that finishes in a notch with a small tree.

31. Pinhead (5.10– PG / R) Begin 3 feet left of *Divining Rod* at a thin vertical crack. Lurch upward on awkward holds to the left side of a left-facing overlap. Pull through and continue slightly right to the top of the cliff.

32. Divining Rod (5.9+ R ★) Begin 5 feet to the left of *Small Pine*, at overlapping flakes. Follow crack systems straight up, passing just right of a left-facing overlap. Follow either of two crack systems above the flake.

33. Small Pine (5.7 PG) Begin at the left edge of the boulder field. Follow the left-leaning crack on good holds and finish straight up the face.

If you really wish to explore, the Whitestone Cliff system continues. From the far left end of the cliff, a short walk downhill will bring you to the top of the "Lower Cliff." The rock is broken up and has a couple routes in the 5.7 range. Below and to the right of the Lower Cliff is the LL Cliff (Lower Lower Cliff). To reach the LL Cliff, instead of making the step up onto the Whitestone Slab area off the unmarked trail along the base of the cliff, continue down the slope for 1 minute and you will encounter a 40-foot wall with a clean right-facing corner (*Stealth*) and a shallow left-facing corner about 10 feet to the left (*Grand Finale*). For even more rock, bushwhack and scramble up the hill to the left of *Stealth* (west), continue past the base of the Lower Ledge, and after a few minutes there is a ledge system with a variety of short, steep roofs.

MATTATUCK STATE FOREST, WATERTOWN

Located in the Mattatuck State Forest in Watertown, just off the blue-blazed Jericho Trail, this steep 75-foot gneiss crag has several interesting climbs where positive edges seem to appear just when needed. Although the rock is textured, many of the routes are poorly protected. Bolt anchors (missing 2015) mark the top of two of the more popular climbs. Please note that some sections contain fragile flakes and edges that can snap off. Also, bees tend to congregate in some of the cracks and can be an unwelcome surprise. The Jericho Cliff is separated from the Biker Crag, which seems to amplify the sound of motorcycles, on the right by a narrow descent gully. There are small crags northwest of the Biker Crag, but they are located on private property. As far as route history, climbers have been exploring the crag for many years. Maybe the next edition will contain more history. Many of the routes, even though listed as TR, have probably been led, but the protection would be poor. In the late 1990s Robert Desocio and friends spent much time toproping most of the routes listed.

Directions: From I-84 East or West, take Route 8 North to exit 37 (Route 262). At the end of the ramp, take a right onto Route 262 East to Echo Lake Road (at the Route 8 overpass). Go left (west) on Echo Lake Road. (If coming from Route 8 South, take a right at the end of the ramp.)

From the Route 8 overpass, drive 0.8 mile on Echo Lake Road to a small pullout (south side of road) across from the gated entrance to state access roads. Please carpool due to limited parking.

Approach: From the pullout on the south side of Echo Lake Road, head back (east) on Echo Lake Road for 0.1 mile to the blue-blazed Jericho Trail entrance on the north side of the road. Hike for 5 minutes up the Jericho Trail to a lookout with views of commercial buildings (blue-blaze arrow painted on the rock). When facing the cliff from below, this is the left end of Jericho Crag. Continue on the trail for about 35 feet then drop right to a trail / gully descending to the base of the crag.

There are climbs on the far left and far right of the main Jericho Cliff as well as on the Biker Crag that are not listed—have an adventure.

Kristina Kern climbing at the Jericho Cliff PHOTO JARED INCILLO

Jericho Cliff

Jericho Cliff

1. Rumor Mill (5.8– R) Sighting a protruding block at the left end of the cliff, on top, helps to figure out the start (which is directly below). Start off a ledge and climb through a wide crack. Follow a seam to an overhang, head left around the overhang, and finish on the final overhang. Variation (5.9 TR): Instead of moving left at the overhang, follow the seam to join *Heaven and Earth* to the top. FRA: Robert Desocio, Dennis Generalli, 1998.

2. Heaven and Earth (5.9 R) Start 6 feet right of *Rumor Mill* and climb up the face, trending left to the small overhang. Climb the overhang at a thin crack and up the face to a slanting finger crack. Continue up the face to a steep finish just left of a corner at the top. FRA: Robert Desocio, Dennis Generalli, 1998.

3. Eyes for You (5.9 ★ TR) Boulder up steep rock just left of the gulley / crack. Climb straight up, aiming for undercling hold just right of a crack / seam. Continue up the face, passing just right of a crack / seam. Bolt anchors (missing 2015) mark the top. FRA: Robert Desocio, 1998.

4. YOS (Year of Strength) (5.9+ TR) Start on *Eyes for You*, but trend right and climb over a small roof at a crack. Up the crack / seam and face to the top.

5. Torchlight (5.9– TR) Start on the block just right of the base of the gulley crack, then step onto the main wall. Up the face to the crack / corner in the middle of the small roof. Follow the crack / corner and face to the top.

6. Gemstone (5.8+ ★ TR) Start on *Torchlight*, but follow the gulley / crack for a few feet. Then ascend the face up to the left end of the large roof. Over the roof at the corner / crack and face to the top. Very cool moves on positive edges.

7. Summer Air (5.9+ R) Start on the pointed boulder / flake. Up the face to the diagonal gulley / crack. Traverse left across and over the overhang then up to, and through, the wide crack past the large roof. Large, but potentially loose, holds provide an airy adventure.

8. White Dragon (5.10– ★ R) (Protection exists but is difficult to locate and place.) Great route. Start on the pointed boulder / flake. Onto the face and trend right over the roof following a crack. Climb past the gulley / crack system at the right end of a block and up to the roof at a shallow right-facing corner and crack. Up the overhanging corner to the top. Bolt anchors (missing 2015) mark the top.

9. Ripshot (5.10+ TR) Climb up to the left slanting crack through the roof. Climb through the roof at the crack and up the face above to the right of the gully / crack. Finish on the face and right-facing corner.

10. Echo (5.10+ TR) Climb up to, and past, the small left-facing corner through the roof. Trend right and up the face near the arête. Finish up the face just right of *Ripshot*.

11. Timeline (5.7 PG) Start on *Echo*, but follow the crack system up right and to the top.

ST. JOHNS LEDGES, KENT

This area is named after Timothy St. Johns, who owned the property in the 1800s. The Stanley Works Company of New Britain purchased the property in 1910 in order to build a dam on the Housatonic River. In 1976 the Stanley Works donated the land to the Nature Conservancy. The Nature Conservancy sold this land to the National Park Service in 1985 as part of the Appalachian Trail Corridor, which is managed and maintained by the Connecticut Chapter of the Appalachian Mountain Club. The Appalachian Trail (AT), linking Georgia to Maine, traverses the base of what is commonly known as the Upper Ledges. If you are climbing on the Upper Ledges in the summer, you will more than likely see a through-hiker. Sharing drinks and snacks with through-hikers is a good way to create some trail magic.

St. Johns Ledges is composed of several ledges. What is commonly referred to as the Lower Ledges is 15 to 30 feet in height, and the Upper Ledges is a friction slab up to 100 feet high. Located near Kent, St. Johns Ledges is a popular climbing destination for colleges, camps, and youth groups. From late June through August, expect to find one of these groups climbing at the Upper or Lower Ledges on any given day. CT AMC Trails Committee volunteers and staff members of user groups have helped to maintain access, cleared fallen trees and brush from the ledges, as well as constructed the retaining walls and terraces at the top of the Upper Ledges, which help to manage erosion and minimize loose rockfall. St. Johns Ledges has seen activity for decades and most of the route names are not from the first ascent. Please note camping is not permitted in this area. The nearest designated campsite is the Stewart Hollow campsite and shelter located about 4 miles north on the AT.

Directions: From the center of Kent at the intersection of Route 341 and Route 7, head west toward New York on Route 341. Immediately after crossing the Housatonic River, turn right on Skiff Mountain Road. Kent School will be on your left, and the river on your right. Follow the road (about 1 mile) until you come to a fork; take the right fork onto a dirt road (River Road) marked with a wooden sign reading "Appalachian National Scenic Trail." Follow the dirt road for 1.6 miles until you see a small Appalachian Trailhead parking area on your left. Please carpool due to very limited parking.

Fred Wilk on *Trail Magic* PHOTO DAVID FASULO

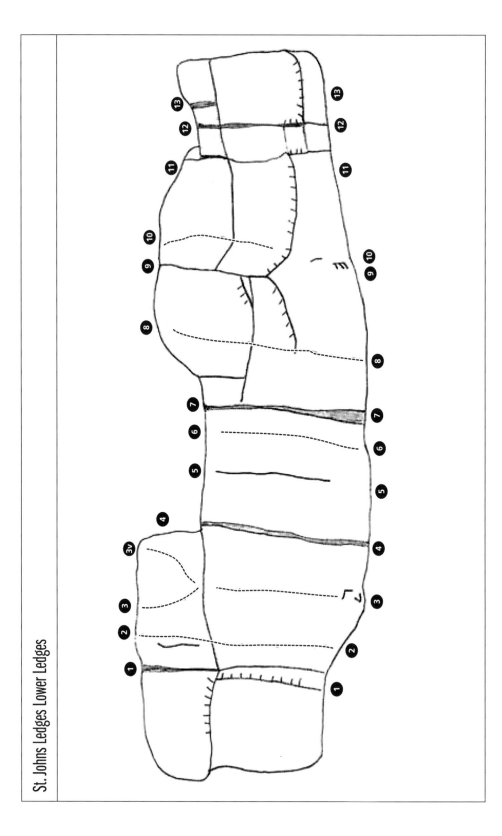

St. Johns Ledges Lower Ledges

Lower Ledges

To reach the Lower Ledges, follow the white-blazed Appalachian Trail south for about 150 feet to an obvious unmarked trail on your left. This trail leads to the Lower Ledges in about 100 yards. Climbs are described from left to right.

1. Workout in the Woods (5.6) Just to the right of the overhang, on the left end of the crag, is a thin seam that widens to 6 inches. Follow the seam and large crack to the top.

2. Seamstress (5.7+ TR) Start a few feet right of *Workout in the Woods* and ascend the face and vertical seam.

3. Little Jewel (aka *The Graduate*) (5.10– TR) Ten feet left of *Wilderness Crack* start at triangle steps. Straight up the face to a small ledge. Continue up the face just right of a thin seam to the top. *Undergraduate* variation (5.7+ TR): From the ledge step right and finish up the face and outside corner right of *Little Jewel*.

4. Wilderness Crack (5.3) The wide crack with a large boulder at the top.

5. Gumby to Greatness (5.10 TR) Eight feet left of *Try*, and just to the right of the lichen-covered slab, is a thin seam that starts about halfway up. Climb face moves to the seam, then follow it to the top.

6. Pokey's Revenge (5.10 TR) Climb the face just left of *Try* using a variety of thin vertical edges.

7. Try (5.2) Up the broken crack and steps to a large ledge.

8. Kick Start (5.9+ TR) Climb the clean face halfway between *Try* and *Try or Fly*. Finish up the face right of the arête.

9. Try or Fly (5.7) Climb a diagonal crack that goes left up a small ramp and continues straight up to the top.

10. Flail (5.10 TR) Climb up *Try or Fly* a few feet to the small overhang. Up the face and finish at the top of *Try or Fly*. Variation (5.11): Instead of finishing left, finish up and right.

11. Fly (5.9– TR) Three feet left of *First Timer*, climb a thin seam ending with a short 1-inch crack near the top.

12. First Timer (5.5) About 7 feet left of the right edge of the cliff is a crack climb. Start at the short left-facing inside corner, and follow the crack for 15 feet to the top.

13. Fly Trap (5.7– TR) Climb the face between *First Timer* and the right outside edge of the cliff. Finish up the wide crack.

Upper Ledges

To reach the Upper Ledges, do not bear left on the trail to the Lower Ledges. Instead, continue on the Appalachian Trail uphill for about 0.25 mile (5 minutes). The trail traverses the base of the Upper Ledges. These cliffs may not appear to be 100 feet tall, but they are indeed. If you plan to set up a slingshot toprope belay, only a 60-meter rope will reach the ground, and even then it may come up short on some parts of the cliffs. Otherwise you can belay from the top.

If you plan to toprope, there are a couple of options to gain the top of the cliffs. The first way is to lead one of the following routes. The most common way is to ascend a gulley on the right as the AT meets the right (north) end of the cliffs. This gully is bordered by a rock wall on its right and a rock-pinched slot, blocked by a tree. Squeeze through the slot, ascend the gully, and near the top continue left to gain the top of the cliff at some erosion-control terraces. Do not attempt to gain the top of the slabs by hiking farther south uphill on the Appalachian Trail. This takes you way out of the way to the very top of the ledges. The only way back to the climbs is a long, horrendous bushwhack back down and north.

Climbs are described from left to right.

1. Quartz Wall (5.8+ TR) On the far left end of the cliff, start left of a low overhang / corner. Up the steep scoop on quartz edges. Continue up the face and arête to the top.

2. Trail Snack (5.9 TR) Start at the right edge of the low overhang and left of the *Half Bling / No Gear* crack to a horizontal break. Continue more or less straight to the top.

3. Snake Eyes (5.7+ TR ★) One of the most pleasant face climbs in Connecticut. Start a few feet to the right of *Trail Snack* and 10 feet left of *Half Bling / No Gear*. Straight up the face to a vertical seam and to a horizontal crack. Move a bit right and then up to the top.

4. Half Bling (aka *No Gear*) (5.8+ R ★; bolt missing 2015) Start up the beautiful shallow crack that diagonals up and right. When it starts to traverse right, head straight up the blank face, and a thin move past a bolt (missing 2015) leads to the top. *Note:* 30 meters in length so toprope anchors may need to be extended.

5. Crack n Up (5.10- R / X) Start between small corners between *Half Bling* (aka *No Gear*) and *Trail Magic*. Follow the shallow left diagonal crack to the horizontal crack. Climb the face between *Half Bling* (aka *No Gear*) and *Trail Magic* to the top. Crack n Ups were a type of gear for thin seams popular in the 1970s and 1980s.

6. Trail Magic (5.9– PG ★) Ten feet right of *Crack n Up* and 30 feet left of the *Blisters* crack is a small overhang, about 15 feet up, with a crack running straight up to the top. Follow the crack system and thin face to the top. A 70-meter rope is best if toproping.

7. Magic Face (5.10– TR) Start on *Trail Magic,* move right under the small overhang about 4 feet then up the face aiming for a thin seam. Up the face 4 to 8 feet to the right of *Trail Magic* to the top.

8. Blisters (5.8 R) Fifty feet uphill from the first series of slab climbs, left of *Athlete's Feat*, is a steep crack with a small overlap and a left-facing inside corner several feet up. Climb up to the small corner (wet), pull the overlap, and then follow the crack. The crack eventually ends for a scruffy finish. The start can be difficult to protect.

St. Johns Ledges Upper Wall

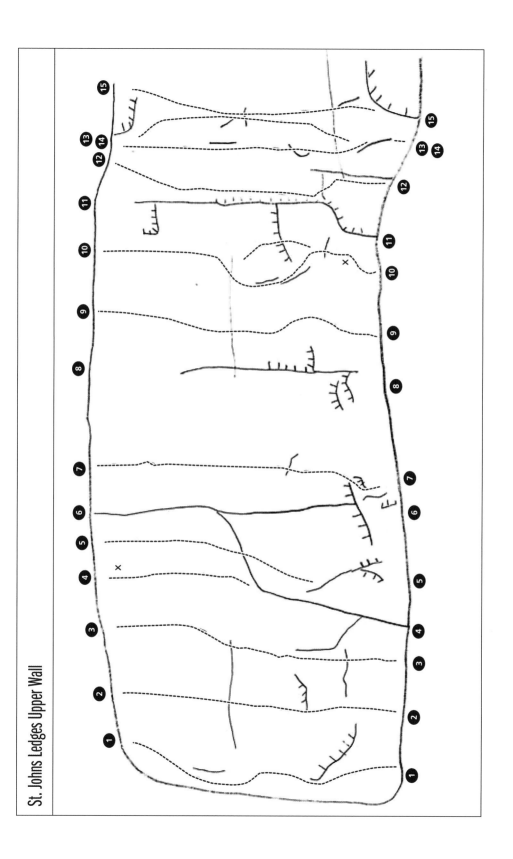

9. Slickrock (5.10+ TR) Fifteen feet left of *Athlete's Feat* bolt is a black water streak whose bottom is 6 feet above the ground. Climb to the black streak, and pass it on the right to a small sloping stance. Step left and climb directly above the streak on the steep face, over a small overlap, to lower-angle face climbing. Continue directly upward through trees branches to the top. FA: Don Pelletier,1986.

10. Athlete's Feat (5.11+ R) Just to the left of *Arch of Delight* is a smooth face with a bolt (missing 2015) about 10 feet up. Climb up the smooth face, past the bolt, to a stance below an overlap. Follow a left-slanting seam, then up and right to a horizontal seam. Up the sustained face to the top. *Super Feat* 5.11+ (rating not confirmed) variation: Once past the crux, climb over the overlap / small roof above and wander up the slabs to the top. FA: Sam Slater.

11. Arch of Delight (5.7 PG) On the left end of *Super Slab* is a 20-foot, left-facing corner above a small ledge. A tricky start up the corner past the overlap and then small roof. Step right and wander up the face and cracks to the top. The top is dirty (2015) and can be toproped using a directional anchor (trees midway up) from *Cornerstone*.

12. Cornerstone (5.9– TR) A few feet to the right of *Arch of Delight*, climb a vertical crack to a horizontal crack / seam. Climb left to the outside corner / arête formed by the *Arch of Delight* corner and climb this corner / arête and face a few feet to the right above the overlap. Trend right to finish between *Arch of Delight* and *Falling Bodies*.

13. Falling Bodies (5.6 TR ★) Start at a left-slanting seam right of *Cornerstone* and left of *Rackless*. Up the seam to a horizontal crack. Up and slightly left to small right-facing corners and up right to a vertical seam, then straight to the top.

14. White Hollow (5.7 TR) Start on *Falling Bodies* (left-slanting seam right of *Cornerstone* and left of *Rackless*). Up the seam a few feet then straight up the face, passing a hollow flake, and finish left of the final corner.

15. Rackless (5.6) Start just above a left-facing corner / ledge on the left end of the open slabs. Up the 10-foot left-slanting crack, then up the face to a horizontal. Trend up and left to the *White Hollow* flake and up *White Hollow* about 10 feet. Then trend right and finish up the face right of the overlap / corner.

16. Thrills and Skills (5.4 TR) On the right end of the slabs is a clean 25-foot-wide section of rock. Wander up the clean rock to the top. Popular with school groups.

17. Stranger Danger (5.1 R) The left-slanting gulley / crack system starting on the right end of the crag that leads to the top.

WOLF ROCK, MANSFIELD

Wolf Rock is a nice destination if climbing with beginners. The approach is short, but so are the cliffs—30 to 40 feet. Wolf Rock is accessed by the blue-blazed Nipmuck Trail, which, at least leading to Wolf Rock, is located on Joshua's Tract Conservation and Historic Trust property.

The route names are referenced from *A Climbing Guide for the 'Monks'* by Robert Perzel (Sugarhill Studios, 1994). With regard to rock climbing, Joshua's Trust does not explicitly permit or deny rock climbing on Wolf Rock.

Directions: Make your way to Route 32, just north of Willimantic. Go east on Mansfield City Road to the intersection with Browns Road. Go left (east) on Browns Road. Take a left on Crane Hill Road. After 0.1 mile there is a pullout on the right.

Approach: Across the street from the pullout, the blue-blazed Nipmuck Trail heads uphill and is marked by the sign "Joshua's Conservation and Historic Trust." Follow the trail for 5 minutes, and you will reach an overlook with a boulder perched on top of the cliff. The boulder marks the top of the Upper Tier. A trail descends to the left side of the Upper Tier. A trail from the center of the Upper Tier descends to the Lower Tier.

Upper Tier

The Upper Tier is short, sunny, and clean. Climbs are described from left to right.

1. Lady Bug (5.2 TR) The start is marked by a short "corner" that gains the base of the left side of the crag. Climb up the face just right of the "corner" to the top. A huge eyebolt marks the top.

2. Beach Party (5.5 TR) Climb the slab to the right of Lady Bug and to the left of the hairline crack.

3. Blanket Party (5.6 TR ★) Climb up the center of the clean slab, following the hairline crack.

4. Cleanup Party (5.4 TR) The face between *Blanket Party* and *Star Fire*.

5. Star Fire (5.1) Climb either of the short cracks to the left of the gully.

6. Tiger Kitty (5.5 TR) Start at the base of the gully, step left onto the face, and climb the blunt arête to the top.

7. Toe Crack (5.6 ★) Follow the prominent crack through the small overhang and up the slab above.

8. Jokers Are Wild (5.5) Climb up the center of the face, passing a large pocket, to the overhang. Climb over the overhang and up the face above.

9. Parental Vision Obscured (5.5) Start on the right side of the wall at the rounded corner / arête. Climb up the face, step left at the overlap, and continue up the face.

Johanna Wolkoff descends the Upper Tier slab. PHOTO DAVID FASULO

Lower Tier

Here you'll find steeper climbs and a little more shade than on the Upper Tier. Follow the trail downhill from the center of the Upper Tier to the right end of the Lower Tier. Climbs are described from left to right.

1. Lurch (5.9– TR) Start up the clean face to the left of the main corner. Crank up to the horizontal, then continue straight up the face above.

2. Pebble Beach (5.2 ★) Hop up the corner and cracks to the ledge at the base of the huge right-facing corner. Climb up the corner to the roof, traverse right, and climb up the corner and large crack to the top.

3. The Whale (5.6) Climb up Pebble Beach to a stance on the ledge to the left. Step right and "bear hug" the crack with your left hand and the corner with your right. Continue over the overhang and up the wall to the small roof. Finish on the crack to your right.

4. Eraser Head (5.9+ R) Climb up the center of the face between *The Whale* and *Lil' Abner*. Start by bouldering the left edge of the wall and then working right to the horizontals. Continue up the center of the face.

5. Lil' Abner (5.8 R ★) Start behind a tree and follow a thin crack / seam past a couple of horizontal cracks to the top.

6. Reachy (5.8+ R) Climb up the face past horizontals 3 feet to the right of *Lil' Abner*.

7. Mossy Crack (5.7) The short, dirty crack on the right side of the crag that passes through a 1-foot roof.

FIFTY-FOOT CLIFF PRESERVE, MANSFIELD

Fifty-Foot Cliff is actually a 35-foot crag located on the 102-acre Fifty-Foot Cliff Preserve. Rock climbers, mostly from UCONN, have been frequenting Fifty-Foot cliff on a regular basis since the 1970s, and several popular climbs can be found on the steep Canterbury Gneiss. The Fifty-Foot Preserve is currently (2015) open to the public, and the Mansfield Parks & Recreation provides up-to-date maps. Prohibited park activities include: unleashed dogs, mountain / motor biking, camping / camp fires, and horseback riding. With regard to rock climbing, Mansfield Parks & Recreation does not explicitly permit or deny rock climbing on the Fifty-Foot Cliff. To help preserve access to this hidden gem, do your part by helping to keep the area pristine. The route names are referenced from *A Climbing Guide for the 'Monks'* by Robert Perzel (Sugarhill Studios, 1994). Some routes seem to be much harder than the original grades and are rated differently from the original guide (some are just guesses).

Directions: Make your way to Route 195 in Mansfield. If coming from the center of Willimantic, take a right on Chaffeeville Road.

Access 1: After 1.5 miles there is a parking area on the left (if you have gone too far, go to Mulberry Road and backtrack 0.2 mile). Take a left on the white-blazed trail, then a quick right on the trail to the base of a moss-covered cliff after about 6 minutes. Where the trail splits, continue straight / left for 1 minute to the base of the Fifty-Foot. The trail on the right will take you to the top.

Access 2: After 1.2 miles there is a pullout on the left and a trailhead. Park at the pullout (other pullouts are located down the road if it is crowded). Just south of the pullout is a trailhead for the blue-blazed Nipmuck Trail. Follow the blue-blazed trail west for 9 minutes to the white-blazed trail on the right (easy to miss). Follow the white-blazed trail for 2 minutes to the base of the cliff. Reach the top of the cliff from the left side of the cliff. To go directly to the top, continue past the white-blazed trail and hike up the blue-blazed trail for 3 minutes to an unmarked overlook trail on the right. This will lead to the top of the Fifty-Foot crag.

The top of the crag can be quickly accessed from the left side, or a little longer from the right side.

Main Wall

1. Left Hook (5.7 TR) Just above the right corner of the mossy ledge, climb up to a large hold and follow the seam to the top.

2. Lefty (5.9+ TR) A few feet right of the mossy ledge, start on good holds and up steep horizontal cracks past a bolt (bolt missing 2015) and edges to the top.

3. Burnout (5.9 TR) Start on good edges / flakes. Work up and right to a horizontal crack, then up and right to a left-facing corner / flake. Climb left then up to the top. 5.10– variation: After going to the first horizontal, continue straight / left up the face.

4. Hang Time (5.9 ★ TR) Start on the right-facing corner / flake. Long reaches to horizontals lead to the left-facing corner and the top. Good climbing start to finish.

5. RPEF (5.10+ TR ★) Start at the "eye" 4 feet right of *Hang Time*. A dynamic move up the steep face, then stay left of the black water streak and crack on pumpy moves to top.

6. Malevolent Eye (5.10 TR) Start on the *RPEF* "eye" and up to the horizontal crack. Traverse right 4 feet, then up the steep face to the top.

7. Chocolate Party (5.11? TR) Climb the left side of the prominent water streak. Steep, with a key edge partway up. Feels much harder than the original 5.10 rating. Rating not confirmed.

8. Nose Tweezers (5.11? TR) Start at a good edge 7 feet right of *Chocolate Party*. Gain the horizontal, then up edges to a dirty top-out. Feels much harder than the original 5.10 rating. Rating not confirmed.

9. The Shield (5.11+ TR) Boulder over the overhang on small edges and up past the "shield" to a bucket, and up the face to the top. Variation (5.10+ TR): Climb *Nose Tweezers*, then traverse right to *The Shield*. Finish on *The Shield*.

10. Waging War on Thieves (5.11+ TR) Over the center of the cave aiming for a large pocket. Trend left then up to the next pocket and finish above.

11. Surprise Party (5.11 TR) Over the right end of the cave on good holds, pass a technical face to a horizontal and the top.

12. American Mouse (5.10 TR) Over the right edge of the cave and midway up the face, traverse right about 4 feet then up to the top. *American Cat* variation (5.10 TR): Start on the right edge of the boulder / flake on the ground. Work straight up the face to join *American Mouse*.

13. Birdie Party (5.10 TR) Start just left of the water mark and up the face.

14. The Flying Spatula (5.10 TR) Start just right of the water streak and up the steep face.

Fifty-Foot

SELDEN NECK STATE PARK, LYME

According to the Department of Energy and Environmental Protection (DEEP) website, "This island park is accessible only from the water. Formerly home to a farm and a stone quarry, it was cut off from the mainland by the powerful runoff in the spring of 1854. As an island, this unique park offers four boating camp site areas." Climbers have been exploring the island for decades. More recently, mixed climbs (natural and fixed protection) have been added to some of the crags. Circumnavigating the island by kayak, day or night, is also a popular outing. Launches include the Deep River town dock or Pratt Cove in Deep River. One of the more interesting cliffs in Connecticut, Joshua Rock is located just south of Selden Neck on the east side of the Connecticut River. Once a popular outing, Joshua Rock is now closed to climbing.

Access: It is difficult to anchor a powerboat near the approach to the climbs, so it is best to paddle a kayak or canoe to the island. The best launch is the Deep River Town Dock. However, on weekends in the summer, they may charge a fee. The other option is Pratt Cove, but navigating through the bridge and the marsh at certain tides can be difficult.

Directions: Deep River Town Dock: Take Route 9 to exit 5. If heading south, take a left off the exit. If heading north, take a right off the exit. Continue on Route 80 / West Elm Street to the second intersection (Deep River center). Continue straight on River Street for 0.8 mile and the town dock will be at the end of the road.

Pratt Cove: Go to the second intersection as above, but take a right on Route 154. After 0.5 mile take a left on Essex Street.

Pratt Cove Parking will be on your right after 0.5 mile.

Approach: Paddle to the southern end of Eustasia Island (directly across from the launch in the Connecticut River). Then paddle directly across the Connecticut River to Selden Island. Land on the bank of the island. Just north of that area is a campground with an outhouse that may be a good landmark if new to the area. From the campground there is a junction with the Red Trail and Blue Trail. If you head up the hill on the Blue Trail, you will reach a small crag (Quarry Knob). However, follow the Blue Trail south along the shore of the river (from the Red / Blue Trail junction) for 5 minutes. The trail splits at a stone wall; follow the Blue Trail into the woods (east) up to cairns and the base of the Quarry Wall.

Shadow Crag: This is the 50-foot-high crag located left of the Quarry Wall.

1. Snafu (5.10+ mixed) On the left end of the main wall, just before a section of mossy / wet rock, there is a mixed route (two bolts) to fixed anchors (sporty getting to anchors). FA: Ryan Richetelli, 2013.

2. Bringing Back the B (5.11; mixed) Start to the climber's right of the large crack on opposing crimps. Difficult move off the ground (harder if you are short) to attain the rail above. Climb past the first two bolts to attain the ledge above. Use traditional protection as you traverse right on underlings along the roof. At the right side of roof place protection and pull through the roof on crimps and good holds above. Climb up to a bolt and past thin climbing to the fixed anchors. FA: John Peterson, Ryan Richetelli, 2015.

3. Shadow Wall (5.9) To the right of *Sanfu* is a prominent corner / roof system that traverses right and then finishes up the steep corner.

Jeff Laggis on the Quarry Wall PHOTO DAVID FASULO

Quarry Wall

The routes are not long, about 45 feet, but are high quality on solid granite. A nasty gully separates the Shadow Crag from the Quarry Wall. If attempting to access routes from the top, it is best to hike around the south side of the Quarry Wall and pick up the blue-blazed trail that skirts across the top. The top of the cliff lines up with the channel marker just south of Eustasia Island. A safety rope is prudent to reach the tops of the climbs.

1. Magic Hat (5.10; sport) To the right of the gully, follow the corner and crack past a bolt and tricky mantle onto the ledge. After the second bolt, traverse right over the arête and join *Hot Chicks in Hammocks* to the top. FSA: Chris Beauchamp, 2014.

2. Hot Chicks in Hammocks (5.11; sport) Stick-clip the first bolt. Work up just to the right of the arête on the left, and traverse right past the first bolt and onto the face at the shallow arête. Trend back left and follow two more bolts to finish on *Roundabout*. FSA: Chris Beauchamp, 2014.

3. Roundabout (5.11; sport) Climb the steep face to the left of the prominent arête past bolts to fixed anchors. Even with the bolts, the route can be nerve-racking due to the off-balance moves. FSA: John Peterson, 2012.

4. 3-Hour Tour (5.9; mixed) The easiest route on the wall. Climb the right side of the prominent arête past two bolts and place gear (small / medium camming units) to fixed anchors. FRA: Chris Beauchamp, 2013.

5. Granum (5.9; mixed) This routes climbs the central face of the clean Quarry Wall.

6. Super Power (5.9 PG) Climb the large left-facing corner using holds on the face to the left. Contrived, as one can simply step left and get on *Granum*. Finish on *Granum*. A high-power leaf blower was used to clean the route. FRA: Rick Kraft, 2013.

7. C.O.D. (5.10; mixed) After a difficult start on perfect granite, follow the face to the right of the arête past bolts. Clear a roof after the ledge (gear) to fixed anchors. FRA: Christopher Beauchamp, 2013.

PACHAUG STATE FOREST, NORTH STONINGTON

Not a crag destined for any major write-ups, but if you are in the area, it can be a fun afternoon climb. This is a small crag that is best climbed on a warm winter day. The surrounding area is wet and should be avoided in midsummer due to bugs. The right end faces southeast and is relatively warm in the winter. The rock is a lighter color, however, so come prepared. The left end of the cliff, approximately 35 feet high, has some good beginner climbs but they are somewhat dirty. Some cleaning could yield many new routes. The right end of the cliff, Little Rumney, is marked by a stone cave and steep wall approximately 35 feet high.

Directions: Take I-95 North to exit 92. Go left off the exit and follow Route 2 West. After 2 miles veer right onto Main Street (Stonington Village). After 0.3 mile veer right onto Wyassup Road. After 3 miles take a left on Wyassup Lake Road. After 0.7 mile there will be a boat ramp on your right. Proceed 0.1 mile and park just past the gated trail on the left.

Approach: From the parking area hike up the blue-blazed trail / dirt road for 5 minutes. The road goes left—continue on the trail for another 9 minutes (an unmarked trail goes straight). Hike for 6 more minutes up the steep hill, then drop down the trail for 2 minutes to a junction with the unmarked trail. Take a left on the unmarked trail (ravine near a stream) for 2 minutes to the base of *Pistol Whip*.

High Ledge

The largest cliff (right end) has a vertical crack going through a roof, *Pistol Whip* (5.8+). The roof can be avoided by going out left (5.6). The arête to the right is *Trigger* (5.5). Fifty feet farther to the right is an overhanging cliff with a bolted route called *Tough Schist* (5.10–; six bolts to anchor); FRA: Brian Phillips. Ascending the multiple roofs on the left, aiming for a blade of rock projecting near the top, is *Roller Blade* (5.10+); FA TR: Ken Nichols, 1999.

DIAMOND LEDGE, WEST GRANBY

Diamond Ledge (aka Broad Hill) is a 60-foot crag located in West Granby on property owned by the Granby Land Trust. As of 2002 the Granby Land Trust allows access to this area and states, "There are no restrictions regarding climbing." The name Diamond Ledge comes from the sparkle of the mica at certain times of day. This area was one of the Granby Land Trust's first properties, donated in the early 1970s by Mary Edwards. It abuts the 37-acre Frances Peterson Preserve on one side and the 320-acre town-owned Holcomb Farm on another.

The rock is a mixture of gneiss and quartz, making for some interesting climbing. Many of the holds are actually protruding quartz crystals. The climbing at Diamond Ledge is more for the advanced climber. There are only a couple moderate climbs, with all the other climbs being 5.9 or higher.

Directions: Take I-91 to Route 20 West (exit 40 traveling northbound), or Route 10, to Granby. From Granby take Route 20 West toward West Granby. You will pass the fire station and then the post office to come to a Y junction. Take a left at the Y on West Granby Road. At its end take a left on Simsbury Road. Take your first right onto Broad Hill Road. After 0.3 mile you will see a small parking area / trailhead on the left. Carpooling is highly recommended.

Approach: Travel up the gated road for 2 minutes, and there is an old parking lot on your left with a "Welcome Holcomb Farm Trails" sign. The unmarked trail to Diamond Ledge is across the street from this parking area. A short march brings you to the base of Diamond Ledge.

Most of the climbs at Diamond Ledge are toproped. Some of the climbs have been lead from the ground up, but you must be an expert with traditional protection to lead these routes.

As with all Connecticut crags, maintaining a low profile is the key to continued climbing at Diamond Ledge. Be courteous to others, keep the noise down, leave before dark, and leash all dogs. Also, cars should travel slowly on Broad Hill Road.

Main Wall

The route information for Diamond Ledge was described to the author by Ken Nichols in 2014.

1. Sunnyside (5.11 R) The face going up the short clean wall on the far left end of the cliff. FA: Ken Nichols, 1989.

2. Night Shade (5.10 TR) The short, clean arête on the far left end of the cliff. FA (toprope): Chuck Boyd. FA solo: Ken Nichols, 1985.

3. Powder Forrest (5.6) The clean corner / wide crack / flake system on the left end of the cliff. This was the first route to be climber at the cliff. FA (toprope): Bill Ryan, 1970s. FA: Marco Fedrizzi, Ken Nichols, 1984.

4. Out of Balance (5.10+ TR) The prominent arête on the left edge of the *Withywindle Wall*. Start on *Powder Forrest*, then move right onto in-cut flakes and up the arête. FA: Chuck Boyd, 1986.

5. Withywindle Wall (5.10 PG) Use the same start as *Out of Balance*, then up and right, climbing the left side of the steep clean face to the top. FA: Ken Nichols, Marco Fedrizzi, 1984. *Weeping Willow Start* (5.11+ R): Start just right of the corner and climb straight up to join *Withywindle Wall*. FA: Ken Nichols, 1985.

6. Pronghorn (5.11– R) Up the face a few feet right of *Withywindle Wall* past overlaps and a horn. FA: Ken Nichols, 1989 (5.10 when led—holds have broken off). FA (toprope): Bob O'Brien, 2004.

7. Jungle Jim (5.10) The prominent right-diagonaling crack on the right edge of the *Withywindle Wall*. FA: Sam Slater, Ken Nichols, 1982.

8. Mountain Laurel (5.7) Start at a point where a crack angles down left to the ground 3 feet left of a triangular detached block. Up the face to the ledge. Follow the steep ramp up and right 15 feet to a steep headwall. Straight up the steep headwall to the top. FA: Ken Nichols, Doug Chapman, 1985.

9. Broadwalk (5.9+ R) Start at the large detached triangle block at the base of a diagonal crack. Up the crack to its end. Then finish up a small left-facing corner. FA: Marco Fedrizzi, Ken Nichols, 1985.

The next few climbs start on the steep wall to the right of the central buttress.

10. Crystals (5.12– TR) Start on the face 4 feet right of a large triangular block. Climb straight up a prominent bulge, and after intersecting *Broadwalk*, climb up and left into small right-facing corners. FA: Ken Nichols, 1987.

11. Crazy Diamond (5.11 TR) Start on the face 13 feet right of the large triangular detached block, 3 feet left of an oak tree. Up the face, then step right up a shallow scoop and small right-facing corner. After the corner, traverse a few feet left and up to the top. FA: Marco Fedrizzi, 1985.

12. Quartz Jester (5.11+ TR) Start just opposite of the right side of a large oak tree, 4 feet downhill and left of a large detached block. Up to and slightly right to an arching overlap. Continue straight up past a 12-inch-deep overlap to bulging rock. Traverse left 3 feet and follow the line of good holds diagonaling up right over the bulge to the top. FA: Ken Nichols, 1989.

13. Saturn V (5.9+ R) Start on the face of the large detached block. Twenty feet uphill from a large oak tree. Up to a stance on the top of the block (below the lower left end of the large diagonal roof). Hand-traverse left on quartz crystals for several feet, then climb over the obvious bulge. Reach left to a short right-facing corner, then finish over the left end of the roof. FA: Marco Fedrizzi, Chuck Boyd, 1986.

ORENAUG PARK, WOODBURY

Orenaug Park has some very good climbs—however, access has been a problem. The 1988 edition of *Woodbury Climber's Guide* by Bill Ivanoff and Ken Nichols describes 121 established routes. Twenty-one of these routes are to the left of the portion of the crag that is currently (2015) closed. One hundred routes, many of which were the best on the crag, are currently off-limits. The Ragged Mountain Foundation, Appalachian Mountain Club (AMC), Access Fund, and local climbers are working on access to this area. It is hopeful that the town, climbers, and landowners can come to an agreement that allows for responsible recreational access.

A little access history according to an Access Fund position paper dated December 25, 2000:

> In 1892, Susan B. Shove conveyed land to the town of Woodbury, to be used as a park. The Orenaug Park has been owned and maintained by the Town for the benefit and use by the public since that time. The Park contains cliffs along one edge in an undeveloped recreation area. The cliffs are within walking distance of the Town Hall. The cliffs, and the access trails below them, have been used by the public for rock climbing for many years.

The following information is from *Access Notes*—Vol. 12 Winter 1995.

> On October 14, 1995, the Woodbury Board of Selectman voted unanimously to re-open Orenaug Park to rock climbing. The area, one of Connecticut's most popular cliffs offering climbs in a variety of grades, was closed to climbing last

Spring after several accidents. The vote occurred after a thorough and careful examination of the nature, history, and realities of rock climbing.

> Woodbury Selectman Mark Alvarez gathered information for this decision from the Access Fund, the American Alpine Club, the Mohonk Trust, the Ragged Mountain Foundation, local public safety officials, the Woodbury Parks and Recreation Commission, and the town's insurance carrier and legal council.

> Alvarez also researched the Connecticut Recreational Use Statute and a state regulation covering rock climbing on state property. This regulation was positively modified as a result of testimony by the Ragged Mountain Foundation at a public hearing three years ago.

> The town's main concern was liability. Connecticut's Recreational Use Statute (Title 52, Section 557 [g]), was upheld by the State Supreme Court, and was determined by council to provide "substantial protection." The state of Connecticut based its regulation on climbing on state property upon this statute, recognizing that climbers pursue their sport at their own risk.

The Ragged Mountain Foundation, as of January 2001 states:

> Climbing at Orenaug Park in Woodbury is currently under a partial closure. The central section of the crag is affected, including the most popular routes in The Viewing Wall area. The adjacent landowner has closed the section of the cliff base trail that crosses his property. Although the actual cliff faces are owned by the town of Woodbury, the landowner has been asking climbers to leave and has

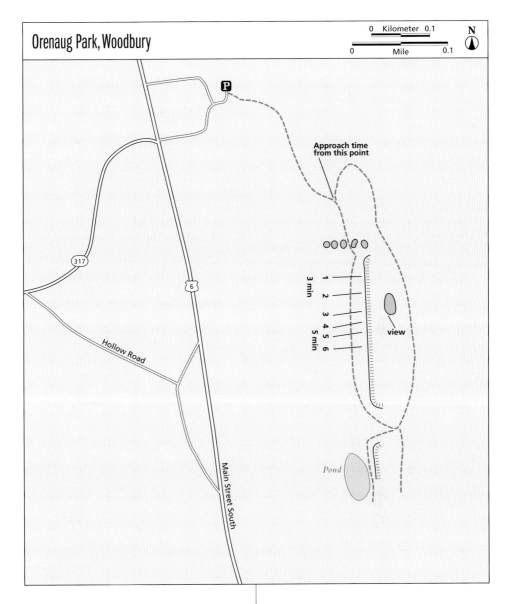

Orenaug Park, Woodbury

0   Kilometer 0.1

0   Mile   0.1

N

Approach time from this point

317

6

Hollow Road

Main Street South

3 min

1
2
3
4
5
6

5 min

view

Pond

called the police to remove climbers if they do not leave voluntarily. The closed area is bounded on the southern (pond) end of the crag by a short stonewall and a concrete marker. The northern boundary of the closure is the route "20th Century Fox." Routes outside this area are still open. The RMF and the Access Fund are trying to work out a compromise. In the meantime, while negotiations continue, please avoid climbing on the closed section of the crag.

Directions: Take I-84 to exit 15. Follow Route 67 North / Route 6 East for about 4.5 miles to the junction of Route 317 at a light. Take a right at the light (marked with a sign for the library). Pass the library and park in the upper lot for Orenaug Park.

Approach: From the park sign follow the orange-blazed trail, past a meadow and into the woods. After 3 minutes of hiking, the trail swings left and there is a climbers' trail heading right, to the left end of the cliffs.

Note: There are at least twenty-one established routes to the left of *20th Century Fox*. The most obvious lines are included below.

Left End

1. Clenched Fist (5.8) On the brown wall, this is the prominent crack on the left with a roof midway. FA: Greg Newth, Bruce Dicks, 1975.

2. Flying Feet (5.9–) The crack in the middle of the wall, cutting through the overhang. FA: Sam Slater, Ken Nichols, 1982.

3. Guard Tower (5.9) Climb up the face, undercling out a roof, and continue up the large right-facing corner. FA: Ken Nichols, 1982.

4. Suffering Sassafras (5.4) Scramble up the left-facing corner / outcrop to a ledge. Climb up the blocky right-facing corner to the top. FA: Bill Ivanoff, Dave Fengler, 1987.

5. Right Diagonal (5.8+) This is marked by a large overhang with a right-diagonaling crack through the roof. It starts at a left-facing corner and follows the crack on the right past the roof and up the face. The crack on the left is 5.7. FA: Landon, Fake, 1979.

6. 20th Century Fox (5.6) Climb up the left-leaning crack through the overhang. Continue up the right-facing corner to a ledge. Move left and finish up the face. FA: Jack Rankin, Dave O'Connell, 1975.

As of 2015 the area to the right of *20th Century Fox* is closed.

BOULDERING

Bouldering—climbing up rock boulders without the use of a rope or harness—has become very popular. Boulder problems are typically safe enough to fall from if using a bouldering pad, unlike free solos. Minimal equipment needs and lots of potential for exploration and difficult climbing are some of the motivating factors. Connecticut has some of the best boulders—and bouldering—to be found anywhere. Glaciers that halted in Connecticut dropped off several large erratics throughout the state. Unfortunately, many of the best boulders lie on private property and are off-limits.

Considering the vast number of boulder problems in Connecticut, it is best to use the Internet to locate and gather information on the various bouldering areas.

SOURCES OF INFORMATION

A Century of American Alpinism. Fay, Bent, Palmer, Thorington, Kauffman & Putnam. The American Alpine Club, 2002.

"A Chop for a Bolt," by Nancy Pritchard. *Rock & Ice*, May / June 1991.

A Climbers Guide to Chatfield Hollow: The Best Climbs of Chatfield Hollow. John Biehn and Toby Stegman. Self-published, 2000.

The Climber's Guide to North America: East Coast Rock Climbs. John Harlin III. Chockstone Press, 1986.

Climber's Guide to Ragged Mountain, 2nd ed. Marvin Johnson, Alan Long, and Simon Whitney. Yale Mountaineering Club, copyright 1973 by Simon Whitney.

A Climber's Guide to Sleeping Giant State Park. William Ivanoff, 1986.

A Climbing Guide for the 'Monks' Along the Nipmuck Trail in Connecticut. Robert Perzel, Sugarhill Studios, 1994.

Climbing Guide to Chatfield Hollow. Jim Wilcox. Self-published, 1990s.

Connecticut Chapter of the Appalachian Mountain Club, www.ct-amc.org/ mountain / index.shtm.

CT Rock Climbers Unite, www.facebook .com / groups / 135140383177882 /.

Connecticut Sport Climbing. Brian Phillips. Self-published, 2013.

Connecticut Walk Book: A Trail Guide to the Connecticut Outdoors. Connecticut Forest & Park Association, 1984.

Country Walks in Connecticut: A Guide to the Nature Conservancy Preserves, 2nd ed. Susan D. Cooley. Appalachian Mountain Club Books, 1989.

Devil's Tower National Monument: A Climber's Guide. Steve Gardiner and Dick Guilmette. The Mountaineers, 1986.

Fifty Hikes in Connecticut: A Guide to Short Walks and Day Hikes in the Nutmeg State. Gerry and Sue Hardy. Backcountry Publications, 1984.

Guidebook to Sleeping Giant. Alex Catlin. Self-published, date unknown.

A Guide to the Main and Small Cliffs at Ragged Mountain, Southington, Connecticut. John Reppy and Sam Streibert. Yale Mountaineering Club, 1964.

Hooked on Ragged: Rock Climbing at Ragged Mountain. Ken Nichols, 1997.

Hooked on Traprock Rock Climbing in Central Connecticut. Ken Nichols. Amereon House, 1995.

"In the Middle of Everywhere: Mother Nature at Its Rawest," by Fred Musante. *New York Times Magazine*, June 25, 2000.

Joshua Land Trust, www.joshuaslandtrust.org.

Mashantucket Pequot (Western) Tribal Nation, www.mptn-nsn.gov / tribalhistory.aspx.

Meriden's Hiking Trails. Joseph A. Zaborowski and the Meriden Land Trust. The Meriden Land Trust Inc., 1997.

Mountain Project, www.mountainproject.com.

"Quick Hits," by Aaron Black. *Climbing*, December 2001, p. 208.

Ragged and Free: Selected Climbs in Central Connecticut. The Ragged Mountain Foundation, 1994, 1999.

Ragged Mountain 1974 Supplement. Ken Nichols. Copycat, 1974.

Ragged Mountain Foundation, www .raggedmtn.org.

Rockclimbing.com, www.rockclimbing.com.

Rock Climbing New England. Stewart M. Green. Globe Pequot Press, 2001.

Rock Climbs in the White Mountains of New Hampshire, 2nd ed. Ed Webster. Mountain Imagery, 1987.

Rock 'n' Road, Connecticut section, 2nd ed. Tim Toula. Globe Pequot Press, 2002.

The Talcott Mountain Foundation Guide to Rock Climbing on Talcott Mountain. Ian Howat and Alec Eakins. The Talcott Mountain Foundation, 1994.

Traprock: Connecticut Rock Climbs. Ken Nichols. American Alpine Club, 1982.

Traprock Ridges of Connecticut: A Naturalist's Guide. Diana V. Wetherell. Connecticut Department of Environmental Protection, 1997.

"Tunxis Trail, Mile of Ledges," by Michael Kodas. Crux Northeast, Issue 7, August / September 1994.

Woodbury Climber's Guide. Bill Ivanoff and Ken Nichols, 1988.

Yankee Rock and Ice: A History of Climbing in the Northeastern United States. Laura and Guy Waterman. S. Peter Lewis Photography, Stackpole Books, 1993.

INDOOR CLIMBING GYMS

Carabiner's Indoor Climbing Gym
85 Mill Plain Rd.
Fairfield, CT 06824
(203) 416-5500
carabiners.com

Central Rock
259 Eastern Blvd.
Glastonbury, CT 06033
(860) 659-8260
centralrockgym.com

City Climb
342 Winchester Ave.
New Haven, CT 06511
(203) 891-7627
cityclimbgym.com

Prime Climb
340 Silversmith Park, Building 28
Wallingford, CT 06492
(203) 265–7880
primeclimb.com

Stone Age Rock Gym
195 Adams St.
Manchester, CT
(860) 645-0015
stoneagerockgym.com

Nicole DeLisi on *Broadway,* Ragged Mountain PHOTO DAVID FASULO

CONNECTICUT RECREATIONAL USE ACT REVISED 2011

The Connecticut Recreational Use Act, essentially, Connecticut General Statues sections 52-557f through 52-577i, was amended in 2011 by Public Act 11-211. This was in response to the court finding the Metropolitan District Commission (MDC) liable for injuries to a bicycle rider on MDC property. The amendment specifically includes municipalities, political subdivisions, and water districts, among others, among entities immune from liability for recreational use of their property. This amendment, it is hoped, will be a useful tool to renegotiate access to various climbing areas in Connecticut.

Sec. 52-557f. Landowner liability for recreational use of land. Definitions. As used in sections 52-557f to 52-557i, inclusive:

(1) "Charge" means the admission price or fee asked in return for invitation or permission to enter or go upon the land;

(2) "Land" means land, roads, water, watercourses, private ways and buildings, structures, and machinery or equipment when attached to the realty, except that if the owner is a municipality, political subdivision of the state, municipal corporation, special district or water or sewer district: (A) "Land" does not include a swimming pool, playing field or court, playground, building with electrical service, or machinery when attached to the realty, that is also within the possession and control of the municipality, political subdivision of the state, municipal corporation, special district or water or sewer district; and (B) "road" does not include a paved public through road that is open to the public for the operation of four-wheeled private passenger motor vehicles;

(3) "Owner" means the possessor of a fee interest, a tenant, lessee, occupant or person in control of the premises. "Owner" includes, but is not limited to, a municipality, political subdivision of the state, municipal corporation, special district or water or sewer district;

(4) "Recreational purpose" includes, but is not limited to, any of the following, or any combination thereof: Hunting, fishing, swimming, boating, camping, picnicking, hiking, pleasure driving, nature study, water skiing, snow skiing, ice skating, sledding, hang gliding, sport parachuting, hot air ballooning, bicycling and viewing or enjoying historical, archaeological, scenic or scientific sites.

Sec. 52-557g. Liability of owner of land available to public for recreation; exceptions. (a) Except as provided in section 52-557h, an owner of land who makes all or any part of the land available to the public without charge, rent, fee or other commercial service for recreational purposes owes no duty of care to keep the land, or the part thereof so made available, safe for entry or use by others for recreational purposes, or to give any warning of a dangerous condition, use, structure or activity on the land to persons entering for recreational purposes.

(b) Except as provided in section 52-557h, an owner of land who, either directly or indirectly, invites or permits without charge, rent, fee or other commercial service any person to use the land, or part thereof, for recreational purposes does not thereby: (1) Make any representation that the premises are safe for any purpose; (2) confer upon the person who enters or uses the land for recreational purposes the legal status of an invitee or licensee to whom a duty of care is owed; or (3) assume responsibility for or incur liability for any injury to person or property caused by an act or omission of the owner.

(c) Unless otherwise agreed in writing, the provisions of subsections (a) and (b) of this section shall be deemed applicable to the duties and liability of an owner of land leased to the state or any subdivision thereof for recreational purposes.

Sec. 52-557h. Owner liable, when. Nothing in sections 52-557f to 52-557i, inclusive, limits in any way the liability of any owner of land which otherwise exists: (1) For willful or malicious failure to guard or warn against a dangerous condition, use, structure or activity; (2) for injury suffered in any case where the owner of land charges the person or persons who enter or go on the land for the recreational use thereof, except that, in the case of land leased to the state or a subdivision thereof, any consideration received by the owner for the lease shall not be deemed a charge within the meaning of this section.

Sec. 52-557i. Obligation of user of land. Nothing in sections 52-557f to 52-557i, inclusive, shall be construed to relieve any person using the land of another for recreational purposes from any obligation which he may have in the absence of said sections to exercise care in his use of such land and in his activities thereon, or from the legal consequences of failure to employ such care.

Referenced from: http:// / www.cga.ct.gov / current / pub / chap_925.htm#sec_52-557f.

AN ACT CONCERNING PROTECTION OF RIDGELINES

HISTORY: 1971, P.A. 249, S. 6.

PUBLIC ACT NO. 95–239

AN ACT CONCERNING PROTECTION OF RIDGELINES.

Section 1. (NEW) As used in section 8–2 of the general statutes, as amended by section 2 of this act:

(1) "Traprock ridge" means Beacon Hill, Saltonstall Mountain, Totoket Mountain, Pistapaug Mountain, Fowler Mountain, Beseck Mountain, Higby Mountain, Chauncey Peak, Lamentation Mountain, Cathole Mountain, South Mountain, East Peak, West Peak, Short Mountain, Ragged Mountain, Bradley Mountain, Pinnacle Rock, Rattlesnake Mountain, Talcott Mountain, Hatchett Hill, Peak Mountain, West Suffield Mountain, Cedar Mountain, East Rock, Mount Sanford, Prospect Ridge, Peck Mountain, West Rock, Sleeping Giant, Pond Ledge Hill, Onion Mountain, The Sugarloaf, The Hedgehog, West Mountains, The Knolls, Barndoor Hills, Stony Hill, Manitook Mountain, Rattlesnake Hill, Durkee Hill, East Hill, Rag Land, Bear Hill, Orenaug Hills;

(2) "Traprock ridgeline" means the line on a traprock ridge created by all points at the top of a fifty per cent slope, which is maintained for a distance of fifty horizontal feet perpendicular to the slope and which consists of surficial basalt geology, identified on the map prepared by Stone et al., United States Geological Survey, entitled "Surficial Materials Map of Connecticut";

(3) "Ridgeline setback area" means the area bounded by (A) a line that parallels the ridgeline at a distance of one hundred fifty feet on the more wooded side of the ridge, and (B) the contour line where a ridge of less than fifty per cent is maintained for fifty feet or more on the rockier side of the slope, mapped pursuant to section 8–2 of the general statutes, as amended by section 2 of this act;

(4) "Development" means the construction, reconstruction, alteration, or expansion of a building; and

(5) "Building" means any structure other than (A) a facility as defined in section 16-50i of the general statutes or (B) structures of a relatively slender nature compared to the buildings to which they are associated, including but not limited to chimneys, flagpoles, antennas, utility poles and steeples.

INDEX

ABOUT THE AUTHOR

David Fasulo grew up in Southington, Connecticut, home of Ragged Mountain, and has been climbing in Connecticut since 1984. He has climbed throughout the East Coast, Argentina, Brazil, Mexico, the French Alps, Spain, and Canada. He has climbed big walls in Yosemite Valley and Zion Canyon and has made several climbing trips throughout the American West. David has been a member of the American Mountain Guide Association since 1989 and is currently an AMGA-certified single-pitch instructor and New York State licensed guide specializing in self-rescue courses. In 1996 David wrote the first edition of *Self-Rescue* in the How to Rock Climb Series. The first edition was well received, being used as reference material for a number of technical-climbing books and manuals, and was translated to three other languages. David wrote the second edition of *Self-Rescue* in 2011, greatly expanding upon the first edition. Aside from climbing adventures, David is a full-time educator, certified American Canoe Association sea kayak instructor, certified emergency medical technician, and experienced ocean sailor and racer. David has served as the treasurer and president of the Ragged Mountain Foundation.

PROTECTING CLIMBING **ACCESS** SINCE 1991

Jonathan Siegrist, Third Millenium (14a), the Monastery, CO. Photo by: Keith Ladzinski

THE RAGGED MOUNTAIN FOUNDATION

www.raggedmtn.org

The idea is simple. If you would like to preserve access and responsibly manage your recreational resources, you need to participate actively in the stewardship—i.e., owning the property or working in partnership with the landowner. Perhaps the best example in the country of local climbers taking an active role in the management of their recreational resources is the Ragged Mountain Foundation (RMF).

The RMF is a 501(c)(3) nonprofit organization whose mission is to preserve Connecticut's scenic ridgetops for responsible recreational use. The RMF was formally established in 1991, and the first defining project for the foundation was the preservation of Ragged Mountain in Southington. The 55-acre parcel was previously owned by the Nature Conservancy and managed by the RMF. After completing a trial stewardship process, the Ragged Mountain Foundation accepted the deed to the former Stanley Hart property on July 9, 1999.

The RMF's work goes beyond the scope of Ragged Mountain and is committed to improving access for outdoor enthusiasts throughout the state.

The Ragged Mountain Foundation is composed of volunteers. The commitment comes from the heart. The reward is a beautiful vista for the use of future generations. If you are a Connecticut climber, join the RMF to help manage the Ragged Mountain property and improve access to Connecticut's high and wild places.

To become a member, either mail your tax-deductible donation ($15 as of January 2015) to: Ragged Mountain Foundation, P.O. Box 948, Southington, CT 06489, or join/renew online at www.raggedmtn.org.